Understanding Multinationals from Emerging Markets

Why have relatively poor and underdeveloped countries been able to spawn so many global firms in the last two decades? Are emerging market multinational companies (EMNCs) really different from successful multinationals from developed economies? This book tackles these and other fundamental theoretical questions about EMNCs. A distinguished group of researchers assesses the unique strategies and behavior of successful EMNCs, from the Chinese telecommunications firm Huawei to the Indian conglomerate Tata, to the South African beverages firm SABMiller. They address a range of topics, such as the drivers of internationalization by EMNCs; their distinctive process capabilities; how they catch up with established rivals on technology; how state ownership or business-group affiliation affects their behavior; and why they sometimes relocate their headquarters to advanced economies. This book will appeal to scholars and graduate students in global strategy and international business, as well as consultants of multinational companies, looking for state-of-the-art analysis of EMNCs.

ALVARO CUERVO-CAZURRA is Professor of International Business and Strategy at Northeastern University's D'Amore-McKim School of Business. He studies the internationalization of firms, with a special interest in developing-country multinationals, and his geographical area of expertise is Latin America. He also analyzes governance issues, with a focus on corruption in international business. He teaches and consults on global strategy and sustainability. For more information, please visit www.cuervo-cazurra.com.

RAVI RAMAMURTI is D'Amore-McKim Distinguished Professor of International Business and Strategy, and Director of the Center for Emerging Markets at Northeastern University's D'Amore-McKim School of Business. His research and consulting have focused on companies operating in, or from, emerging economies. This is his third volume with Cambridge University Press, the others being *Emerging Multinationals in Emerging Markets* (2009, edited with J.V. Singh) and *The Competitive Advantage of Emerging Market Multinationals* (2013, edited with P.W. Williamson, A. Fleury, and M.-T. Fleury).

Understanding Multinationals from Emerging Markets

Edited by

ALVARO CUERVO-CAZURRA

RAVI RAMAMURTI

CAMBRIDGE
UNIVERSITY PRESS

CAMBRIDGE
UNIVERSITY PRESS

University Printing House, Cambridge CB2 8BS, United Kingdom

One Liberty Plaza, 20th Floor, New York, NY 10006, USA

477 Williamstown Road, Port Melbourne, VIC 3207, Australia

314-321, 3rd Floor, Plot 3, Splendor Forum, Jasola District Centre, New Delhi - 110025, India

79 Anson Road, #06-04/06, Singapore 079906

Cambridge University Press is part of the University of Cambridge.

It furthers the University's mission by disseminating knowledge in the pursuit of education, learning and research at the highest international levels of excellence.

www.cambridge.org
Information on this title: www.cambridge.org/9781107064539

© Cambridge University Press 2014

First published 2014
First paperback edition 2015

A catalogue record for this publication is available from the British Library

Library of Congress Cataloging in Publication data
Understanding multinationals from emerging markets / edited by
Alvaro Cuervo-Cazurra and Ravi Ramamurti.
  pages   cm
Includes bibliographical references and index.
ISBN 978-1-107-06453-9 (hardback)
1. International business enterprises – Developing countries.   2. Competition –
Developing countries.   3. Globalization – Developing countries.   4. International
cooperation.   I. Cuervo-Cazurra, Alvaro, editor of compilation.   II. Ramamurti,
Ravi, editor of compilation.
HD62.4.U5298 2014
338.8′891724–dc23
2014011298

ISBN   978-1-107-06453-9   Hardback
ISBN   978-1-107-69832-1   Paperback

To
Sebastian and Annique
Meena, Bharat, Paige, Gita, and Arjun

Contents

Figures

Tables

Contributors

YAIR AHARONI was the Daniel and Grace Ross Professor of International Business and later the Issachar Haimovic Professor of Business Policy, both at Tel Aviv University in Israel. He received his Doctorate from Harvard Business School. Professor Aharoni's publications include more than 30 books and monographs. He has authored or edited more than 100 papers in various journals and chapters in books as well as more than 150 case studies. Professor Aharoni is a Fellow of the Academy of International Business and of the International Academy of Management and an Israel Prize in Management Science Laureate.

HELENA BARNARD is an associate professor at the Gordon Institute of Business Science at the University of Pretoria in South Africa. She completed her PhD at Rutgers University with a dissertation on how emerging multinationals use investment in more developed countries as a way to access new capabilities. She is interested in how knowledge flows from more to less developed contexts, both through emerging multinationals and through individual linkages such as the diaspora and scientific collaborations.

KRISTIN BRANDL is a PhD Fellow at Copenhagen Business School in Denmark. She received her MSc in International Business and Trade from the University of Gothenburg, School of Business, Economics and Law and will receive her PhD in International Management from Copenhagen Business School. Her research interests are the sourcing of knowledge-intensive and value-adding services from emerging market economies and the catch-up strategies of firms from these economies.

ALVARO CUERVO-CAZURRA is a Professor of International Business and Strategy at Northeastern University's D'Amore-McKim School of Business. He received a PhD from the Massachusetts Institute of Technology and another from the University of Salamanca. He studies the internationalization of companies, with a special interest in emerging market multinationals. He also analyzes governance issues, with a special interest in corruption in international business. He is Reviewing Editor of the *Journal of International Business Studies* and serves on the Executive Committee of the International Management Division of the Academy of Management.

AFONSO FLEURY is a Professor in the area of Work, Technology and Organisation at the University of Sao Paulo and (former) head of the Production Engineering Department. His research work focuses on different industries such as Aeronautics, Automobile, Capital Goods, Computing and Information, Digital Games, Machine-tools, Shoes, Software, Telecommunications, and Textile/Apparel. He is currently engaged in research about International Operations and coordinates a large project about the internationalization of firms from emerging economies at the Centre for Technology Policy and Management at USP. He is Associate Editor of the *Journal of Manufacturing Technology Management* and Regional Editor of *Operations Management Research*.

MARIA TEREZA LEME FLEURY is Dean of FGV-EAESP (Escola de Administração de Empresas de São Paulo da Fundação Getulio Vargas) and a professor at FEA-USP (Faculdade de Administração, Economia e Contabilidade – University of Sao Paulo) in Brazil. From 1998 to 2006 she was Dean and deputy-Dean of FEA-USP. She has a PhD in Sociology from the University of Sao Paulo. She is Director of ANPAD, a member of FAPESP, and a member of the research board of EUROMED in France. Her research and professional experience are in the areas of international management, competency management, and culture and learning.

ANDREW GODLEY is a Professor of Management and Business History and Director of the Henley Centre for Entrepreneurship at the Henley Business School, University of Reading, in the UK. He has a PhD from the London School of Economics and Political Science. His research interests lie in the area of business history and the economics of entrepreneurship and innovation, with a particular focus on the international food and pharmaceutical sectors. He has been a consultant to several leading companies and government departments and is a frequent commentator in the broadcast and written media on industry trends.

DONALD LESSARD is the EPOCH Foundation Professor of International Management Emeritus at the Sloan School of Management, Massachusetts Institute of Technology, in the USA. He earned his PhD in Business Administration from Stanford University. His research interests are on global strategic management and project management, with an emphasis on managing in the face of uncertainty and risk and in the energy sector. A leader in international management education, he is a Fellow, past Dean of the Fellows, and past President of the Academy of International Business.

KLAUS E. MEYER is a Professor of Strategy and International Business at China Europe International Business School (CEIBS) in China, and Adjunct Professor (honorary) at Copenhagen Business School in Denmark. He received a PhD from London Business School. Professor Meyer's current research focuses on strategies of multinational enterprises in emerging economies. He is Deputy-Editor-in-Chief of *Management and Organization Review*, a consulting editor of the *Journal of International Business Studies,* and is serving as a vice president of the Academy of International Business. He is also a Fellow of the Academy of International Business.

RAM MUDAMBI is a professor at Temple University in the USA. He completed his Master's degree at the London School of Economics and Political Science and his PhD at Cornell University. Professor Mudambi's current research focuses on technology and innovation management, studying both multinational as well as entrepreneurial companies, and the geography of innovation is one of his main research interests. He has published over 80 refereed journal articles and six books. He has served as an associate editor of *Global Strategy Journal* (2010–13) and a department editor of the *Journal of International Business Studies* (2013–16). He was elected a Fellow of the Academy of International Business in 2012.

RAJNEESH NARULA is a Professor of International Business Regulation and Director of the John H. Dunning Centre for International Business at the Henley Business School, University of Reading, in the UK. He obtained his PhD in Management from Rutgers University. Professor Narula's research and consulting focus is on the internationalization of innovation, R&D alliances, and the role of multinational companies in industrial development. He consults regularly for UNCTAD,

UNIDO, the European Commission, the Inter-American Development Bank, and the OECD.

QUYEN T. K. NGUYEN is a Lecturer of International Business and Strategy at Henley Business School, University of Reading, in the UK. She received her PhD from the University of Reading. Her research focuses on multinational subsidiary strategy and subsidiary performance. Before joining academia, she had 13 years of professional and managerial experience in accounting, finance, and business administration, working for German, US, and New Zealand multinational enterprises in Southeast Asia and Canada.

TORBEN PEDERSEN is a Professor in Global Strategy at Bocconi University, Italy. He received his PhD from the Copenhagen Business School. His research interests are located at the interface between strategy and international business, and focus mainly on globalization, organizational design, offshoring/outsourcing, knowledge management, and subsidiary strategies. He has published more than 100 journal articles and books on these topics. He is Co-editor of the *Global Strategy Journal* and serves on several editorial boards. He is a Fellow of the Academy of International Business and a past vice-president of the Academy of International Business and the European International Business Academy.

RAVI RAMAMURTI is a D'Amore-McKim Distinguished Professor of International Business and Strategy, and Director of the Center for Emerging Markets at Northeastern University's D'Amore-McKim School of Business. He obtained his BSc in Physics from St. Stephen's College, his MBA from the Indian Institute of Management, and his Doctorate in Business Administration from Harvard Business School. Professor Ramamurti's research and consulting have focused on companies operating in, or from, emerging economies. He served on the Executive Committee of the Academy of Management's International Management Division, and in 2008 he was elected a Fellow of the Academy of International Business. He works on innovation and the international competitive advantage of emerging market firms. He has done research in or consulted with companies and governments in more than 20 emerging economies.

ALAN M. RUGMAN is a Professor of International Business and Head of the School of International Business and Strategy at the Henley

Business School, University of Reading, UK. He earned his PhD in Economics from Simon Fraser University. He published his first article in *JIBS* in 1976 and many subsequent papers on the theory of the MNE and its regional strategy, both in *JIBS* and in other leading journals. From 2004 to 2006 he served as President of the Academy of International Business (AIB). Currently he is Dean of the Fellows of AIB.

TAMARA STUCCHI is a Postdoctoral Fellow in the Management Engineering Department at the Technical University of Denmark. She has an MS in Management Engineering from Politecnico di Milano University and a PhD in Economics and Management from Copenhagen Business School. Her research is focused mainly on emerging market firms' internationalization.

PETER J. WILLIAMSON is a Professor of International Management at Judge Business School and Fellow of Jesus College, University of Cambridge, in the UK. He earned his PhD in Business Economics from Harvard University. He has worked with companies in China since 1983 and co-authored two of Asia's best-selling business books: *Dragons at Your Door: How Chinese Cost Innovation Is Disrupting Global Competition* and *Winning in Asia: Strategies for Competing in the New Millennium.*

Foreword

This book is the result of a long journey. During research trips through emerging markets, we noticed that some domestic companies were attaining international levels of competitiveness, despite the many handicaps of their home countries, and venturing into unfamiliar foreign markets. There was understandably a lot of skepticism about whether these firms could compete successfully with established multinational enterprises from advanced economies and become truly global players. Nevertheless, the firms persisted because many of them saw it as vital for their survival, and eventually some grew big enough to join the top-5 or top-10 list of global firms in their respective industries.

Traditional theories of the multinational, which were developed by studying companies in advanced countries, predicted that developing economies could not produce such firms. However, as we learned more about the firms, we realized that studying these firms was actually a powerful way to improve our understanding of multinational enterprises more generally. In other words, EMNCs should not be dismissed as exotic species found only in strange countries (emerging economies), but viewed as the latest wave of globalizing firms through which theories of the multinational enterprise could be revisited.

This book is the result of the Third Conference on Emerging Market Multinationals organized by the Center for Emerging Markets at the D'Amore-McKim School of Business, Northeastern University, on August 4, 2012. That conference followed two previous ones – in 2007 with the Wharton School of the University of Pennsylvania, and in 2011 with the Judge Business School of the University of Cambridge – which led to the publication of *Emerging Multinationals in Emerging Markets* (Ramamurti and Singh, 2009) and *The Competitive Advantage of Emerging Market Multinationals* (Williamson, Ramamurti, Fleury, and Fleury, 2013), both published by Cambridge University Press.

For the third conference, we invited 17 leading scholars to present their views on the topic or to serve as chair-cum-discussants. Panelists were asked to be bold in their thinking and to present new arguments that had not been addressed properly or at all in the literature, rather than present a narrow research study. The discussants for each session critiqued the presenters and offered their own insights, and facilitated a lively debate with the 90-strong audience of senior and junior faculty members from around the world who work on EMNCs. After the conference, authors submitted draft chapters that responded to the questions and comments raised by chairs, discussants, and the audience. Two presenters at the conference were unable to participate in this book (Jean-François Hennart and Robert Hoskisson), and one who did not attend the conference (Andrew Godley) accepted our invitation to write a chapter on a specific topic for the volume.

The book is a synthesis of all these ideas, including deliberations at the conference and feedback provided by the editors in several rounds of review. We hope the ideas presented in the book provide an objective and nuanced view of how the rise of EMNCs relates to the existing literature and our understanding of the multinational firm.

A book like this is the result of a team effort. First and foremost, we owe a deep debt of gratitude to our distinguished contributors, who responded sportingly to our request to take a broad view of the EMNC phenomenon and the literature, including highlighting topics and concepts that did not fit neatly with existing frameworks and models. We also appreciate the contributions of the scholars who served as chairs and discussants at this conference and the faculty who participated actively in the deliberations. The August 2012 conference at Northeastern University was made possible by grants from the D'Amore-McKim School of Business and the Center for Emerging Markets. We would like to thank Dean Hugh Courtney and Senior Associate Dean Margie Platt for financial and moral support throughout the project. Kayne Bordes, Lacey Bradley-Store, Anne Claire Ramsey, and Caitlin Riley provided invaluable logistical support for the conference. Subsequently, we had the good fortune of working yet again with Paula Parish of Cambridge University Press, who guided us in developing the manuscript and was, as usual, very responsive to our questions and requests. Kat Wilson helped polish the manuscript. Last but not least, we are grateful to our families for their support not just with this project but throughout our academic careers. We dedicate this book to them.

1 | Introduction

ALVARO CUERVO-CAZURRA AND
RAVI RAMAMURTI

The aim of this book is to improve our understanding of emerging-market multinational companies (EMNCs) in particular, and how their study contributes to a better understanding of multinational companies (MNCs) in general. Most of the foundational models and theories explaining MNCs were based initially on firms from the advanced economies of North America and Europe, and later Japan. These explanations implicitly assumed that for a domestic firm to invest abroad and become an MNC, it had to be from a country with strong technological and institutional infrastructures and a relatively affluent home market. These conditions were believed to improve its technological and marketing capabilities to the point where it could compete abroad effectively, despite the challenges of operating across borders. Thus, a lot of the initial research on MNCs was focused on understanding how such firms transferred their competitive advantages across borders and leveraged their worldwide presence.

EMNCs were rarely the object of researchers' attention, and their behavior was not considered when the foundational models of the MNC were developed. EMNCs were actually relatively rare firms on the world stage until the 2000s. Except for some state-owned firms in natural resources, many of which had emerged from nationalization processes in the middle of the twentieth century and expanded abroad to ensure access to resources or markets, developing country firms engaged mostly in international trade rather than international investment, importing advanced technologies and exporting raw materials and low-tech manufactures. Many governments in developing countries followed a program of import-substituting industrialization, discouraging inbound foreign direct investment (FDI) and sheltering local firms from international competition, which limited their international competitiveness. Similar conditions prevailed to an even greater extent in Communist bloc countries. The Asian Tigers

1

(Hong Kong, Singapore, South Korea, and Taiwan) were exceptions to this rule and followed export promotion models of economic development even in the 1960s and 1970s, but even they engaged in relatively little FDI. As a result, in 1970, EMNCs represented only 0.35 percent of the world's flows of outward foreign direct investment (OFDI).

Nevertheless, the pro-market reforms that swept through much of the world in the 1980s and 1990s induced, and in some cases led, many governments to open their markets to foreign competition and reduce constraints on local firms. The exposure to foreign competition, and the domestic economic crises that some countries suffered, led the best-managed firms to upgrade their international competitiveness, ramp up exports, and invest in foreign facilities. As a result, the share of EMNCs in the world's OFDI flows rose from 5.05 percent in 2000 to 24.39 percent in 2012. Some EMNCs even became leaders in high-tech industries, such as Huawei of China in telecommunications equipment or Embraer of Brazil in regional jets. Others made bold acquisitions in advanced economies, such as the purchase of the US brewer Miller by the South African firm SAB or the acquisition of the British tea company Tetley by the Indian firm Tata Tea.

This proliferation of EMNCs in the 2000s perplexed managers, consultants, and international business scholars alike, with two questions often arising. Why have relatively poor and underdeveloped countries been able to spawn so many global firms in the last two decades? And second, in what ways are EMNCs different from earlier MNCs that came from Europe, North America, or even Japan?

Before going further, we should clarify what we mean by emerging economies, a popular term coined in 1980 that has taken on a life of its own, displacing old labels such as developing countries, transition economies, and Third World nations. Today, the term often refers to relatively poor countries with high levels of growth that have undertaken pro-market reforms (Wright et al., 2005). However, the term is sometimes used to include countries that are in fact backsliding on reforms, such as Argentina or Venezuela, or countries that are already quite developed, such as Singapore, Taiwan, South Korea, and Hong Kong, whose firms are technologically sophisticated and in many cases indistinguishable from advanced-country MNCs. For the purposes of our discussion, we will use "emerging markets" to mean all countries except the 28 that the International Monetary Fund classified in 2000 as "developed countries."[1]

Given the novelty of the EMNC phenomenon, the first step in answering these questions was to gather basic facts about their origin and evolution. By 2013, that task had been largely accomplished, thanks to several descriptive studies of EMNCs in the business press (e.g., BCG, 2006, 2008, 2009, 2011, 2013; Economist, 2008) and by multilateral organizations (e.g., ECLAC, 2006; UNCTAD, 2006). Several books also discussed how EMNCs were turning into serious competitors of MNCs from advanced economies, based on case studies of leading EMNCs and analyses of their business models for internationalization (e.g., Casanova, 2009; Chattopadhyay et al., 2012; Fleury and Fleury, 2011; Goldstein, 2007; Guillén and Garcia-Canal, 2012; Larçon, 2009; Panibratov, 2012; Ramamurti and Singh, 2009; Santiso, 2013; Sauvant, 2008; Sauvant et al., 2010; van Agtmael, 2007; Yeung et al., 2011; Williamson et al., 2013; Zeng and Williamson, 2007).

This volume was motivated by a very specific goal. While prior work on EMNCs, including our own, often concludes with a discussion of implications for theory, the raison d'être of this book is to improve our theoretical understanding of EMNCs. We believe the time is ripe to take stock of how the field is developing, so that future research by scholars and consultants can be directed at under-studied topics and lead eventually to a deeper understanding of the internationalization process and the behavior of multinational enterprises (Cuervo-Cazurra, 2012; Ramamurti, 2012).

We aim to do this in three ways. The first is by comparing and contrasting EMNCs with advanced-economy MNCs, whose experiences were the basis for extant theory of the MNC. Specifically, we ask how existing arguments and theories need to be modified to account for differences between advanced-country MNCs and EMNCs. Second, we strive to compare and contrast EMNCs from different countries with one another, looking for explanations for observed variations, including country-of-origin effects. And, finally, we identify a research agenda that identifies topics deserving more attention from

---

[1] These are: Australia, Austria, Belgium, Canada, Denmark, Finland, France, Germany, Greece, Hong Kong, Iceland, Ireland, Israel, Italy, Japan, Luxembourg, Netherlands, New Zealand, Norway, Portugal, Singapore, South Korea, Spain, Sweden, Switzerland, Taiwan, United Kingdom, and the United States.

scholars and consultants than they have received so far, in the hope that these topics will be picked for research in the future. Each of these approaches in order is illustrated by a research question below:

- How are EMNCs able to compete globally when, unlike advanced-country MNCs, they lack sophisticated technology? It is often the case that advanced-country MNCs were technological pioneers and leaders in their industries and used that advantage to internationalize. In contrast, most EMNCs are technological laggards, and yet several of them have been able to compete globally. Why has this been possible, and what does it imply for the nature of competitive advantages firms must possess in order to internationalize?

- How does a firm's home country affect its internationalization? Many studies look at how characteristics of the host country affect a firm's choice of target markets and modes of entry, but relatively few look at how an MNC's home country affects its competitive advantages and internationalization strategy. The diversity of emerging economies covered by contributors to this volume provides an excellent opportunity to understand how a firm's country of origin affects its internationalization.

- Why do some EMNCs relocate their headquarters from an emerging economy to an advanced economy, and what does that mean for an MNC's "nationality"? Some EMNCs have moved their headquarters to advanced economies to escape the limitations of their home countries, or to overcome the negative connotations of their emerging-market roots in the mind of customers. This is an example of an under-explored topic, because advanced-country MNCs seldom shifted their headquarters to another country as part of their evolution, whereas several EMNCs have done so.

Overview of the book

This volume consists of 12 chapters clustered into three sections on different facets of EMNCs. The first section consists of chapters that take a historical view of EMNCs or argue for more research that extracts the lessons of history. Going back into the past with a critical view helps evaluate the newness of EMNCs in a more objective manner.

Yair Aharoni reviews the literature on the MNC in general and on the EMNC in particular, identifying several distinct features of EMNCs that warrant additional study. First, it is intriguing how quickly some EMNCs have become dominant players in their industries, and what the sources of their competitive advantage are. EMNCs do not appear to have the same sources of advantage as advanced economy MNCs, which were mostly based on innovative products, and instead appear to have developed new innovations in organization and management. Second, there is a need to better understand the influence of the government as owner of some EMNCs. State ownership raises new questions about some of the reasons behind the foreign expansion of these firms and about their ability to compete with advanced economy MNCs and with private EMNCs. Third, the notion of the home country of the firm is crucial in the study of EMNCs, since it is not fully clear how the home country affects the behavior and internationalization of firms. Fourth, EMNCs bring to the fore the ability of a firm to buy rather than build international management teams, and the role of these managers in the internationalization and performance of the firm. Finally, there are several factors that warrant more detailed analysis as they modify not only existing theories of the MNCs but also conclusions driven from analyzing EMNCs: the industry of operation, the level of technology required to compete, the size of the firm, differences in market structures, and differences in institutions across countries.

Andrew Godley complements this analysis from a historical vantage point by cautioning that some of the distinctive features of EMNCs are not so new after all, because they have occurred in the past in different guises. First, the rapid catch up of these firms to global leaders is not a particularly unique feature, as the catching up of the then-backward German firms to the more advanced British ones in the nineteenth century illustrates. Second, developing sources of competitive advantage despite operating in countries with limited supporting infrastructure does not appear to be a unique feature of EMNCs, but it is nevertheless important to analyze them in more detail. Third, coordinating operations across borders via networks that some EMNCs appear to be using is also a feature that was present in the nineteenth and early twentieth century among MNCs from advanced countries, although many of these firms later adopted hierarchical structures.

The second section analyzes the mechanisms that facilitate or hinder EMNCs' efforts to upgrade their capabilities to international levels in order to compete in global markets. Among other things, the underdeveloped nature of innovation systems and institutions in developing countries creates special challenges for these latecomers to upgrade their capabilities to international levels.

Alan Rugman and Quyen Nguyen kick off this section with a skeptical view of the competitive advantages of EMNCs. They argue that, despite the increasing attention paid to the internationalization of emerging market firms, most EMNCs are still quite heavily focused on their domestic markets, and many EMNCs are underperforming financially, even when they have grown and internationalized rapidly. They argue that a better understanding of the capabilities for international expansion of EMNCs requires an understanding of how firms' specific capabilities are built on a country's comparative advantage, and that EMNCs are mostly building their international expansion on their home country's comparative advantages.

Rajneesh Narula dwells deeper into the concept of location advantage. He questions whether all firms have access to a home-country's location advantage, and what causes some firm-specific advantages to be location bound. He argues that access to the comparative advantage of the home country, which in many cases is the foundation of EMNCs' firm-specific advantages, is not as straightforward as assumed by many authors. The advantage of a location needs to be thought of as being a club good, with limited access, rather than a public good, with open access to all. He argues that firms are locally embedded and encounter significant barriers to change as the environment changes, which also limits their ability to enter new locations abroad. This reconceptualization adds a useful twist to the challenges EMNCs face in upgrading their capabilities.

Donald Lessard challenges the notion that EMNCs lack capabilities to compete in global markets. He argues that changes in the operational environment have resulted in new phenomena, such as EMNCs, and new ways of organizing cross-border economic relationships, such as Global Value Chain Enterprises (GVCEs) that use relational arrangements instead of ownership to compete globally. He introduces the Relevant-Appropriable-Transferable and Complementary-Appropriable-Transferable framework for the identification and accumulation of advantages through a continuous self-reinforcing process of exploitation and enhancement of capabilities by EMNCs and GVCEs. Thus, the study of EMNCs offers the basis for understanding different bases of competitive advantage.

Kristin Brandl and Ram Mudambi identify how catch-up processes followed by EMNCs vary across industries. To successfully internationalize, firms need to start catching up with the capabilities of their advanced-country rivals. As latecomers, EMNCs have the advantage of being able to follow in the footsteps of advanced-economy firms, but the specifics of the catch-up process seem to vary across industries. Brandl and Mudambi's comparison of catch-up processes by Indian firms in the auto component, pharmaceutical, filmed entertainment, and wind turbine industries following the country's pro-market reforms reveals interesting differences driven by the level of technological sophistication of the industries and the interaction between local firms and advanced-economy MNCs.

The third section focuses on distinctive aspects of the internationalization processes of EMNCs. Advances in communication and transportation technologies and the economic liberalization that has accompanied pro-market reforms have created a more hospitable global environment for internationalization by EMNCs. However, many of their actions are driven not just by these environmental conditions, but also by unique aspects of EMNCs.

Peter Williamson identifies three areas in which research on EMNCs can yield new insights by challenging the assumptions of existing theoretical arguments. The first is exploring the differing sources of competitive advantage that support EMNCs' internationalization, based partly on the distinctive kinds of comparative advantage enjoyed by their home countries. Some of these advantages are especially relevant in a world where developing countries are becoming increasingly important markets and consumers even in advanced countries are looking for value for money. The second area is to understand how the easier movement of goods and information across countries helps firms internationalize, establish global value chains to help create new sources of advantage, organize production across borders differently, and achieve leadership in mature industries. The third line of inquiry is to understand how EMNCs rely on learning as a leading driver of internationalization, in contrast to the traditional approach of advanced-country MNCs, which is to exploit existing capabilities in new markets abroad. In other words, EMNCs often internationalize to overcome deficiencies at home rather than to exploit pre-existing advantages abroad. This has implications for how they enter new markets, transfer advantages across borders, and integrate resources and capabilities.

Klaus Meyer goes deeper into the internationalization of EMNCs by arguing that EMNCs follow a logic in their internationalization process that differs from the traditional model of expanding abroad in incremental steps to minimize risk. He proposes that the crucial role of learning in such an incremental process can also be applied fruitfully to understand the international expansion of EMNCs, albeit with modifications to reflect the changed global conditions under which EMNCs are globalizing.

Helena Barnard introduces the concept of the migrating multinational as a novel explanation of the internationalization of EMNCs. She argues that EMNCs may encounter some negative discrimination by foreign consumers and governments because they hail from emerging economies. To overcome this disadvantage, some EMNCs have moved their headquarters to advanced countries, to disguise their country of origin. In turn, this challenges our understanding of what is meant by the "nationality" of MNCs, because, as Barnard points out, multiple criteria can be used to determine the nationality of firms: their place of incorporation, stock market listing, principal market for products and services, historical roots, nationality of senior management, and so on. Not only does this make it difficult to identify the nationality of EMNCs, it also creates difficulties in establishing legitimacy in various markets.

Torben Pedersen and Tamara Stucchi argue that business groups and pro-market reforms have led to particular patterns of global expansion of EMNCs. Business groups, or collections of legally independent firms that coordinate operations in diverse industries, are a notable feature of emerging markets and some advanced economies. As emerging economies have engaged in pro-market reforms, business groups have helped member firms internationalize by leveraging the group's experience, resources, and connections, but in other ways they have hindered the internationalization of member firms, because they are so deeply embedded in the home country.

Afonso Fleury and Maria Tereza Fleury explain how the home country institutions and macroeconomic policies have affected the capabilities, internationalization trajectories, and global value chains of EMNCs, drawing on the experience of Brazilian MNCs. They argue that the historical development and conditions of the country have resulted in firms that compete abroad using process and business model innovations; that seek other countries with weak institutions and prefer to achieve a high degree of control over the operations; and that configure global value chains differently depending on the location of the subsidiaries, with those in developing countries exploiting existing advantages and those in advanced economies learning, although they still face coordination challenges.

In the concluding chapter, we abstract from these themes and provide an overview of our understanding of the EMNC phenomenon, literature, and unique drivers of the internationalization of EMNCs. We provide a critical review of the relative importance of EMNCs in the context of increased OFDI in the twenty-first century, showing that the large increase in OFDI from emerging economies is part of a general trend of OFDI growth. We review the literature on EMNCs, identify factors that have been argued to be unique to EMNCs, and caution that in reality many of these factors affect EMNCs and advanced economy MNCs alike. We then provide a framework to help identify unique aspects of EMNC internationalization, focusing particularly on the role of a firm's country of origin on its international behavior. We propose that the economic and institutional under-development that characterizes developing countries leads to distinctive internationalization behavior by EMNCs. Both contextual factors have positive implications for how these firms innovate at home and use those innovations to expand abroad, but they also have negative implications, inasmuch as they force EMNCs to internationalize to overcome the limitations of the home country.

We hope this book not only addresses an important phenomenon in international business but also paves the way for high-quality research of value to academics, consultants, and managers. Towards that end, in the concluding chapter we offer a research agenda on EMNCs that could only have been developed through the collective effort of a distinguished group of scholars such as our contributors. Pursuing such a research agenda should improve our collective understanding of not just EMNCs, but the multinational enterprise in general.

References

BCG. 2006. *The New Global Challengers: How 100 Top Companies from Rapidly Developing Economies Are Changing the World*. Boston, MA: Boston Consulting Group.

2008. *The 2008 BCG 100 New Global Challengers: How Top Companies from Rapidly Developing Economies Are Changing the World*. Boston, MA: Boston Consulting Group.

2009. *The 2009 BCG 100 New Global Challengers: How Companies from Rapidly Developing Economies Are Contending for Global Leadership*. Boston, MA: Boston Consulting Group.

2011. *2011 BCG Global Challengers. Companies on the Move: Rising Stars from Rapidly Developing Economies Are Reshaping Global Industries*. Boston, MA: Boston Consulting Group.

2013. *Allies and Adversaries: 2013 BCG Global Challengers*. Boston, MA: Boston Consulting Group.

Casanova, L. 2009. *Global Latinas: Latin America's Emerging Multinationals*. Fontainebleau, France: Insead Business Press.

Chattopadhyay, A., Batra, R., and Ozsomer, A. 2012. *The New Emerging Market Multinationals: Four Strategies for Disrupting Markets and Building Brands*. New York: McGraw Hill.

Cuervo-Cazurra, A. 2012. How the analysis of developing country multinational companies helps advance theory: Solving the Goldilocks debate. *Global Strategy Journal*, 2: 153–167.

ECLAC. 2006. *Foreign Investment in Latin America and the Caribbean 2005*. Santiago de Chile: ECLAC.

Economist. 2008. Emerging-market multinationals: The challengers. *The Economist*, January 10th. www.economist.com/node/10496684. Accessed February 19, 2013.

Fleury, A. and Fleury, M. T. L. 2011. *Brazilian Multinationals: Competences for Internationalization*. Cambridge University Press.

Goldstein, A. 2007. *Multinational Companies from Emerging Economies: Composition, Conceptualization and Direction in the Global Economy*. New York: Palgrave MacMillan.

Guillén, M. and Garcia-Canal, E. 2012. *Emerging Markets Rule: Growth Strategies of the New Global Giants*. New York: McGraw Hill.

Larçon, J. P. 2009. *Chinese Multinationals*. Singapore: World Scientific.

Panibratov, A. 2012. *Russian Multinationals: From Regional Supremacy to Global Lead*. London: Routledge.

Ramamurti, R. 2012. What is really different about emerging market multinationals? *Global Strategy Journal*, 2: 41–47.

Ramamurti, R. and Singh, J. V. (eds.). 2009. *Emerging Multinationals in Emerging Markets*. Cambridge University Press.

Santiso, J. 2013. *The Decade of the Multilatinas*. Cambridge University Press.

Sauvant, K. 2008. *The Rise of Transnational Corporations from Emerging Markets: Threat or Opportunity?* Cheltenham: Edward Elgar.

Sauvant, K., Maschek, W., and McAllister, G. 2010. *Foreign Direct Investments from Emerging Markets: The Challenges Ahead.* New York: Palgrave MacMillan.

UNCTAD. 2006. *World Investment Report 2006: FDI from Developing and Transition Economies: Implications for Development.* Geneva: United Nations Conference on Trade and Development.

van Agtmael, A. 2007. *The Emerging Markets Century: How a New Breed of World-Class Companies Is Overtaking the World.* New York: Free Press.

Williamson, P., Ramamurti, R., Fleury, A., and Fleury, M. T. (eds.). 2013. *The Competitive Advantage of Emerging Market Multinationals.* Cambridge University Press.

Wright, M., Filatotchev, I., Hoskisson, R. E., and Peng, M. W. 2005. Strategy research in emerging economies: Challenging the conventional wisdom. *Journal of Management Studies,* 42: 1–33.

Yeung, A., Xin, K., Pfoertsch, W., and Liu, S. 2011. *The Globalization of Chinese Companies: Strategies for Conquering International Markets.* New York: John Wiley.

Zeng, M. and Williamson, P. 2007. *Dragons at Your Door.* Boston, MA: Harvard Business Press.

EMNCs *in historical perspective: what is new?*

2 | Theoretical debates on multinationals from emerging economies

YAIR AHARONI

For several decades, the theory of international business assumed that MNCs "concentrated mainly in knowledge-intensive industries characterized by high levels of research and development (R&D) expenditure and advertising expenditure, and by the employment of skilled labor" (Buckley and Casson, 2009: 1563). Firms in emerging markets do not have the capabilities to compete against these MNCs and should concentrate on being production workshops. In contrast to this view, a spate of firms from emerging market economies increasingly expanded their operations by foreign direct investments in other countries, including the advanced economies. These developments call for a reflection from both historical and theoretical viewpoints – was the theory wrong? Do these firms have firm-specific advantages? If so, what are they? How different is the internationalization process of these firms? Further, many of these firms are state-owned. Does ownership matter and, if so, how? What are the ramifications of government involvement in business operations to the international economic order?

I start with a brief survey of the historical evolution of theories explaining the existence of international production, and then turn to the case of emerging market multinationals. I then suggest areas I consider to be important for future research. In keeping with the purpose of this volume, I try to be provocative.

Birth of theories of MNCs

The phenomenon of multinational companies (MNCs) was an enigma for classical economists. There was no satisfactory explanation for their existence. Why do some firms erect plants in foreign countries and others not? Indeed, international economic textbooks chose for many years to ignore the phenomena of foreign direct investment (FDI) and MNCs, and concentrated instead on international trade.

While most international economists likewise ignored FDIs, there were a few exceptions. John Dunning studied American investment in the British manufacturing industry (1958). In the 1960s, Raymond Vernon directed the Multinational Enterprise Project at Harvard Business School that assembled data on US-based multinationals. Because his major concern was the relations of governments and MNCs, Vernon defined a firm as being a multinational if it was listed in the Fortune 500 and had subsidiaries in at least six countries (Vernon, 1971). Vernon's doctoral candidates looked at these organizations in terms of finance, organization, production, marketing, and business–government relations. His own interest was in the relations between these firms and the nation-state.

Stephen Hymer's doctoral thesis of 1960, published in 1976, was one of the first to offer a theory of why a firm produces abroad rather than simply exports from its home country. His explanation assumed that such firms have some monopolistic advantage that allows them to overcome the additional costs of foreign operations and compete successfully against domestic firms. It stands to reason that prior investments in R&D and marketing resulted in these disproportional advantages. Since his seminal work, firm specific advantages (FSAs) or ownership advantages have become a cornerstone of international business (IB) theory.

In 1977, John Dunning published the first statement of the ownership-location-internalization (OLI) paradigm (Dunning, 1977). He identified three potential sources of advantage that may explain a firm's decision to become a multinational. Ownership advantages, following Hymer, explained why some firms but not others were MNCs: these firms possessed some firm-specific advantages that allowed them to overcome the costs of operating in a foreign country. Location advantages, later called country-specific advantages, focused on the question of where an MNC chooses to locate. Finally, internalization advantages explain why certain activities are carried out within firms while others are done through arm's-length transactions. Since the 1977 paper, Dunning has refined and extended his paradigm in many other papers (Narula, 2010). Other researchers analyzed MNCs through different lenses. Forsgren (2013) analyzes and compares six theoretical perspectives of the MNC used by different researchers to explain it as an actor in the global economy. The first perspective is that of Hymer, in which the MNC is portrayed as dominating because of its market power. The second perspective is the coordinating MNC, which is based on transaction cost theory. It emphasizes the ability of the firm to internalize such transactions and coordinate them across borders. The third perspective emphasizes the knowing MNC: a tale of value creation. This perspective is rooted in the resource-based view of the firm. It emphasizes the process of creation of unique knowledge. A fourth view, according to Forsgren, is the designing multinational. This approach stresses the ability of MNCs to adapt their organization and control systems to changes in the environment. A fifth perspective is the networking multinational: a tale of business relationships. It is based on resource dependence theory and emphasizes business relationships with customers, suppliers, and other counterparts. The business network, in which each subsidiary is embedded, has a profound impact on the strategic decisions of the multinational firm. The sixth and final perspective emphasizes legitimacy and power, as well as the political side and role of the MNC.

The initial attempts to explain the existence of the MNC and the way that it behaves seem to have ignored several issues. First, while Raymond Vernon defined an MNC as operating in at least six countries, UNCTAD and most scholars today accept the definition of an MNC as operating in two or more countries. This difference in definition is particularly important when the MNC–government relations are considered. The more spread out the MNC, the greater its ability to avoid single state regulations. Second, MNCs were defined as giant firms, but size does not determine their nature as MNCs. Third, until very recently most academic work on MNCs analyzed the "greenfield" mode of FDI. However, according to UNCTAD, cross-border mergers and acquisitions (M&As) accounted for over 80 percent of worldwide FDI in the 1990s; the motives for M&A may be synergy or gains from absorbing a rival. Further, many FDIs are not accounted for in the official statistics. Thus, code sharing agreements and other forms of strategic alliances are excluded. Finally, until the 1980s it was taken for granted that MNCs were firms from advanced economies. The activities of these MNCs were assumed to enjoy firm-specific advantages, mainly because of brands and high levels of R&D expenditure.

MNCs from emerging economies

The first wave of recognition for the existence of emerging market multinational companies (EMNCs) appeared in the 1980s. Lou Wells published his book on Third World multinationals (Wells, 1983), and a few other scholars researched or discussed these firms as well (Ghymn, 1980; Kumar and McLeod, 1981; Lall, 1983; Lecraw, 1977).

These researchers attempted to explain how it was possible for EMNCs to compete against rivals from advanced economies. Two sets of explanations were suggested. First, these firms used outdated and simple technologies, produced low-priced products, and focused on labor-intensive production because of the abundance of inexpensive labor in their home countries. Second, EMNCs enjoyed a greater capability for adapting products to the specific demands of import-protected emerging markets. In other words, these firms enjoyed advantages because they were under-developed. Since the advantages were related to operations in emerging markets, it was taken for granted that EMNCs could not compete against firms from advanced economies or in free-market economies.

Since the 1990s, however, EMNCs have competed quite successfully in advanced and free-market economies, and some of them are becoming world leaders in their respective industries. They are challenging some of the world's most accomplished advanced-economy multinationals in a wide variety of industries, thus changing the competitive landscape. Moreover, these EMNCs have grown very fast both in numbers and as a percentage of global FDI outflows. Whereas the share of emerging markets in global stock of outward FDI was zero in 1969, it soared to 12.7% in 1980, declined to 8.3% in 1990, and recovered to 15.9% in 2009. In terms of outward FDI flows, the share of emerging markets – excluding transitional economies – out of global OFDI flows zoomed from almost zero in 1970 to 1.9% in 1975, 6.2% in 1980, 6.4% in 1985, 15.3% in 1995, 27.6% in 2010, and 22.3% in 2011. Figure 2.1 illustrates this fast growth.

In addition, in what might be termed the second wave of EMNCs, many of these firms were state-owned. Two-thirds of emerging-market companies listed in the *Fortune* 500 are state-owned. So are many of the new MNCs. Ian Bremmer, an analyst of political risk, argues that what we term "State Capitalism" is growing (Bremmer, 2010). In this regime, governments use markets to achieve political goals. Politics lead governments to establish national oil and gas corporations, as well as other types of state-owned enterprises (SOEs). Governments also subsidize "National Champions." These are privately owned firms that are expected not only to seek profit but also to advance the interests of the nation. Governments subsidize such firms to achieve

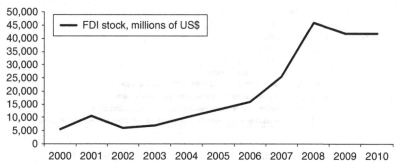

Figure 2.1 Outward FDI from selected emerging markets to advanced economies.
Source: OECD.Stat.

national objectives. This policy has been practiced by many countries, most recently in Russia. A final tool is the Sovereign Wealth Funds, which controlled about $4.8 trillion in assets in the early 2010s. By the end of this decade, that figure is likely to rise to $10 trillion. The concentration of power in an inner circle of SOEs has been gathering pace over the past decade: China's 121 biggest SOEs, for example, saw their total assets increase from $360 billion in 2002 to $2.9 trillion in 2010 (though their share of GDP has declined). This was given an extra boost by the 2007–08 financial crises: in 2009, some 85 percent of China's $1.4 trillion in bank loans went to state-owned companies. Figure 2.2 shows the share of state-controlled companies in the MSCI emerging market index by industry.

The proliferation and tremendous growth of the EMNCs have taken IB scholars by surprise. The unexpected rise to prominence of these EMNCs has raised several interesting issues. First, how can these firms compete? In other words, do they enjoy ownership advantages, and if so what are they? Several researchers believe these firms do not have any ownership advantages and therefore will soon perish (e.g., Rugman and Li, 2007). Still, if they do not have any ownership advantages, how do they compete? Others suggest that companies from emerging markets have pursued distinctive approaches to internationalization and they enjoy different specific advantages than advanced-economy MNCs. As one example, a study of the global white goods industry (Bonaglia, Goldstein, and Mathews, 2007) posits that Haier (China), Mabe (Mexico), and Arçelik (Turkey) have internationalized

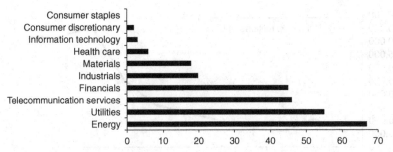

Figure 2.2 Share of national/state-controlled companies in MSCI emerging-market index by industry sector (June 2011, percentage).
Source: Deustche Bank as reported in the *Economist* (2012).

in ways that do not simply recapitulate the experiences of the earlier MNCs that are the incumbents today. Rather, they leveraged their strategic partnerships with established MNCs to upgrade their operations, evolving from the production of simple goods into new product lines developed through their own design, branding, and marketing capabilities. The recipe for their success has been "the ability to treat global competition as an opportunity to build capabilities, move into more profitable industry segments, and adopt strategies that turn latecomer status into a source of competitive advantage" (Bonaglia, Goldstein, and Mathews, 2007: 380–381). The authors of this study conclude that "their experiences show that there are many strategies and trajectories for going global" (369). In other words, these EMNCs did not exploit existing firm-specific advantages. Instead, they all internationalized very rapidly, and succeeded in their internationalization not through technological advantage, but through organizational innovations that successfully adapted to the circumstances of the emerging global economy. More generally, several researchers suggest that EMNCs developed strategic innovations that enabled them to exploit their latecomer and peripheral status. These firms have many different types of advantages, which are different from the traditional advantages analyzed in MNCs from advanced economies. For example, they are said to have better political capabilities, or superior abilities to operate in harsh institutional environments in other developing countries. These EMNCs are said to be more used to dealing with unstable governments in their home country. Therefore, they are able to succeed in foreign countries characterized by a weak institutional environment

(Cantwell and Barnard, 2008; Cuervo-Cazurra and Genc, 2008; Dunning and Lundan, 2008). Williamson and Zeng (2009) suggest that EMNCs leverage home country-specific advantages such as natural resources and cheap labor. Buckley et al. (2007) stress privileged access to cheap capital, either because of government subsidies or as a result of imperfections in the domestic capital market. Others argue that EMNCs do not go abroad to exploit existing firm-specific advantages, but rather to explore new ones. In other words, they internationalize in order to build their advantages and engage in knowledge asset seeking in foreign markets – a reversal of the traditional perspective (Dunning, 2006; Dunning, Kim, and Park, 2008; Goldstein, 2007; Hoskisson et al., 2000; Luo and Tang, 2007; Mathews, 2002). For useful discussions on the debate see Cuervo-Cazurra (2012) and Ramamurti (2012).

A related question is: Can the existence of EMNCs be explained by extant theories, or does their rise imply the demise of these theories? OLI theory posits that MNCs must possess FSAs that allow them to overcome the liability of foreignness. These FSAs are assumed to be based on technological or marketing capabilities. An extreme position already mentioned is that these new MNCs do not possess these classic FSAs and therefore will perish (Rugman and Li, 2007). The other side of the extreme is that these firms represent a new species and so new theory is needed (Mathews, 2002). In between are those that claim the core explanation for the existence of MNCs is valid. The new MNCs do possess valuable but nonconventional FSAs, e.g., political and networking skills. For example, "firm specific advantages originate from, or are reinforced by, home country institutions" (Wang et al., 2012: 671). Another issue is whether the expertise of these firms is replicable. If a firm learns, for example, what the Mexican cement producer CEMEX did to become a giant, can it replicate that to also become a multinational?

Some basic issues

Having briefly surveyed the existing research on EMNCs, I would like next to raise certain basic issues. The first one is, what is the meaning of an MNC's "home country"? And does it really matter for the operations of the MNC and for the home country's government? The first dimension of this issue is whether an MNC's home market needs to be large. Many theories of international business came from the United States, which happens to be a relatively large country in terms of population – not as large as China, but certainly much larger than Israel, for instance. Therefore, most of my friends in the United States believe that you have to have a big home market in order to be multinational. Michael Porter, in his discussion of the competitive advantage of nations, certainly emphasized the necessity of a large home market in his "diamond" (Porter, 1990). But I come from a small country, Israel, which also has many multinationals. How and why were they successful? Obviously, I was very interested in this issue and wrote extensively on small countries. Some of my specific conclusions on Israeli MNCs are discussed, e.g., in Aharoni (2009). Here, it is enough to note that that they were successful despite coming from a small country. One possibility is that firms from small countries establish positions in a large country such as the United States, taking advantage of what Rugman and D'Cruz (1993) called the "double diamond." In other words, the MNC from the small country establishes a base in a large country such as the United States. As a general observation, the Israeli firms were extremely successful when they focused on a very clear segment that they were able to dominate – starting with a small segment and growing to a larger one. They developed a global supply chain in which each country specialized in the part of the product or service for which it enjoyed a comparative advantage. Finally, developing FSAs requires a deep understanding of the environment, but also of the strengths and weaknesses of the firm. In this sense, it is important to avoid dogmas of "generic strategies." The industry analysis is crucial, but a firm would be much more successful creating a new industry, or defining a well-differentiated segment within an industry that it can dominate, and avoiding direct competition with established firms.

A second dimension of the home-country issue is how an MNC's home country is defined. Specifically, what are the consequences for the home economy of having multinationals? As one example, if China were to use its foreign exchange reserves to buy American firms, will the acquired firms now become Chinese? And if indeed they are now Chinese, exactly what does that mean or imply? What is the meaning of being home-based? An interesting reference to this question is Reich (1990), who claimed that Ford Motor was not an American company but Toyota was, because Toyota created more jobs in the United States than Ford. This is one way of looking at it, but there are other possible criteria. One possibility is to identify whether the top management team is composed of home-country citizens. Yet the real question is how the home base affects the strategic decisions of the firm. Will the firm invest more in China? And so on. Basically, I suggest that we do not know very much about the meaning of an MNC's home country and we should study this issue much more thoroughly than we have up to now.

A second basic issue is whether a firm's top management can be acquired. My inclination is to assume that if an EMNC has money, it can acquire advanced-economy firms. Through such an acquisition it will enjoy excellent management, with all the firm-specific advantages and ownership advantages of the acquired firm. My friend Ravi Ramamurti argued when we discussed this question that you have to be a good manager to be able to acquire other management teams or companies. In other words, emerging market firms may not possess the knowledge as to who or what should be acquired, but I think such expertise can also be bought. At this juncture, the issue is not settled. Anyway, it is still a very interesting question. Can a Chinese firm, for example, simply acquire foreign firms in other countries and then these firms would by definition thus instantly become Chinese multinationals? Think of the Chinese computer manufacturer Lenovo becoming a multinational simply by acquiring the personal computer division of the American information technology firm IBM in 2004. The issue is of course broader than that single computer business. This question has broad ramifications and is extremely important.

A third basic issue is the role of governments. Governments are becoming more sophisticated in using the market to the advantage of their nations as well as owners. As I argued before, SOEs can be managed well. Governments can protect and leverage what Alan Rugman calls country-specific advantages, allowing only certain firms to benefit from these advantages. Several researchers are interested more in the effect of state ownership on the strategy and competitive advantage of these SOEs. Unfortunately, too often their conclusions are based on ideological beliefs, not facts. For example, the *Economist* published a special report on state-capitalism (*Economist*, 2012) that concluded that SOEs should be privatized because they were not doing well. But this conclusion was based on values about how societies should be run, not on any economic or business theory. In fact, most studies of the performance of SOEs compare these firms to an ideal of perfect market with full information (Aharoni, 1986, 2000). My view is that ownership *per se* does not matter. I have spent dozens of years studying SOEs and concluded that what matters is how managers and directors are nominated and chosen. If they are chosen and nominated for political reasons, then you have political influence in the firm, the managers are more politically oriented, and you have a problem. If they are chosen because of their professional qualifications, however, there is no difference between an SOE and any well-managed, private investor-owned firm. These are of course important topics for research. To be sure, in some economic activities such as oil and other energy sources, governments tend to interfere in the operations of the markets. However, the intervention is not restricted to SOEs, but also and equally so affects investor-owned firms. Even the ardent believers in unfettered markets tend to agree that governments should regulate certain economic activities, be it for security reasons or because of market failures. Governments have many tools of intervention, of which ownership is one. The relations between governments and managers of SOEs can be structured to achieve efficiency rather than political power (Aharoni and Ascher, 1998). As a recent example, the UK created the UK Financial Investments Limited on November 3, 2008. UKFI is set up as a company under the Companies Act with the Treasury as the sole shareholder. The stated goal of the structure is to adopt institutional arrangements for keeping UKFI at arm's-length from the government, centered on a heavyweight UKFI board to make all major decisions (HM Treasury, 2008).

A last basic point I would like to make is to revive the explanation of MNCs put forward by Robert Aliber (1970, 1971). According to him, the competitive advantage of an MNC was its access to hard currencies and therefore lower financial costs. This theoretical contribution seems to have been neglected and forgotten since then by IB scholars as finance theory moved to the efficient markets assumption. However, one reason why some countries may spawn more MNCs than others is that their firms have access to hard currency and can use that advantage to acquire other firms in other countries.

A provocative critique

In the embryonic stage of management theory it was believed that there were universal rules of the game, which should be followed by all firms. Then came the Hawthorne experiments, through which we found out that human beings also mattered. Since the 1960s, management theory has moved from the rigid universal rules to a contingency theory.

Unfortunately, IB theory still attempts to function based only on universal rules. My view is that we should think about which variables make a difference and develop a contingency theory of international business. One such variable is industry. For example, the airline industry is governed by a regulatory regime designed after World War II that prevents airlines from globalizing through international acquisitions. They also cannot take off or land wherever they like, and so on. As another example, despite much talk about the globalization of health care, in most countries it is still tightly regulated by governments. The only globalization of health care is some so-called medical tourism. A final example is accountants, which I studied and found not to follow the theory about manufacturing MNCs (Aharoni, 1999).

A second variable may be the level of technology: it seems that high-tech industries are different in important ways from low-tech industries. For example, high-tech industries need a high level of research and development expenditures, and the life cycle of their products is very short.

A third important variable is the size of firms. When Ray Vernon designed his study of multinationals, all 187 firms in his sample were from the *Fortune* 500 list. When I pointed out to him that a firm called International Flavors and Fragrances was more multinational than most firms in his sample, his response was, "This is not part of my sample because it's not in the *Fortune* 500." As a result, the 187 multinationals he studied were not a sample representative of all multinationals. They represented only firms that were a part of this one list of large publicly traded firms, and they controlled a very significant part of the world economy. However, Vernon's sample ignored small multinational firms.

Two other possible contingency variables are market structure and institutions, which differ across countries, possibly because of differences in national culture. Thus, one problem of a small country is that the probability of just a few firms dominating the national economy is very high. Such domination often results not only in economic consequences but also in political influence of these firms. Institutions in the United States are based on a strong ideological belief in the superiority of the individual. Other countries' cultures cherish reciprocal aid of individuals as a part of the community. The culture of *guanxi* (connections) in China leads to yet different institutions. Countries also differ in the degree to which their citizens rely on trust, loyalty, and authority relations. Members of the diamond exchange move millions of dollars without any legal documents – based on a trust in other members of the clan.

Another issue for our consideration is the research methods used in our field. Personally, I like field studies; I like thinking outside the box, and I like our studies to be relevant for policy makers. But, most of all, I like it when scholars recognize the limitations of their studies. On the other hand, I do not like what I call baroque studies, which summarize that A said this, B said that, C said that, and so on. The study's main contribution then is to add another brick on this wall, arguing that maybe there is a difference between A and B. This is a very good way to get published – in fact, it is often difficult to publish if you do not adopt this style – but I do not think it adds much to what we know about the real world of MNCs.

The tendency I really fight against all the time is that of making unfounded generalizations. Let me illustrate through the parable from China and India about blind men and an elephant. In China they had a parable about three blind men and an elephant. One blind man said the elephant was a rope, another said it was like a wall, and so on. Why? Because not one of them could see the whole elephant, and each based his assessment on touching a different part of the elephant's body. A few centuries later the parable moved to India and because of inflation, I suppose, there were now six blind men, who describe the elephant variously as a snake, a wall, a rope, a tree, and so on. Not being able to see, each reached general conclusions based on partial evidence of what they felt. I think many of our studies suffer from exactly the same problem. We focus on a certain part, touch it, and decide that this part truly represents the whole.

Let me come back to the point I made about strategy based on domination of a well-defined segment and avoiding competition on an industry basis. Such a strategy is not confined only to firms from small countries. The French mineral water company Perrier exported water from France to the United States. Take any theory you like and show me why the United States needs water from France. Coming from a desert country, Israel, the one thing I find amazing is how much water there is in the United States. In this case, the water was transported at a high cost in small glass bottles. So why was Perrier successful? Because it did not attempt to compete in the water industry but rather in a totally different sector. Based on that and other examples, I wrote a paper called *In Search of the Unique*, which argued that strategy is all about being unique (Aharoni, 1993). With all due regard to Michael Porter, it is not about competing in an industry. A firm that has a really good strategy does not work within the industry; it creates its own industry. I do not mean being high-tech. To create your own industry you can take water and call it the taste of life. One of our problems is that we try to help populations of firms, but a successful firm does not want to be part of a population. It wants to be unique, because that is the best way to be successful in this very competitive world. The best way is not to compete against ten other firms in the same industry with the same product. I hope IB scholars will keep this point in mind as they look for the firm-specific advantages of MNCs from emerging markets – or any firm, for that matter.

References

Aharoni, Y. 1986. *The Evolution and Management of State Owned Enterprises*. Cambridge, MA: Ballinger.

1993. In search of the unique: Can firm specific advantages be evaluated? *Journal of Management Studies*, 30: 31–49.

1999. Internationalization of professional services: Implications for accounting firms. In D. Brock, M. Powell, and C. R. Hinings (eds.), *Restructuring the Professional Organization*: 20–40. London: Routledge.

2000. The performance of state owned enterprises. In P. A. Toninelli (ed.), *The Rise and Fall of State-Owned Enterprise in the Western World*: 47–72. Cambridge University Press.

2009. Multinationals from Israel. In R. Ramamurti and J. Singh (eds.), *Emerging Multinationals from Emerging Markets*: 352–396. Cambridge University Press.

Aharoni, Y. and Ascher, W. 1998. Restructuring the arrangements between government and state enterprises in the oil and mining sectors. *Natural Resources Forum*, 22: 201–213.

Aliber, R. Z. 1970. A theory of foreign direct investment. In C. P. Kindleberger (ed.), *The International Corporation*: 17–34. Cambridge, MA: MIT Press.

1971. The multinational enterprise in a multiple currency world. In J. H. Dunning (ed.), *The Multinational Enterprise*: 49–56. London: George Allen & Unwin.

Bonaglia, F., Goldstein, A., and Mathews, J. 2007. Accelerated internation-
    alization by emerging multinationals: The case of white goods sector.
    Journal of World Business, 42: 369–383.
Bremmer, I. 2010. *The End of the Free Market: Who Wins the War between
    States and Corporations?* New York: Portfolio/Penguin Publishers.
Buckley, P. J. and Casson, M. C. 2009. The internalization theory of the
    multinational enterprise: A review of the progress of a research
    agenda after 30 years. *Journal of International Business Studies*, 40:
    1563–1580.
Buckley, P. J., Clegg, L. J., Cross, A. R., Liu, X., Voss, H., and Zheng, P.
    2007. The determinants of Chinese outward foreign direct investment.
    Journal of International Business Studies, 38: 499–518.
Cantwell, J. and Barnard, H. 2008. Do firms from emerging markets have to
    invest abroad? Outward FDI and the competitiveness of firms. In K. P.
    Sauvant (ed.), *The Rise of Transnational Corporations from Emerging
    Countries: Threat or Opportunity?* Cheltenham, UK: Edward Elgar.
Cuervo-Cazurra, A. 2012. How the analysis of developing country multi-
    national companies helps advance theory: Solving the Goldilocks
    debate. *Global Strategy Journal*, 2: 153–167.
Cuervo-Cazurra, A. and Genc, M. 2008. Transforming disadvantages into
    advantages: Developing-country MNEs in the least developed coun-
    tries. *Journal of International Business Studies*, 39: 957–979.
Dunning, J. H. 1958. *American Investment in British Manufacturing
    Industry*. London: Allen & Unwin.
    1977. Trade, location of economic activity and the MNE: A search for an
    eclectic approach. In B. Ohlin, P.-O. Hesselborn, and P. M. Wijkman
    (eds.), *The International Allocation of Economic Activity*: 395–418.
    London: Macmillan.
    2006. Comment on dragon multinationals: New players in 21st century
    globalization. *Asia Pacific Journal of Management*, 23: 139–141.
Dunning, J. H. and Lundan, S. 2008. *Multinational Enterprises and the
    Global Economy*. Cheltenham, UK: Edward Elgar.
Dunning, J. H., Kim, C., and Park, D. 2008. Old wine in new bottles: A
    comparison of emerging-market TNCs today and developed-country
    TNCs thirty years ago. In K. P. Sauvant (ed.), *The Rise of Transnational
    Corporations from Emerging Countries: Threat or Opportunity?*
    Cheltenham, UK: Edward Elgar.
Economist. 2012. Special report: State capitalism. January 21. www.econo-
    mist.com/node/21543160. Accessed November 13, 2012.
Forsgren, M. 2013. *Theories of the Multinational Firm. A Multidimensional
    Creature in the Global Economy* (2nd edn.). Cheltenham, UK: Edward
    Elgar.

Goldstein, A. 2007. *Multinational Companies from Emerging Economies: Composition, Conceptualization and Direction in the Global Economy*. London: Palgrave Macmillan.

Ghymn, K.-I. 1980. Multinational enterprises from the third world. *Journal of International Business Studies*, 11: 118–122.

HM Treasury. 2008. Establishment of UK Financial Investments Limited (UKFI). London: National Archives. http://webarchive.nationalarchives. gov.uk/+/http://www.hm-treasury.gov.uk/uk_financial_investments_limited.htm. Accessed January 8, 2013.

Hoskisson, R. E., Eden, L., Lau, C. M., and Wright, M. 2000. Strategy in emerging economies. *Academy of Management Journal*, 43: 249–267.

Hymer, S. 1976. *The International Operations of National Firms: A Study of Direct Foreign Investment*. Cambridge, MA: MIT Press.

Kumar, K. and McLeod, M. G. (eds.). 1981. *Multinationals from Developing Countries*. Lexington, MA: Lexington Books.

Lall, S. 1983. *The New Multinationals: The Spread of Third World Enterprises*. New York: Wiley.

Lecraw, D. 1977. Direct investment by firms from less developed countries. *Oxford Economic Papers*, 29: 445–457.

Lessard D. and Lucea, R. 2009. Mexican multinationals: Insights from CEMEX. In R. Ramamurti and J. Singh (eds.), *Emerging Multinationals in Emerging Markets*: 280–311. Cambridge University Press.

Luo, Y. and Tang, R. L. 2007. International expansion of emerging countries enterprises: A springboard perspective. *Journal of International Business Studies*, 38: 481–498.

Mathews, J. A. 2002. *Dragon multinationals: A new model of global growth*. New York: Oxford University Press.

  2006. Dragon multinationals: New players in 21st century globalization. *Asia Pacific Journal of Management*, 23: 5–27.

Mathews, J. A. and Cho, D. S. 2000. *Tiger Technology: The Creation of a Semiconductor Industry in East Asia*. Cambridge University Press.

Narula, R. 2006. Globalization, new ecologies, new zoologies, and the purported death of the eclectic paradigm. *Asia Pacific Journal of Management*, 23: 143–151.

  2010. Keeping the eclectic paradigm simple. *Multinational Business Review*, 18: 35–50.

  2012. Do we need different frameworks to explain infant MNEs from developing countries? *Global Strategy Journal*, 2: 188–204.

Porter, M. 1990. *The Competitive Advantage of Nations*. New York: The Free Press.

Ramamurti, R. 2009. What have we learned about emerging market MNEs? In R. Ramamurti and J. Singh (eds.), *Emerging Multinationals in Emerging Markets*: 399–426. Cambridge University Press.

2012. What is really different about emerging market multinationals? *Global Strategy Journal*, 2: 41–47.

Reich, R. B. 1990. Who is us? (The changing American corporation). *Harvard Business Review*, 68: 53–64.

Rugman, A. M. and D'Cruz, J. R. 1993. The "Double Diamond" model of international competitiveness: The Canadian experience. *Management International Review*, 33: 17–39.

Rugman, A. M. and Li, J. 2007. Will China's multinationals succeed globally or regionally? *European Management Journal*, 25: 333–343.

Vernon, R. 1971. *Sovereignty at Bay: The Multinational Spread of U.S. Enterprises*. New York and London: Basic Books, Inc.

Wang, C., Hong, J., Kafouros, M., and Wright, M. 2012. Exploring the role of government involvement in outward FDI from emerging economies. *Journal of International Business Studies*, 43: 655–676.

Wells, L. 1983. *Third World Multinationals: The Role of Foreign Direct Investment from Developing Countries*. Cambridge, MA: MIT Press.

Williamson P. J. and Zeng, M. 2009. Chinese multinationals: Emerging through new global gateways. In R. Ramamurti and J. Singh (eds.), *Emerging Multinationals in Emerging Markets*. Cambridge University Press.

3 | What does history add to EMNC research?

ANDREW GODLEY

Is there an intellectual case for using historical studies in EMNC research?

How to explain the rapid growth in emerging market multinational corporations (EMNCs) has become one of the most controversial topics of international business scholarship in recent years. As global economic integration proceeded in the 1980s, 1990s, and into the 2000s, so increasingly more firms from emerging markets began to pursue outward foreign direct investment (FDI) strategies. Much of this economic activity is entirely consistent with the established canon of international business (IB) theory. But the observations by John Mathews (2002, 2006) that several EMNCs (what he tellingly called 'dragon multinationals') were acquiring global competitive advantage, and that they were increasingly able to leapfrog advanced economy incumbent MNCs' technologies, has acted as a catalyst for this important debate.

The subsequent discussion about the relative merits of EMNCs has shown that it is important to differentiate between different kinds of FDI pursued by different EMNCs. Ramamurti's typology of generic strategies adopted by EMNCs (Ramamurti, 2009, Table 13.1) includes natural resource integrators, local optimisers, low-cost partners, global consolidators, and global first movers. Of these five generic strategies only the last one represents a significant deviation from the traditional IB theoretical framework, which privileges advanced country technologically derived firm specific advantages (FSAs). Ramamurti's survey acknowledges that among the population of EMNCs, global first movers are only a very small minority. But it is these – Mathews' 'Dragon Multinationals' – that pose such a challenge to IB theory. How have developing economies with such poorer knowledge bases been able to create such advanced human capital endowments that even a handful of EMNCs have acquired advanced FSAs at the technological frontier (Rugman, 2010)?

The question at the heart of this debate is not whether a few EMNCs have acquired advanced technological capabilities, nor whether they are able to out-compete advanced economy incumbents. With the number of case studies piling up, the evidence here is unambiguous. EMNCs are clearly capable of out-competing advanced economy incumbents in high technology sectors. The very great controversy that remains, however, is about whether this is economically sustainable or not. For this to be the case, some rather heroic assumptions have to be maintained. For example, the evidence that the Chinese EMNC Lenovo is globally successful is undeniable (to take a well-known exemplar of a 'dragon multinational' [Mathews, 2006]). But to go from this observation to an explanation that its success is derived from acquiring competitive advantage through superior investments in (using Mathews' LLL framework): 'linkage' (or accelerated internationalisation through networks), 'leverage' (through strategic asset seeking FDI, for example), and 'learning' (acquiring fundamental technological capabilities) requires the assumption that both the incumbent and latecomer firms are competing within broadly similar economic contexts. For competition (and its derivative concepts of competitive advantage and technological capabilities) to be a meaningful economic construct, the market participants must be playing in a field that is recognisably level. But almost all the home economies from which EMNCs are emerging are pursuing development paths that privilege capital-intensive exporting firms over consumers. Michael Pettis' magisterial explanation of China's development path is one that emphasises the role of the Chinese Government pursuing the policy of 'financial repression' of the household sector (through restricting the interest rate on deposits and savings accounts) in order to subsidise the borrowing of the industrial sector (Pettis, 2013). He estimates that this subsidy represents a transfer from households to firms on the order of 5–6 per cent of Chinese GDP per year. This has important implications for how we interpret the emergence of global first movers like Huawei and Lenovo. If their success is really a product of a subsidy stream that is denied to their advanced economy competitors, then the fact that they have acquired global competitive advantage is not to be explained by superior strategic behaviour. In this scenario, EMNCs like Lenovo may have acquired global competitive advantage, but they are not yet economically sustainable.

Given the opacity of such subsidising behaviour, it remains impossible to estimate how much EMNC competitiveness is derived solely from the subsidy, and by implication how much is derived from superior management behaviour. In principle the emergence of 'dragon multinationals' may be entirely a product of the financial repression of the domestic household sector rather than any superior 'linkage', 'leverage', or 'learning' effects (Mathews, 2002, 2006). It follows, then, that only once the subsidies in China have been withdrawn (or matched in advanced economies) will IB scholars truly be able to judge whether such 'dragon multinationals' have genuinely acquired sustainable FSAs that enable them to compete in high technology markets. And that is unlikely to happen anytime soon.

It is in precisely this situation, where IB scholars are faced with an irresolvable controversy of great public moment, that the possibility of using historical studies to generate some further insights may prove to be a particularly powerful methodological approach. Economic history confirms that there was an earlier period when globalisation was at least as important in the world economy as today, when FDI and MNCs were as significant, and when flows of outward FDI began to accelerate from what were then emerging economies. This was the period of globalisation from around 1870 to 1929, which business historians have referred to as G1 (Godley and Hang, 2012; Jones, 2005), in order to contrast it with G2, the post-1980 to the present era of globalisation.

Systematic research of firms that were the equivalent of today's EMNCs in G1 may provide important evidence that might go some way to resolving the current controversy. This chapter discusses how historical frameworks may help IB scholars, and does so by first reviewing the place of history in the leading international business theories more generally, then going on to illustrate that the dominant theoretical framework used to explain EMNCs is, in fact, explicitly historical. This theoretical framework was first developed by the Austrian-born Harvard economist and economic historian Alexander Gerschenkron (Gerschenkron, 1962). It is Gerschenkron's explanation of the advantages that latecomer economies may possess in economic development that has been so usefully adapted to offer the potential explanation of the rise of global first-mover, but latecomer, EMNCs. Gerschenkron's application of latecomer advantages was thought to be most relevant in explaining the rapid economic development of Germany from 1850 to 1914. While historical studies have been notably rare among IB scholarship in recent years, if IB scholars want to pursue comparative research across different historical periods in order to better understand EMNCs today, rather than examining whether there were indigenous MNCs emerging from the BRIC nations (or other home economies of EMNCs today) during G1, a more theoretically robust comparison is likely to be with patterns of outward FDI from Germany before 1914. This may seem a somewhat surprising deduction for many IB scholars. But systematic and theoretically coherent historical comparisons are renowned for being able to produce counter-intuitive results. Before returning to the possible historical precedent of EMNCs in Imperial Germany, it is apposite to review more clearly just how significant a role historical studies have played in the canon of IB scholarship.

The IB canon and history

In recent years it has become commonplace for IB scholars to prioritise ahistorical, cross-sectional analyses. There is nevertheless a widespread agreement among the IB community that history is important. Even the merest acquaintance with the canonical works will reveal a deep regard for the chronological development of MNCs. Dunning and Lundan (2008) devoted an entire section of their overview to the history of IB. For example, Peter Buckley recently asked how IB theory can be advanced by incorporating 'time' more explicitly as 'a key variable in any analysis of MNCs' (Buckley, 2009: 18). IB scholars are therefore far from unaware *that* history matters; that is obvious. History provides additional layers of robustness to any general theory, in particular through revealing sequencing and causality far better than any cross-sectional analysis can do (Morck and Yeung, 2011). Jones and Khanna observed in 2006 that 'at least one-third' of the total of all articles published in *Journal of International Business Studies* since 1990 mentioned the word 'history', yet not a single one employed historical data or was devoted to the history of international business. But although 'there is a widespread acknowledgement that history matters, there is still a search for *how* it matters' (Jones and Khanna, 2006: 453, emphasis supplied).[1]

Jones and Khanna (2006) identified four conceptual channels where history might matter in IB research. Firstly, and most obviously, there

---

[1] Historical data was defined there as time series data stretching back more than one decade.

is the additional value of time series analysis to supplement the initial correlations that cross-sectional analysis documents. Secondly, historical comparisons will expose spurious claims of novelty by documenting that there were in fact earlier examples of such phenomena. Thirdly, detailed historical case studies of key firms reveal a better understanding of the roots of 'resources' – or the origins of FSAs – and so, given their path-dependency, offer a richer explanation of how 'resources' in truly important examples have actually developed. Finally, according to Jones and Khanna, any attempt to answer really big questions must take account of history in order to be considered valid.

When John Dunning first began to assemble his empirical data for what became *American Investment in British Manufacturing Industry* (1958), which is widely considered to be the foundation work of the IB discipline, his approach was explicitly historical and entirely consistent with Jones and Khanna's recommendations. His analysis of the population of entrants began with understanding their rationale for entry, their subsequent development and impact, and the relationship between the two. In 1958, his was explicitly an evolutionary and highly empirical approach. Dunning's underlying data set has continued to be expanded, extrapolated, and analysed by business historians in the years since (Bostock and Jones, 1994; Jones and Bostock, 1996; Fletcher and Godley, 2000, 2001; Godley and Fletcher, 2000; Godley, 1999, 2003, 2013).

Dunning's observation that US FDI was concentrated in relatively high tech sectors (for the time) strongly influenced the first, and still highly influential, theoretical model of FDI: Vernon's product cycle theory (Vernon, 1966, 1979; extended by Magee, 1977). Here the explanation for FDI is couched in terms of how the standardisation of a given technology leads to the more optimal location for manufacturing being a lower cost country, compared with the high wage economy of initial innovation. This is a strong explanation of observed events, with historical causality clearly driven by a trade-off between the diminishing returns to technological innovation and the differential costs of labour. The theory appeared to explain much of the pattern of post-war US FDI into Europe, which of course was not surprising given that this episode represented most of the total universe of observations open to Vernon. As MNC behaviour began to exhibit greater heterogeneity during the 1970s and 1980s, however, Vernon's model was seen as increasingly partial (Cantwell, 1995).

While the major theoretical contributions of the 1970s – Hymer (1970),[2] Buckley and Casson (1976), and Dunning's first version of the OLI-paradigm (1979) – advanced the analytical content of IB, in contrast to Vernon they give little attention to sequence or time, either explicitly or implicitly. That firms possess some technological advantage is a given. That overseas markets possess some form of imperfection is a given. Firms are simply responsive, optimising their contractual behaviour in any given conditions. Buckley and Casson used internalisation theory to explain past MNC behaviour (and of course Casson has contributed enormously to IB history). But in the absence of spillovers, feedback loops, or other features of evolutionary behaviour, there is little room specifically for history as a key variable in internalisation theory.

It was rather in the writings of the Uppsala school of the 1970s and 1980s that history (in the form of time and sequencing) re-emerged as an important feature (Johanson and Vahlne, 1977). The Uppsala model holds that what firms internalise is knowledge, and that the process of internationalisation adds to the stock of this knowledge; past experiences inform decision making and so confer a strong advantage to those with previous international experience. The Uppsala school's model was based on close observation of the experiences of European – especially Scandinavian – MNCs, and so, of course, appeared to explain this historical behaviour. But the general theories with the strongest emphasis on sequence and time only partially account for observed behaviour. The overarching general theory of IB – the transactions costs approach – is of course historically applicable, but it contains no special role for time or sequencing outside the steps associated with short term optimisation. (And as an aside, this may help to explain why business history is still considered a core element of IB in Scandinavian business schools, where the Uppsala model remains dominant, but not in North American business schools, where the transaction costs framework is dominant.)

John Mathews' *Dragon Multinationals* is another example of an IB theory that, like the Uppsala school, explicitly uses historical sequencing. As noted, Mathews draws explicitly on the explanatory framework of

---

[2] Hymer's PhD preceded Vernon's contribution, and so is now generally accepted as the first modern general theoretical statement, but it was only published some years later.

Gerschenkron, whose *Economic Backwardness in Historical Perspective* (1962) has proven to be so influential in development studies. Gerschenkron was not, however, concerned with explaining FDI. He was solely focused on trying to account for how less developed economies had been able to divert scarce capital into cutting edge technological developments, and hence compete in world markets.

Gerschenkron's dilemma was that investing in new technology requires capital, and that backward nations have a relatively smaller domestic supply of finance. Gerschenkron's solution was to suggest that banking systems might evolve that could allocate capital into relatively more productive purposes. While he invoked the examples of late nineteenth century Austria–Hungary, Italy, and Russia, the empirical support he developed most fully to support his bank-led development model was the case of Germany from 1850 to 1914.

Germany 1850–1914: historical precedent for EMNCs?

Compared to Britain, the country of the Industrial Revolution, Germany was economically backward in 1850. Yet by 1914 the German shipbuilding, coal, iron, and steel industries had larger outputs than their British competitors. Furthermore, the German firms in chemicals and pharmaceuticals and in electrical engineering had developed world-leading technological capabilities. This technological catch-up and then leapfrogging by German firms over formerly leading British firms occurred, according to Gerschenkron, because of the development of a universal banking model in Germany, where banks developed close ties to specific industrial interests. German banks were therefore able to channel investment funding into new technologies and demand superior rationalisation of practices compared to their UK equivalents. Thus, according to Gerschenkron, German firms acquired global supremacy by 1914.

Mathews' use of Gerschenkron's historical framework needs to be teased out. Gerschenkron's principal mechanism for explaining German firms' advancement was German banks' allegedly superior ability to channel funding. While there have been criticisms of this development model, Pettis has recently and forcefully argued that it is consistent with the most recent East Asian and Chinese development (Forsyth and Verdier, 2003; Pettis, 2013). But even allowing that there may be times when nations depend solely on domestic sources of funding for economic development and are able to exert sufficient pressure on savers that the interests of infant industry borrowers are privileged, the purest version of the Gerschenkronian development model still does not account for all EMNCs. To be more precise, it may help to explain how some emerging market firms with privileged access to finance may invest in acquiring overseas natural resources, or in market-seeking investment in neighbouring developing econo- mies, all complementary to the Solow-type technical progress model (where productivity and growth come as a result of specialisation and incremental investment in capital goods and mechanisation) at the heart of this version of the Gerschenkronian model (Solow, 1957). But this cannot account for the emergence of EMNCs with FSAs strong enough to compete in advanced markets. Global first movers among EMNCs have to have acquired some sort of technological advantage, often initially from overseas ('linkage'), and exploited it through some sort of superior 'learning' and 'leverage', features which are closely associated with the human capabilities of the individuals within the organisation. The closest Gerschenkron gets to anticipating the new growth models (Romer, 1994) and invoking the significance of human capital is in the occasional references to cultural development, civilisa- tion, and worker discipline.

Gerschenkron's fascination with the German case is illustrative here, because while his focus on German rapid industrialisation, world export-share, and technological catch-up was centred on the coal, iron, steel, and ship-building sectors, German FDI – which increased dramatically from 1880 to 1914 – was concentrated in chemicals and pharmaceuticals, electrical engineering, and, to a lesser extent, food and beverages (Chandler, 1990; Jones, 1996, 2005). In some of these sectors, notably chemicals and pharmaceuticals, German FSAs went from being those of small, local producers to those of globally domin- ant producers. These producers responded to failures in international markets for their products by adopting internalisation strategies, so becoming MNCs. If Gerschenkron is correct in identifying Germany as a backward economy that caught up and overtook the industrial leader during the 1850–1914 period, then the historical equivalents of the EMNC global first movers are surely to be found in the German syn- thetic pharmaceuticals and dyestuffs producers (Athreye and Godley, 2009). But the source of these companies' FSAs was not to be found in their close links with banks. Rather, the standard explanation for the rise of the German chemicals and pharmaceuticals industries typically emphasises the German investment in civic education and higher education institutions and the development of corporate research and development capabilities to further exploit human capital advantages (Beer, 1959; Haber, 1958).

Mathews does not try to adapt the Gerschenkron framework by incorporating human capital endowments leading to technological innovation, growing FSAs, and FDI to internalise international markets. Nor does he emphasise the primitive Gerschenkron model of privileged investment in infant industries. Rather, for Mathews the key contribution of Gerschenkronian development was the identification of some institutional solution to a specific problem in the local environment, a solution which inadvertently then led to a global – albeit location-bound – FSA. In Gerschenkron's Germany it was the creation of universal banks, which channelled funding and information and took on the role of co-ordinating activity efficiently. The investments ended up conferring a strong advantage over global competition. The specific institutional adversity that conferred the latecomer advantage need not be restricted to finance. Clearly there are examples that support the 'adversity advantage' argument more generally. Japanese MNCs, for example, developed internal labour markets because of the absence of any meaningful national labour market. The knock-on effect of the dormitory system was for Japanese corporate culture to support flexible manufacturing systems, and hence confer a strong and durable FSA (Fruin, 1992; Womack, Jones, and Roos, 1990). Equally, the Greek business groups headquartered in a handful of Ionian islands controlled world freight before 1914 (Harlaftis, 1993). Their adversity was the absence of national statehood over many generations giving rise to an investment in very strong cultural ties, which suited the networking peculiarities of global shipping at the time and so gave rise to strong and persistent FSAs in that sector.

Returning to Gerschenkron's fascination with Germany between 1850 and 1914, and the evidence of early German MNCs that became global first movers in chemicals and pharmaceuticals, recent historical research has refined the earlier consensus that FSAs here depended on the creation of firm R&D laboratories and easy access to highly qualified workers. In particular, recent research on the emergence of the German pharmaceuticals and dyestuffs firms' technological capabilities has identified changes to the German patent law in 1870, which forced German owners of IP to commercialise patents or lose them (Burhop, 2009; Godley and Leslie-Hughes, in press). The changes were not introduced with the specific intention of increasing technological productivity, but rather to increase the duties paid by inventors to the state at a time when increasing general taxation was politically unpopular. An apparent institutional disadvantage, in other words, led to a specific institutional solution which in turn indirectly conferred great advantages on German chemicals and pharmaceuticals producers in global markets.

Of course, the question remains: Why should these specific 'institutional voids' (Khanna and Palepu, 2000) have led to such strong and durable FSAs among Japanese auto makers or Greek shippers, yet similar levels of adversity from similar institutional voids in, say, the region of the former Ottoman Empire did not lead (as far as we know) to any nascent intangible resource able to be exploited by an infant MNC on the world stage (Owen and Pamuk, 1998)? A series of carefully constructed research questions focusing on specific historical comparisons would reveal much about the creation and durability of FSAs among infant EMNCs, and about the mechanism that relates different kinds of institutional voids to the creation or not of EMNC FSAs. Matthews' dependence on a Gerschenkronian model of development implies that Germany from 1850 to 1914 would be the most suitable historic case study to begin with. But others might be equally insightful.

Possible historical research questions for EMNC scholars

When studying EMNCs today, it is possible to see how a comparative framework that exploits abundant historical data might lead to better theory (Adler, Campbell, and Laurent, 1989). Of course, the difficulties of making historical comparisons, of truly comparing like-with-like over different periods, must not be overlooked. But it is easy to exaggerate the extent of change. For most historians the past seems very familiar, with many similarities to the present. Much of the efforts of economic historians such as Nobel laureate Doug North and Eric Jones impress upon their readers the pervasiveness of market signals over time and the potency of governance regimes to persistently deflect from optimal outcomes.

Sceptics would nevertheless maintain that the effort of investing in assembling and integrating historical data is not worth the candle when it is so much easier to use present-day data. It may well be that historical comparisons might add conceptual rigour to current theory, but perhaps at too great a cost. History matters, as Jones and Khanna asserted, but does it matter enough?

Jones and Khanna identified four areas where history might matter: time series analysis, avoiding spurious claims for novelty, understanding the origins of 'resources' or FSAs, and addressing really big issues. The above discussion of how the historical precedents of EMNCs might be found in the business history of outward FDI from Germany from 1850 to 1914 clearly shows how historical data can address the major issue of interpreting EMNCs from the broader perspective of whether the present-day EMNCs (like Lenovo) are economically viable and whether or not they make a positive contribution to net economic welfare.

Incorporating the earlier discussion of the Gerschenkronian roots of Mathews' approach to EMNCs with these larger net welfare concerns should lead us to conclude that a historical approach could augment our current understanding of EMNCs by asking several specific research questions. Firstly, following the purest form of the Gerschenkron model, we should compare where early German MNCs and present-day EMNCs were and are getting their sources of finance from, and whether this was directly or indirectly via some form of government subsidy. The historic research would then also be able to assess whether such early subsidisation of outward FDI ever led to sustainable FSAs. If such a research project discovered that early German MNCs enjoyed subsidies (as implied by Gerschenkron) and that these directly led to the very considerable FSAs that the German pharmaceutical and chemical MNCs enjoyed after 1900, then that would represent *prima facie* evidence that 'global first mover' EMNCs can indeed develop in an economically sustainable fashion. Given the current controversy, this would represent a major contribution. Secondly, a historical research agenda could focus on early German firms' responses to institutional adversity and whether such responses created conditions for sustainable 'latecomer advantages'. Any empirical findings here of how those early German MNCs were able to acquire such powerful FSAs in the early 1900s as a result of domestic adversity would represent a very important contribution to the wider debate about the potential mechanisms that EMNCs are able to utilise to acquire FSAs.

Perhaps a less significant use of historical data might be Jones and Khanna's second area, of avoiding spurious claims of novelty. For IB scholars interested in better understanding the EMNC phenomenon, one application of historical studies here might be to subject the apparent importance of 'linkage', or accelerated internationalisation among EMNCs, to historical scrutiny. The plausible argument put forward by EMNC scholars here is that technical know-how is concentrated in advanced economies, and so EMNCs are more successful in accessing such knowledge if they internationalise quickly. Thus, accelerated internationalisation is associated with the allegedly novel form of IB, the EMNC.

Unfortunately, this view is predicated on an understanding of the 'normal' model of the MNC, which is historically contingent. This is the view that the MNC normally builds its FSAs in its home location first, before internationalising these FSAs. That may well explain most outward FDI from advanced economies over the past forty years or more, but it conspicuously fails to explain earlier outward FDI from advanced economies during G1. For example, Weetman Pearson (later ennobled as Lord Cowdray) created one of the leading British oil majors of the early twentieth century, the Mexican Eagle Oil Company (which became the biggest division of Royal Dutch-Shell after its 1921 acquisition). Mexican Eagle was the third largest oil company in the world, and the Pearson Group was the UK's largest business by some considerable stretch in 1919 (Bud Frierman, Godley, and Wale, 2010). But Pearson also controlled dozens of other companies – some through equity stakes, some only through exclusive trading relationships – associated with oil and infrastructure development in Mexico and throughout Latin America between 1890 and the 1920s. Most of these UK-headquartered MNCs were established solely for developing economic activity overseas. There was no home base of any significance. The London headquarter location was for board meetings, recruitment of senior personnel, and liaison with outside shareholders. In Mira Wilkins' term, these MNCs, like the Pearson group, were 'Free Standing Companies' (Wilkins, 1988; Wilkins and Schroter, 1998).

The period immediately before World War I was a high water mark for the influence of MNCs in the world economy, compared with any other time in world history up until the very recent past. By the mid-1990s the value of the total stock of global FDI was the equivalent of 8.5 per cent of total world output. By 2001 it had reached 20 per cent, and by 2006 it was 25 per cent (Jones, 1996: 30; UNCTAD, 2007: Table 1.4), confirming that recent years have witnessed the most extraordinary boom in cross-border activities. We now know this era to also have been marked by extreme financial laxity. In 1913 the total stock of global FDI has been estimated to have been the equivalent of 13.5 per cent of world output (Corley, 1994, 1997; Jones, 1996: 30). The most common organisational form before 1914 was the free standing company, responsible for half of the global stock of FDI. In other words, accelerated internationalisation and 'linkage' was a leading strategy of the majority of MNCs from advanced and emerging economies in G1. These early MNCs were highly entrepreneurial and mostly small, but not always. Pearson's Mexican Eagle was also a Free Standing Company. The previous existence of MNCs that pursued such accelerated internationalisation strategies and collaborated in networks focused on overseas markets means, of course, that their re-emergence in the 1990s cannot be described as particularly novel.

This outcome of historical studies is more than simple intellectual point scoring. After all, if there are historical precedents for the 'accelerated internationalisation' of EMNCs today, then these precedents may help to clarify what the underlying economic value is of such accelerated internationalisation. In the literature regarding EMNCs today, such internationalisation is focused on acquiring advanced economy knowledge or strategic assets. By contrast, free standing companies in the 1900s represented a rational organisational choice by entrepreneurs aware that the world economy had abundant supplies of capital for development projects but often weak governance structures in overseas markets. Advanced economy (typically British) entrepreneurs built a track record for exploiting their own knowledge-intensive capabilities and successfully completing complex infrastructure projects. They were then able to leverage this reputation with outside investors, who were typically unsure of the ability or willingness of the government of whichever nation the development was located in to repay bonds. The net result was networks of established entrepreneurs who were able to raise the equivalent of third tier venture capital for overseas infrastructure projects on the London Stock Exchange, typically selling their stakes on completion (Casson, 1998; Corley, 1994). The implication of this historical comparison is that accelerated internationalisation today may not be driven by the need to acquire advanced economy knowledge, but instead may be more a response to weak governance among EMNCs. A systematic historical comparison of a sample of EMNCs today and free standing companies in the past may provide extremely useful research findings and illustrate what the underlying economic logic is of accelerated internationalisation strategies.

Furthermore, such a historical survey would also reveal that accelerated internationalisation strategies have historically led only to very weakly sustainable FSAs for MNCs in overseas markets. When technical knowledge became more evenly distributed, and/or when developing country debt repayment became more reliable (or dependence on outside investors lessened), the returns for this kind of knowledge-intensive, project-based FDI fell. The liabilities of foreignness began to outweigh the diminishing value of the FSA, and indigenous competitors emerged. The rise of the Tata family business in India in the early years of the twentieth century can be explained in this way (Jones and Khanna, 2006). The emergence of the enormously successful Melkonian and Motassian cigarette businesses in Egypt can also partly be accounted for by British American Tobacco's (then the global leader in tobacco – and another large free standing company) diminishing FSA in this market (Cox, 2000; Shechter, 2006). In most developing economies in the 1900s to the 1920s, indigenous competitors were becoming increasingly significant – in India, China, and the Middle East. This indicates that the relative strength of the FSAs of Free Standing Companies – or accelerated internationalisers – in these locations was being eroded.

Conclusion

The emergence of EMNCs poses a distinct theoretical problem for mainstream IB theory. One possible approach to resolve such a dilemma would be to pursue historical comparisons more rigorously. The illustration of how in earlier periods MNCs pursued accelerated internationalisation strategies as the norm, not the exception, suggests that complex contemporary issues in IB may well benefit from more detailed historical analyses. The study of EMNCs would surely also benefit from such an approach, not least because one of the principal authors, John Mathews, uses an explicitly historical explanatory framework, the Gerschenkron development model, when explaining how these EMNCs acquire sustainable FSAs through strategic innovations. The chapter has expounded the Gerschenkronian model and Gerschenkron's favoured empirical support for his framework, the case of Germany from 1850 to 1914, and has developed three areas where future historical comparisons might be profitably focused.

This approach may well come as a surprise to many IB scholars. After all, business history is famously, even stereotypically, a theory-lite discipline (Lamoreaux, Raff, and Temin, 2008). But it would be wrong to conclude that it was theory-free. Mira Wilkins' stage model of the growth of US MNEs' overseas subsidiaries describes how there was typically a change from the initial investment as a simple overseas branch, to the subsidiary developing somewhat autonomously in the host economy, before finally becoming more integrated into the increasingly complex global structure of the now much bigger parent company (Wilkins, 1974: 414–22). Wilkins' stage model implicitly captures many of the most important phenomena of IB, namely the welfare gains from the internalisation of imperfect international markets for knowledge, and the additional innovation, and hence FSA creation, derived from the internationalisation process itself. Wilkins' model may be inductive, but, as Peter Buckley recently stated, her 'theoretical innovations ... anticipate the Uppsala model' (Buckley, 2009: 323).

More generally the longstanding conventions of writing history are that researchers focus on 'big issues' (or 'meta-narratives'). These issues are highly complex by definition, and hence the reductionist approach is viewed with some suspicion by most historians because it may produce overly simplistic results. Of course, what this means is not that historians have little or no theory, but rather that the theories underlying most historical works are implicit rather than explicit, and are typically meta-theories or worldviews such as Marxism, nationalism, Whiggism, and so on (Lamoreaux, Raff, and Temin, 2003, 2004). This can cause considerable confusion for those wanting to navigate their way through, say, the history of MNEs in Latin America who are uninitiated into the finer points of the dependency school. Worldviews do not typically yield much in the way of testable propositions. The selection bias of data presented in works informed by such strong views may therefore be subtly altered, and interpretations need to be treated with caution, challenging even the most persistent of IB scholars. So it has to be acknowledged that there is much in the canon of business history to potentially put off an IB scholar. To adapt Churchill, IB and business history may be disciplines divided by a common language, but there are undoubtedly enormous mutual benefits to investing research time in better translation.

References

Adler, N. J., Campbell, N., and Laurent, A. 1989. In search of appropriate methodology: From outside the People's Republic of China looking in. *Journal of International Business Studies*, 20: 61–74.

Athreye, S. and Godley, A. C. 2009. Internationalisation and technological leapfrogging in the pharmaceutical industry. *Industrial and Corporate Change*, 18: 295–323.

Beer, J. J. 1959. *The Emergence of the German Dye Industry*. Urbana, IL: University of Illinois Press.

Bostock, F. and Jones, G. 1994. Foreign multinationals in British manufacturing, 1850–1962. *Business History*, 36: 89–126.

Buckley, P. J. 2009. Business history and international business. *Business History*, 51: 307–33.

Buckley, P. J. and Casson, M. 1976. *The Future of the Multinational Enterprise*. London: Macmillan.

Bud Frierman, L., Godley, A. C., and Wale, J. 2010. Weetman Pearson in Mexico and the emergence of a British Oil Major, 1901–1919. *Business History Review*, 84: 275–300.

Burhop, C. 2009. Pharmaceutical research in Wilhelmine Germany: The case of E. Merck. *Business History Review*, 83: 475–503.

Cantwell, J. A. 1995. The globalisation of technology: What remains of the product cycle model? *Cambridge Journal of Economics*, 19: 155–74.

Casson, M. 1998. An economic theory of the free-standing company. In M. Wilkins and H. Schroter (eds.), *The Free Standing Company in the World Economy 1930–1996*. Oxford University Press.

Chandler, A. D. 1990. *Scale and Scope*. Harvard, MA: Belknap Press.

Corley, T. A. B. 1994. Britain's overseas investments in 1914 revisited. *Business History*, 36: 71–85.

   1997. Competitive advantage and foreign direct investment: Britain, 1913–1938. *Business and Economic History*, 26: 21–36.

Cox, H. 2000. *The Global Cigarette: Origins and Evolution of British American Tobacco, 1880–1945*. Oxford University Press.

Dunning, J. H. 1958. *American Investment in British Manufacturing Industry*. London: Allen and Unwin.

1979. Explaining changing patterns of international production: In defence of the eclectic theory. *Oxford Bulletin of Economics and Statistics*, 41: 269–95.

Dunning, J. H. and Lundan, S. 2008. *Multinational Enterprises and the Global Economy* (2nd edn.). Cheltenham: Edward Elgar.

Fletcher, S. and Godley, A. C. 2000. Foreign direct investment in British retailing, 1850–1962. *Business History*, 42: 43–62.

  2001. International retailing in Britain, 1850–1994. *Service Industries Journal*, 21: 31–46.

Forsyth, D. J. and Verdier, D. (eds.). 2003. *The Origins of National Financial Systems: Alexander Gerschenkron Reconsidered*. London and New York: Routledge.

Fruin, M. 1992. *The Japanese Enterprise System: Competitive Strategies and Cooperative Structures*. Oxford University Press.

Gerschenkron, A. 1962. *Economic Backwardness in Historical Perspective*. Cambridge, MA: Belknap Press.

Godley, A. C. 1999. Pioneering foreign direct investment in British manufacturing. *Business History Review*, 73: 394–429.

  2003. Foreign multinationals and innovation in British retailing: 1850–1962. *Business History*, 45: 80–100.

  2013. Entrepreneurial opportunities, implicit contracts and market making for complex consumer goods. *Strategic Entrepreneurship Journal*, 7(4): 273–87.

Godley A. C. and Fletcher, S. 2000. Foreign entry into British retailing, 1850–1994. *International Marketing Review*, 17: 392–400.

Godley, A. C. and Hang, H. 2012. Globalization and the evolution of international retailing: A comment on Alexander's 'British Overseas Retailing, 1900–1960'. *Business History*, 54: 529–41.

Godley, A. C. and Leslie-Hughes, D. in press. E. Merck of Darmstadt and the origins of industrial research capabilities in U.S. pharmaceuticals at Merck & Co. *Enterprise and Society*.

Haber, L. F. 1958. *The Chemical Industry during the Nineteenth Century*. Oxford University Press.

Harlaftis, G. 1993. *Greek Shipowners and Greece, 1945–1975. From Separate Development to Mutual Interdependence*. London: Athlone Press.

Hymer, S. 1970. The efficiency (contradictions) of multinational corporations. *American Economic Review*, 60: 441–48.

Johanson, J. and Vahlne, J. E. 1977. The internationalization process of the firm: A model of knowledge development and increasing foreign market commitments. *Journal of International Business Studies*, 8: 23–32.

48   *Andrew Godley*

Jones, G. 1996. *The Evolution of International Business*. London: Routledge.

2005. *Multinationals and Global Capitalism: From the Nineteenth to the Twenty-First Century*. Oxford University Press.

Jones, G. and Bostock, F. 1996. US multinationals in British manufacturing before 1962. *Business History Review*, 70: 207–56.

Jones, G. and Khanna, T. 2006. Bringing history (back) into international business. *Journal of International Business Studies*, 37: 453–68.

Khanna, T. and Palepu, K. 2000. Group affiliation profitable in emerging markets? An analysis of diversified Indian business groups. *Journal of Finance*, 55: 867–91.

Lamoreaux, N., Raff, D., and Temin, P. 2003. Beyond markets and hierarchies: Towards a new synthesis of American business history. *American Historical Review*, 108: 404–33.

2004. Against Whig history. *Enterprise and Society*, 5: 376–87.

2008. Economic theory and business history. In G. Jones and J. Zeitlin (eds.), *Oxford Handbook of Business History*. Oxford University Press.

Magee, S. P. 1977. Multinational corporations, the industry technology cycle and development. *Journal of World Trade Law*, 11(4): 297–321.

Mathews, J. A. 2002. *Dragon Multinational: A New Model for Global Growth*. New York: Oxford University Press.

2006. Dragon multinationals: New players in 21st century globalisation. *Asia Pacific Journal of Management*, 23: 5–27.

Morck, R. and Yeung, B. 2011. Economics, history and causation. *Business History Review*, 85: 39–63.

Owen, R. and Pamuk, S. 1998. *The Economic History of the Middle East in the Twentieth Century*. London: I.B. Tauris.

Pettis, M. 2013. *The Great Rebalancing: Trade, Conflict and the Perilous Road ahead for the World Economy*. Princeton University Press.

Ramamurti, R. 2009. What have we learned about emerging-market MNEs? In R. Ramamurti and J. V. Singh (eds.), *Emerging Multinationals from Emerging Markets*. Cambridge University Press.

Romer, P. 1994. The origins of endogenous growth. *The Journal of Economic Perspectives*, 8: 3–22.

Rugman, A. 2010. Globalization, regional multinationals and Asian economic development. *Asian Business & Management*, 9: 299–317.

Shechter, R. 2006. *Smoking, Culture and Economy in the Middle East: The Egyptian Tobacco Market 1850–2000*. London: I.B. Tauris.

Solow, R. 1957. Technical Change and the Aggregate Production Function. *The Review of Economics and Statistics*, 39: 312–20.

UNCTAD. 2007. *World Investment Report*. New York: United Nations Conference on Trade and Development.

Vernon, R. 1966. International investment and international trade in the product cycle. *Quarterly Journal of Economics*, 80: 190–207.

1979. The product cycle hypothesis in a new international environment. *Oxford Bulletin of Economics and Statistics*, 41: 255–67.

Wilkins, M. 1974. *The Maturing of Multinational Enterprise: American Business Abroad from 1914–1970*. Cambridge, MA: Harvard University Press.

1988. The free-standing company 1870–1914: An important type of British foreign direct investment. *Economic History Review*, 41: 259–82.

Wilkins, M. and Schroter, H. (eds.). 1998. *The Free Standing Company in the World Economy 1930–1996*. Oxford University Press.

Womack, J. P., Jones, D. T., and Roos, D. 1990. *The Machine that Changed the World*. New York: Free Press.

PART II

Unique capabilities of EMNCs: do they exist?

4 | Modern international business theory and emerging market multinational companies

ALAN M. RUGMAN AND
QUYEN T.K. NGUYEN

Introduction

In this chapter we explore the theoretical foundations of international business as they explain the nature and activities of emerging market multinational companies (EMNCs). We demonstrate that EMNCs mainly build upon their home country-specific advantages (CSAs). CSAs are exogenous location factors in a country that represent economic and institutional environments (including geographic location, factor endowments, government policies, national culture, institutional framework, and industrial clusters). The firm-specific advantages (FSAs) that these firms possess are due to recombinations with the complementary assets of home CSAs. FSAs are unique resources, capabilities, and strengths specific to a firm; they are strong when they are superior to those of rivals. In principle, FSAs must be effectively created, deployed, recombined, utilized, and profitably exploited by MNEs through their foreign subsidiaries. Yet, there are few examples of the foreign subsidiaries of EMNCs succeeding in developing FSAs in host economies. We find that EMNCs follow a linear one-way street from home CSAs to home country-based FSAs, but go off the tracks in seeking to develop host country-based FSAs.

In the pursuit of empirical support for this analysis, we reconsider many of the current case studies inhabiting the literature on EMNCs. We find that examples of alleged Chinese FSAs in cost innovation and scale efficiencies are entirely based upon home CSAs and do not transfer into host country-based FSAs. In contrast, many EMNCs are in mid-tech and mature industries, as discussed by Ramamurti (2009), with potential FSAs that might be based upon host CSAs. This chapter examines the specific conditions in the home country which influence the internationalization process of EMNCs. In the second part of the chapter, specific examples of EMNCs' international expansion (or not) will be analyzed.

What is modern international business theory?

Traditional internalization theory examines the interaction between country-specific advantages (CSAs) and firm-specific advantages (FSAs). A neglected aspect of this is the focus upon home CSAs. This leads to a focus upon the dynamic capabilities (FSAs) of parent firms in the home country. Literature based on this stems from Buckley and Casson (1976), Dunning (1958, 1981), Hennart (1982), Rugman (1981), and Vernon (1966). We refer to these as explanations based on "old internalization theory."

Consistent with the interactions between home country CSAs and parent firm FSAs is the eclectic paradigm (Ownership-Location-Internalization or OLI) of Dunning (1981, 1993). This argues that parent MNEs expand abroad through foreign direct investment (FDI) according to three basic motives: market seeking (to secure access to foreign country markets); natural resource seeking (to secure access to minerals, oil, forest products, and other natural resources in foreign countries); and efficiency seeking (to seek lower labor costs in foreign countries). In all three cases, the FSAs of the parent firm are taken abroad through FDI and the foreign subsidiaries of such MNEs operate as dependent branch plants or miniature replicas of the parent firm (Rugman, 1980, 1981). In other words, subsidiaries are not developing new capabilities, as their interactions with host CSAs are entirely driven by centralized and hierarchical strategic decision making by their parents in the home country.

Dunning made the unfortunate theoretical mistake of adding a fourth motive for FDI: asset seeking (sometimes called strategic asset seeking). This is a motive which is inconsistent with the OLI framework, which builds upon MNEs developing FSAs based in their home country where home CSAs matter. With asset seeking, the MNE subsidiary somehow needs to acquire knowledge assets (FSAs) owned by foreign MNEs in their own patch (which is subject to "host" CSAs from the viewpoint of the parent MNE). Well, good luck to these subsidiary managers. Somehow, they need to acquire (steal) FSAs from strong rival MNE parent firms. They shall seek but they shall not find.

Verbeke (2009); Rugman et al. (2011)

Home country-specific advantages Home CSAs	Host country-specific advantages Host CSAs
Location-bound firm-specific advantages **LB FSAs** • Stand-alone • Routines • Recombination capability **Non-location-bound firm-specific** **advantages** **NLB FSAs** ————————→	**Location-bound firm-specific advantages** **LB FSAs** • Stand-alone • Routines • Recombination capability **Non-location-bound firm-specific** **advantages** **NLB FSAs**

Ramamurti (2009); Hennart (2012)

Home country-specific advantages Home CSAs ————————→	Acquire FSAs in host countries
Control of complementary assets in home country (Brazil, Russia, India and China)	

Figure 4.1 Modern international business theory.

Basic internalization theory demonstrates that the rival MNEs will not sell (or yield to the theft) of their FSAs. At best, subsidiaries may have access to host CSAs, but they will not have mechanisms to turn these into FSAs.

Based upon the false notion of asset seeking FDI, an entire theoretically unsound literature has developed assuming that EMNCs can somehow acquire the knowledge assets of advanced Western MNEs. At best, this literature represents wishful thinking as both the MNEs themselves, and sometimes their governments, erect barriers to prevent the loss of their FSAs. The international political economy of interactions between EMNCs and Western MNEs is often distinguished by conflict in which issues of international competitiveness are used as quasi protectionist defense mechanisms. This process of prevention of asset seeking FDI now needs to be better incorporated into the literature.

In order to facilitate this challenge to the literature, we will carefully distinguish between old and new internalization theory. New internalization theory, as developed by Hennart (2009), Rugman and Verbeke (1992, 2001), and Verbeke (2009), distinguishes between FSAs obtained in home and host countries. It builds upon the old internalization theory focus on home CSAs and parent FSAs by explicitly theorizing about host CSAs and subsidiary-specific advantages (SSAs). Figure 4.1 illustrates these differences.

New internalization theory maintains that FSAs can be developed by both parent firms in the home countries and foreign subsidiaries in the host countries. There are three types of FSAs: stand-alone, routines, and recombination capability. Recombination capability is the highest-order FSA, and involves not just recombining the existing resources transferred from the parent firms but also recombining resources in novel ways, usually including new resources and capabilities developed by subsidiaries and accessing complementary resources from external actors in the host countries (Rugman, Verbeke, and Nguyen, 2011; Verbeke, 2009).

FSAs can also be classified by location specificity (Rugman and Verbeke, 1992). A location-bound (LB) FSA is defined as one that benefits a firm only in a particular location (or set of locations), and leads to benefits of national responsiveness. In contrast, a non-location-bound (NLB) FSA is defined as one that can be exploited on a worldwide basis, and leads to the benefits of scale, scope, and exploitation of national differences. SSAs (Rugman and Verbeke, 2001) are unique resources and capabilities owned or accessed by subsidiaries, which are to some extent distinct from those possessed by the parent firms and sister affiliates (Birkinshaw, 2000). We shall now apply this new internalization theory, especially the concept of recombination capability, to EMNCs.

Applying modern international business theory to EMNCs

The current literature on EMNCs (Cuervo-Cazurra and Genc, 2008; Hennart, 2012; Narula, 2012; Ramamurti, 2009, 2012) argues that home CSAs are the basis for FSAs. In the case of Ramamurti (2009), using India's EMNCs as an example, there are FSAs resulting from improvements in intermediate technology and the internalization of skilled labor in the IT sector. In the case of Hennart (2012), these are superior recombinations with home CSAs by EMNCs, as they build on their expertise in their home base. Narula (2012) argues that the initial FSAs of an EMNC tend to be constrained by the CSAs of the home country. Cuervo-Cazurra and Genc (2008) argue that MNEs from emerging markets may face less difficulty when entering host countries with institutional voids due to their home country experience with similar institutional deficiencies. Institutional voids are the gaps in market institutions found in the absence of intermediaries that facilitate a well-functioning market (Khanna and Palepu, 2010). This is an EMNC-type of adversity advantage.

To put these arguments more formally, Cuervo-Cazurra and Genc, Hennart, Narula, and Ramamurti correctly demonstrate that EMNCs can have dynamic capabilities. These are in the form of mainly stand-alone FSAs built through recombinations with the home country CSAs. As their thinking is the most advanced in this area, it is apparent that previous work simply ignored issues of FSAs and the dynamic capabilities of EMNCs. Indeed, as shown previously by Rugman (2009) and by Rugman and Doh (2008) most of the EMNC literature ignores internalization theory and its explanation of the necessity of recombinations between CSAs and FSAs.

What is missing from all the extant literature on EMNCs is the interaction between foreign subsidiaries of EMNCs and the host CSAs. This is the area of recombinations where future theoretical work is required. In this chapter we make a modest first step towards addressing this lacuna. In general, EMNCs need to erect autonomous managerial structures in their subsidiaries in order for the latter to achieve stand-alone recombinations with host CSAs. Yet there is little evidence that EMNCs, especially from China, have the managerial insights required to decentralize strategic decision making to their subsidiary managers. Rather, they are very hierarchical, parent-driven firms. In short, the critical lack of managerial resources in the subsidiaries of EMNCs will likely continue to hinder recombination capabilities with host CSAs.

EMNCs that build upon home CSAs are unlikely to have significant recombination capability in terms of the generation of tacit knowledge. Instead, their FSAs are likely to be stand-alone or characterized by routines and codification. Both types are genuine internalized FSAs, but both tend to be dependent on home CSAs and are thus likely to be LB FSAs. The tacit knowledge FSAs, which are NLB FSAs, are likely to be rare in EMNCs.

In summary, EMNCs are successful as they take home CSAs abroad. They are highly unlikely to develop dynamic capabilities by recombinations with host CSAs. The strength of EMNCs lies in the internalization of home CSAs through their control of complementary assets in their home country. This permits EMNCs to transmit such home CSAs and related FSAs to host countries. This is consistent with the 'late-comer' perspective (Mathews, 2006) and 'springboard' (Luo and Tung, 2007) literature, which correctly diagnose the home CSA sources of many EMNCs' capabilities. However, EMNCs lack internal organizational capabilities in their subsidiaries (which are rarely autonomous) and thereby are unable to develop recombination capabilities in host countries. In this, EMNCs differ from Western MNEs because the latter possess national responsiveness skills in subsidiary managers, leading to the possibility of working with the complementary resources of host CSAs.

Advancing empirical research on EMNCs

We shall focus here on Ramamurti (2009), as he offers an insightful synthesis of the theoretical literature relevant for analysis of EMNCs. Key contributions are by Aulakh (2007); Buckley et al. (2007), Cuervo-Cazurra (2012), Cuervo-Cazurra and Genc (2008), Goldstein (2007), Guillén and Garcia-Canal (2010), Hennart (2012), Lall (1993), Lecraw (1977, 1993), Li (2007), Mathews (2006), Narula (2006, 2012), Ramamurti (2009, 2012), Ramamurti and Singh (2009), Rugman (2009), Tolentino (1993), and Wells (1983). Ramamurti (2009) demonstrates correctly that many of these firms build upon home country CSAs. This analysis, in particular as it applies to Chinese firms, is entirely consistent with Rugman (2009). Ramamurti advances on Rugman (2009) through his innovative discussion of EMNC-type FSAs. Ramamurti (2009) presents examples of EMNCs that have developed five types of FSAs. Examples of such FSAs are: (1) products suited to emerging markets; (2) production and operational excellence; (3) privileged access to resources and markets; (4) diversity advantage; and (5) intangible assets.

The short case examples reported by Ramamurti (2009) generally seem to be plausible. However, (as shown below) the future development of theory will require more rigorous empirical work which examines the *strategy and performance* of EMNCs at a more aggregate and robust level. This takes us into the familiar methodological debate about the nature of empirical research. To assemble sufficient data to meet the requirements of rigorous econometric research, it is necessary to generalize by obtaining multiple observations of firms, possibly within industries or in other groupings. Inevitably, this leads to generalization about strategy and performance which may be invalidated by the heterogeneity of EMNCs. In contrast, specific case studies, no matter how detailed and vivid in description, may not be generalizable. At this stage, the future of research on EMNCs needs to continue to combine both approaches, but needs to move fairly quickly towards the gathering and analysis of large data sets at firm level in order to better align to modern theory.

As noted by Ramamurti, many of the EMNCs are in mid-tech and mature industries (Ramamurti, 2009: 415). This is a useful generalization and is based upon the extension of the CSA/FSA concepts. However, it now requires more detailed analysis. In particular, the performance of mature industries, especially state-owned firms from China, needs to be better analyzed. It is highly unlikely that mature state-owned enterprises (SOEs) perform well in comparison to competitors. We shall examine the composition of the "Global" 500 list of the world's largest firms in the next section.

The firms from emerging economies in the Fortune Global 500

Traditionally, over half of all world trade and approximately 80 percent of all foreign direct investments are made by the 500 largest firms in the world, which appear in the Fortune Global 500 annual ranking. Yet, the current literature on EMNCs has suffered from a basic empirical flaw. There is a commonly ungrounded assumption that once a firm from an emerging economy enters the Fortune Global 500, it is automatically referred to as an MNE (Guillén and Garcia-Canal, 2010: 10). This is not correct for the majority of BRIC (Brazil, Russia, India, and China) firms, as we demonstrate in this section.

A classic definition of an MNE is a firm headquartered in one country but having operations in at least three other countries (Rugman, 1981). These firms have at least 10 percent foreign sales and some foreign production through foreign direct investment (FDI). The foreign production takes place in a wholly owned foreign subsidiary (WOFS). Using these definitions, the majority of firms in the Fortune Global 500 from the broad Triad regions of North America, the European Union, and Asia Pacific qualify as MNEs. In contrast, the vast majority of firms from China entering the Fortune Global 500 in recent years are not qualified as MNEs. Indeed, most of the firms from emerging economies in the Global 500 are not MNEs.

Table 4.1 *Emerging economy firms in the Fortune Global 500 (2007–2012).*

Economies	2007	2008	2009	2010	2011	2012
P.R. China	24	29	37	46	61	73
Korea	14	15	14	10	14	13
Brazil	5	5	6	7	7	8
India	6	7	7	8	8	8
Russia	4	5	8	6	7	7
Taiwan Province of China	6	6	6	8	8	6
Mexico	5	5	4	2	3	3
Singapore	1	1	2	2	2	2
Malaysia	1	1	1	1	1	1
Thailand	1	1	1	1	1	1
Poland	1	1	1	1	1	1
Turkey	1	1	1	1	1	1
Saudi Arabia	1	1	1	1	1	1
Venezuela			1	1	1	1
Hungary			1			1
Colombia					1	1
United Arab Emirates						1
Total	70	78	91	95	117	129

Sources: Authors' calculations using data from Forbes, Fortune Global 500, several issues 2007–2012.

We rely on UNCTAD's *World Investment Report* for a definition of firms from developing and transitional economies, which includes ones from newly industrialized economies such as Korea, Taiwan Province of China, and Singapore. As shown in Table 4.1, the number of firms from emerging economies entering the Fortune Global 500 has increased significantly from 70 firms in 2007 to 129 firms in 2012. Most of these – 104 of the 129 in 2012 – are from the Asia Pacific region. For the 2012 ranking, the largest number of new entries comes from China, whose contribution rose from 24 in 2007 to 73 in 2012. There are thirteen firms from the Republic of Korea, eight from India, six from Taiwan Province of China, two from Singapore, one from

Malaysia, and one from Thailand. There are also eight from Brazil, seven from Russia, three from Mexico, one from Poland, one from Hungary, one from Turkey, one from Saudi Arabia, one from United Arab Emirates, one from Colombia, and one from Venezuela.

Chinese firms are not MNEs

The Chinese firms pose perhaps the greatest challenge as examples (or not) of international business. While the number of Chinese firms entering the Fortune Global 500 has nearly tripled in the past five years, the evidence suggests that few of them are truly internationalized. Indeed, the majority of the 73 large Chinese firms are mainly state-owned enterprises (SOEs) that have most of their total sales within China. They are still largely in protected banking, insurance, natural resources, utilities, telecommunication, land and real estate development, engineering, and construction industries. Such FSAs as they may have are built on home-country advantages like low labour cost, large scale of economies, subsidized capital, and privileged access to government connections, which actually distort the efficiency-based market economy. In short, Chinese SOEs have Chinese CSAs embedded in them.

A closer analysis of sales by geographic segments as required by the new International Financial Reporting Standard *IFRS8 Operating Segments* reveals that these 73 Chinese firms generate on average 94.3 percent of their total sales in Mainland China and Hong Kong. Indeed, 56 out of 73 firms have 100 percent of their total sales within China. Nine firms have some exports between 1 and 9 percent. The majority of these firms state in their annual reports that foreign operations are immaterial compared to those in Mainland China, so they are not subject to disclose geographic activities. Overall analysis of the 73 large Chinese firms reveals that their sales are home-country based, with the strong focus on the Chinese market likely to continue.

In summary, we find that there are only five Chinese firms which meet the basic definition of MNEs. These are (Table 4.2): Noble Group and Hutchison Whampoa (both from Hong Kong); and Huawei Investment & Holding, Lenovo Group, and China Ocean Shipping (all three from Mainland China). Although China Communications Construction (CCC) has foreign sales of 10.9 percent, it is highly likely that such foreign sales are from foreign contracts by the parent firm,

Table 4.2 *The five Chinese firms "Truly MNEs" in the Fortune Global 500 (2012).*

Country rank	Companies	Global 500 rank	Cities	Revenues (US$ m)	Intra-regional sales %	North America	Europe	Asia Pacific	ROW	Industry
8	Noble Group	91	Hong Kong	80,732	22.3	54.7	13.3	22.3	9.7	Trading/investment holding
47	Huawei Investment & Holding	351	Shenzhen	31,543	19.5	0	0	19.5	80.5	Electronics, electronic equip.
48	Hutchison Whampoa	362	Hong Kong	30,023	44.5	0.1	55.4	44.5	0	Trading/investment holding
52	Lenovo Group	370	Beijing	29,574	53.9	25.2	20.9	53.9	0	Computers
53	China Ocean Shipping	384	Beijing	28,797	46.3	14.5	12.2	46.3	27	Water transportation
Average				40,133.80	37.30	18.90	20.36	37.30	23.44	

Notes: Intra-regional sales = home country sales + rest of region sales.
Sources: Authors' calculations using data from the July 23, 2012 issue, Forbes, Fortune Global 500. Companies' annual reports: Data are for 2011. OneSource, *Thomson Reuters,* 2013.

and CCC has only two foreign subsidiaries: one in Japan and one in Indonesia. Weiqiao Pioneering Group has 13.6 percent foreign sales, which are exports by the parent firm. All of Weiqiao's subsidiaries are in Mainland China and Hong Kong. Similarly, China Shipbuilding Industry has 57.2 percent foreign sales, which are exports by the parent firm. Its subsidiaries are in Mainland China. While the current empirical literature on Chinese MNEs typically cites a few firms – namely Huawei, Lenovo, and Haier – Haier is actually not on the Fortune Global 500 list, and the majority of Chinese firms are domestic firms, not MNEs.

Similarly, the majority of Brazilian, Russian, and Indian firms have a strong focus on home-country sales given their large home markets. There are only a few exceptions of potential EMNCs, such as Vale and JBS (Brazil); Lukoil (Russia); and Reliance Industries, Tata Motors, and Tata Steel (India). These already have foreign sales over total sales in the range of 30–50 percent. In short, most firms from Brazil, Russia, India, and China (BRIC) in the Fortune Global 500 are not yet MNEs, and will take a long time to attain that status.

While each of the non-MNE Chinese firms needs to be examined, here we focus upon one which is at the forefront of internationalization. The Chinese SOE Aviation Industry Corporation Group of China (AVIC) operates in the aerospace and defense industry with business activities in military helicopters, commercial aircrafts, regional jets, aviation engines, flight test, and training. AVIC is attempting to internationalize into the commercial aircraft industry and is sending senior executives for management training at Henley Business School in the United Kingdom.

AVIC's strategy has been largely based on sales growth. The firm's sales have nearly doubled from US$21.7 billion in 2009 to US$40.8 billion in 2011. Its growth appears impressive at first glance as it has jumped from the 426th position when it first entered in the Fortune Global 500 in 2009 to the 250th position in 2012. However, a closer analysis reveals that it exhibits poor key performance indicators such as return on assets, return on sales, and especially return on employees (sales-per-employees) in comparison to other major aerospace and defense firms (Table 4.3). Specifically, this table indicates that AVIC currently has comparatively poor financial returns compared with Boeing, EADS, BAE plc, Thales, and Bombardier, and a poor return on employees compared with Mitsubishi and Embraer.

Table 4.3 *Comparative analysis on the performance of AVIC and competitors in the different segments.*

Indicators	Regional jet segment			Defense segment			Aerospace and defense segment	
	AVIC China	Bombardier Canada	Embraer Brazil	Mitsubishi Heavy Industries Japan	British Aerospace The UK	Thales France	EADS Europe	Boeing The US
Sales (US$ billion)	40.834	18.347	5.890	35.725	28.624	18	68.310	68.7
Profits (US$ billion)	0.930	0.837	0.093	0.3108	1.987	0.711	1.436	4.018
Assets (US$ billion)	81.946	23.864	8.908	48.115	35.901	27.374	114.855	79.986
Return on sales (profit/sales %)	2.3	4.43	1.59	0.87	6.9	3.93	2.1	5.8
Sales per employee (US$)	102,087	262,100	306,117	497,056	317,429	247,535	409,171	400,320
Return on assets (%)	1.13	3.49	1.12	0.62	5.53	2.28	1.21	5.02

Sources: AVIC sales data is from Fortune Global 500, employee data is from OneSource, *Thomson Reuters*, 2013; Bombardier, *Annual Report*, 2011; MHI, *Annual Report*, 2012; Embraer, *Annual Report*, 2011; BAE plc, *Annual Report*, 2011; Thales, *Annual Report*, 2011; EADS, *Annual Report*, 2011; and Boeing, *Annual Report*, 2011.

AVIC is an example of a Chinese SOE that is strongly based in its home market but has some opportunity to expand internationally. The key driver for such international expansion is that AVIC cannot develop into a world class modern aerospace and defense firm without being involved in the supply chain with potential airline customers outside of China. It will need to modernize sections of its value chain by introducing innovation and modern system integration on par with major world competitors.

However, unlike many other Chinese SOEs, AVIC has the opportunity to make foreign acquisitions of suppliers across its value chain and thereby leverage innovation, internal management, and other potential FSAs. The basic strategy for AVIC is to supplement home CSAs in financing subsidies and scale with the necessary internal organizational FSAs to develop sustainable product growth and service. Recently, AVIC acquired US aircraft engine manufacturer Continental Motors in 2010.

The major strategy of AVIC is to efficiently develop military technology and to eventually compete with Boeing and Airbus in the civilian airline industry. During the Airshow China 2008, AVIC appeared in public for the first time. In the Singapore Air Show in February 2010, AVIC introduced the COMAC 919 commercial aircraft for the first time outside of Mainland China. The aircraft is designed and built in China and will compete directly against industry stalwarts Airbus A320 and Boeing 737 after completing flight trials in four years. It should be commercially available by 2016 (Rugman and Collinson, 2012).

Alternative analysis of the EMNC case studies

We need to bring the analysis of firms from emerging economies to a more advanced and sophisticated level by scrutinizing their strategy and performance. The performance of specific firms from emerging economies now needs to be benchmarked against their global competitors, not just left in the limbo of the EMNC literature. Once such basic performance indicators are applied across firms from emerging economies, it is highly unlikely that the case examples can be shown to have successful strategies and sustainable performance.

We show here that the literature on EMNCs has reached implausible conclusions by studying a small number of firms from emerging economies. Previous studies (e.g. Mathews, 2006) have attempted to generalize their findings for the whole group of EMNCs by studying outliers, while Narula (2006) has correctly pointed out the selection bias of case studies. A few anecdotes have been repeated endlessly in the current literature, such as Lenovo (China) acquiring IBM's personal computer business, Haier (China) advancing in white goods, Huawei (China) and ZTE (China) succeeding in electronics and computer industries, Tata Motors (India) introducing the breakthrough initiative of "ultra cheap car Tata Nano" and its acquisition of Jaguar Land Rover from Ford Motor in the UK, Geely (China) acquiring Volvo (Sweden), Tata Steel's acquisition of Corus Steel (the UK), Suzlon (India) acquiring European wind turbine firms, South African Brewery's acquisitions of beer companies in Europe, Embraer (Brazil) advancing in regional jets, Mexico's Grupo Elektra, Cemex (Mexico), and Vale (Brazil), among others (Awate, Larsen, and Mudambi, 2012; Cuervo-Cazurra, 2012; Govindarajan and Ramamurti, 2012; Hennart, 2012; Peng, 2012; Ramamurti, 2009; Zeng and Williamson, 2007).

An intensive literature review on EMNCs and a Google search shows that Lenovo, Suzlon, and Tata Motors are among the most frequently cited examples. Below we shall provide alternative analyses of these case studies (Yin, 2003) to clarify whether the acquisition strategy of so-called strategic-asset FSAs improves their performance. We adopt an original and innovative approach by carefully integrating international business with international financial management and thus offer new perspectives.

Verbeke (2013) emphasizes that the real question when contemplating strategy alternatives is how to capture value and retain profits inside the firm. This is not simply how to rearrange a supply chain, nor how to lower costs further, nor how to enter into alliances with other companies, nor even how to specialize. Doing more R&D and having more advertising expenditures, i.e., moving up the smiling curve, both sound like good ideas (Mudambi, 2008). However, the reality is that both R&D and branding may require the allocation of large amounts of scarce resources without necessarily any guarantee of a positive return in terms of value capture at the level of the individual firm trying to move up the value chain, whether upstream or downstream. In other words, the real question is to find out which activities of the value chain FSAs can be developed and protected over the longer term. That means FSAs cannot be emulated by rivals or substituted by other companies, but are associated with a bargaining position strong enough to allow value capture by the firm (Verbeke, 2013).

A new perspective on Lenovo's acquisition of IBM's personal computer business in 2005

Lenovo is a China-based personal computer vendor. Lenovo develops, manufactures, and markets technology products and services. Lenovo acquired IBM's personal computing business on April 30, 2005, amid a backlash in Congress against Chinese companies trying to purchase American businesses. Lenovo paid US$1,750 million for IBM's computer business, which included US$650 million in cash, US$600 million in Lenovo equity, and the transfer of approximately US$500 net liabilities (IBM, *Annual report*, 2005). In a speech about the purchase, Lenovo executive Liu Chuanzhi said, "We benefited in three ways from the IBM acquisition. We got the ThinkPad brand, IBM's more advanced PC manufacturing technology, and the company's international resources, such as its global sales channels and operation teams. These three elements have shored up our sales revenue in the past several years."

To verify this statement, we analyze Lenovo's subsequent key performance indicators compared to global industry average. We find that as of September 30, 2012, Lenovo's performance was far behind industry average standards. Lenovo's five-year sales growth was 16.17%, while the industry average was 27.16%; its net profit margin was very thin at 1.63%, compared to the industry average of 16.98%; and its return on assets (ROA) was 3.28%, whereas the industry average was 19.26% (OneSource, *Thomson Reuters*, 2013).

We traced the annual reports of IBM for the period 2000–2005 and found that the personal computing business and other original equipment manufacturer (OEM) sales slowed dramatically due to pricing pressures and an ongoing downturn affecting worldwide semiconductor and OEM markets. The personal computer and hard disk drive (HDD) markets have much lower margins than other business segments for IBM because personal computers have become commoditized. In 2004, the personal systems group's pre-tax profit margin was 1.2%; it was 1.0% in 2003 and 0.5% in 2002. Other business segments had much higher pre-tax profit margins: global services at 9.4%, systems and technology group at 11.9%, software at 26.9%, and global financing at 38.4% (IBM, *Annual report*, 2004).

So, why did Lenovo buy into a business where FSAs are fading? At the turn of this century, the computer industry was at a mature stage of manufacturing. This means that there was pressure either to be extremely cost competitive or to develop value-added services that build on the computer itself. Thus, the major computer manufacturers have responded to these market changes in different ways. Although IBM invented the personal computer, it was perhaps the first to move strongly toward customer service. Eventually IBM divested personal computers altogether, selling the business to Lenovo. It is possible that Lenovo wanted insights into IBM's brand, distribution system, and marketing skills, but it quickly became a low-cost computer manufacturer. In late 2002, Hewlett-Packard and Compaq merged in order to consolidate production and develop the service end. In Europe, Siemens Nixdorf formed a joint venture with Fujitsu in 1999 and finally divested out of the computing business in 2009. This left Apple and Dell as the firms driven by low cost and technology (Rugman and Collinson, 2012).

By divesting its loss-making personal computing business, IBM has been able to focus on high-profit-margin business segments such as software, services, systems, and technologies. In the US market, IBM has developed a strategy of providing the best service in the industry. In the past, IBM had often referred service problems to its dealers. Now the company is addressing these issues directly, ensuring a higher level of service and reclaiming customers who were lured away by smaller firms with better service, support, and prices. Today, IBM makes very sizeable profits from software and services. IBM is customer-led; its US and international clients ask for what they want from IBM, and IBM produces solutions rather than specific products to link together the complicated global infrastructure. IBM is also making a big push into cloud computing, developing software to move big corporate clients into the cloud and building vast data centers to host them. It is also looking at ways in which technology can make an impact in the health care sector, with sensors to monitor patients remotely (Rugman and Collinson, 2012). It is apparent that Lenovo has not entered into such recombinations with host CSAs; indeed it is not in this type of service industry.

As of December 30, 2012, IBM's key performance indicators were close to industry averages. Its net profit margin was 15.89%, compared to the industry average of 18.27%, and its return on assets of 14.09% was above the industry average of 12.59% (OneSource, *Thomson Reuters*, 2013).

It is possible that Lenovo did indeed acquire certain FSAs related to the manufacturing of PCs in the acquisition, as evidenced by the loyal following of the ThinkPad models by corporate customers. But to what end? As other firms focus on disruptive technologies such as cloud computing and tablets, which are increasingly being adopted by consumers, it seems that any FSAs acquired by Lenovo from IBM are not the type that can deliver sustainable competitive advantage into the future.

In short, when the basic performance indicators are applied to the case study of Lenovo and its performance is benchmarked against international competitors, it is becoming clear that Lenovo is unlikely to realize sustainable and viable strategy and performance. The only two firms making profits in the personal computing business are the US chip maker Intel, with an average net profit margin of 20.63 percent, and the operating software firm Microsoft, with a net profit margin of 20.21 percent. Both firms outperform the industry average (OneSource, *Thomson Reuters*, 2013).

Suzlon and advanced wind power technology

Suzlon Energy Limited (SEL) is an India-based wind power company. The firm is in the business of manufacturing, selling, and installing wind turbine generators (WTGs) of various capacities and components. Its related activities include the sale/sub-lease of land for wind mills, infrastructure development, the sale of gear boxes, and the sale of foundry and forging components. Other activities include power generation operations.

Suzlon is the third-largest supplier of wind power after GE Wind (the US) and Vestas (Denmark), and it is the uncontested leader in India (Ramamurti and Singh, 2009). Suzlon is viewed as a "global innovator" in the advanced wind power technology industry through a series of acquisitions of Western firms (Awate et al., 2012; Hennart, 2012). In 2006, Suzlon paid US$565 million to acquire Hansen Transmission (Belgium), the world's second-largest maker of gearboxes for wind turbines. In 2007, Suzlon paid US$1.6 billion to purchase a controlling stake in REpower Systems AG, Germany's third-largest wind turbine manufacturer. In 2011, Suzlon paid US$85 million to achieve full control of REpower by acquiring the remaining 5 percent stake held by minority shareholders who resisted the takeover. Suzlon has used aggressive acquisitions to gain access to key components and technology (Guillén and Garcia-Canal, 2010).

Suzlon's strategy has been largely built on an aggressive sales growth, with a five-year average at 21.45 percent, which is above the industry of 6.22 percent. However, this strategy has not yet translated into the expected profit, but rather has increased debts, thus placing Suzlon in serious financial distress. Suzlon has recorded a loss in three consecutive years (2010–2012). As of September 30, 2012, Suzlon showed signs of over-trading, as its current ratio was 0.85 versus an industry average of 1.95; its quick ratio was 0.57 versus an industry average of 1.03. Suzlon relied heavily on debt financing, as its debt-to-equity ratio was 3.63 versus an industry average of 0.45. Its interest coverage for 2012 was at a worryingly low 0.37, which is far below the doomsday level of 2. All these ratios signal high gearing with high risk implications. Suzlon had negative working capital in 2012 at US$127.7 million. In fact, Suzlon's working capital has been deteriorating for the five-year period 2008–2012, from a positive working capital of US$2,556.1 million in 2008, declining to US$ 2,017.5 million in 2009, US$1,732.2 million in 2010, US$521.7 million in 2011, and ending up in negative working capital of US$127.7 million in 2012 (Suzlon, annual reports, 2008–2012; OneSource, *Thomson Reuters*, 2013).

Suzlon's net profit margin was extremely poor at −10.07 percent, compared to an industry average of 7.96 percent. The return on assets was at an extremely low level of −7.39 percent, while the industry average was at 8.48 percent (OneSource, *Thomson Reuters*, 2013). Such an aggressive international growth strategy through acquisitions is highly unlikely to lead to sustainable performance.

While international business scholars praise this firm as one of India's global powerhouses taking on the world (Kumar, Mohapatra, and Chandrasekha, 2009) and as a global niche player (Guillén and Garcia-Canal, 2010), a basic analysis of strategy and performance clearly reveals that Suzlon is in serious financial trouble. In 2009, Suzlon decided to sell a 35 percent stake in Hansen Transmission for US$370 million, and in 2009 it sold its remaining stake of 26.06 percent for US$178 million as part of a debt restructuring program.

It has considered selling two of its domestic subsidiaries, including SE Forge, and three foreign subsidiaries, including one in China, in order to reduce long-term debt (Datta, 2010). In short, Suzlon has failed to profitably exploit its newly acquired potential FSAs and has not created shareholder value. The causes of its underperformance are insufficient integration to achieve synergies, agency problems, and inadequate discipline in debt capital (Karnani, 2012).

Tata Motors and the world's cheapest car, Tata Nano

Another frequently cited example is Tata Motors and the world's cheapest car, Tata Nano, which has been hailed as a breakthrough reverse innovation (Govindarajan and Ramamurti, 2012). Tata Motors developed an affordable car that would appeal to many Indians who drive motorcycles after it was successful with low-cost pick-up trucks Ace and Magic. The purchase price of this "no-frills car" was brought down by dispensing with most nonessential features, reducing the amount of steel used in its construction, and relying on low-cost Indian labor. However, the plan backfired when Tata put too much emphasis on the cost savings and not enough on the (limited) sex appeal (Kapoor, 2012).

Tata Nano sales have been disappointingly poor and have been far below expectations since the car was launched in 2009. Sales stuck at 74,521 units for the year 2012, a growth of 5.8 percent over the previous year (Tata Motors, *Annual report*, 2012). However, Tata's planned production capacity was at approximately 250,000 units per year. Analysts have emphasized the need to recover from the marketing gaffe it has been haunted by since its launch in 2009.

"Tata didn't stress the car itself and it played too much on the cost attribute. People didn't want to buy the cheapest car in the world," said Deepesh Rathore, managing director at IHS Automotive in India (Kapoor, 2012). After ironing out a raft of safety concerns, Tata Motors announced its plans to improve the Nano by including a more powerful engine, a rectified exhaust system (which has previously caused fires), better air-conditioning, and a possible electric version (Tata Motors, *Annual report*, 2012).

In July 2012, Tata Group Chairman Ratan Tata asserted that the car has immense potential in the developing world, while admitting that early opportunities were wasted due to initial problems. The Nano is currently being tested for sales in Thailand (Tata Motor, *Annual report*, 2012).

Despite Tata's intention to replace two-wheel and three-wheel motorcycles, the Indian motorcycle segment witnessed record sales of 13.4 million units in 2011–2012, a growth of 14 percent over the previous year. In the same year, a growth in other automobile segments – particularly passenger vehicles and medium and heavy vehicles – slowed to single digits due to declining demand. This was due to rising inflation, high fuel prices, and high interest rates. The medium-term outlook for the motorcycle industry is steady growth, given an underdeveloped public transport system, growing urbanization, and strong replacement demand (ICRA, 2012).

In summary, our analysis of the strategy and performance of the three most cited cases of EMNCs (Lenovo, Suzlon, and Tata Motors) sheds new light on their international expansion strategy; it generally has very poor performance outcomes. We shall now turn to further analysis of the difficulty of internationally enhancing the FSAs of EMNCs, which is at the heart of the debate on EMNCs. We shall conclude with a fourth case example.

Spinning your wheels with "good enough products"

Ramamurti (2009) argues that one important FSA of EMNC is that they develop "good enough" products suited for other emerging markets. He provides the examples of Haier white goods (China), Mahindra and Mahindra SUV (India), Marcopolo bus (Brazil), and Tata Nano (India). Yet, an analysis of Haier's sales by geographic segments, as required by *IFRS8 Operating Segments*, shows that for the three-year period 2009–2012 Haier generated an average of 90 percent of its total sales within China (Haier, *Annual reports*, 2009–2012). In short, Haier white goods products are mainly for sales in China.

Analysis of sales by geographic segments of Mahindra and Mahindra SUV reveals that for the three-year period 2009–2012, it generated an average of 94 percent of its total sales in the domestic market. In short, its products are mainly for sales in India (Mahindra and Mahindra, *Annual reports*, 2009–2012).

Analysis of sales by geographic segments of Marcopolo (Brazil) shows that for the year 2011, Marcopolo generated 85% of its total sales in Brazil, 4% in Mexico, 4% in Colombia, 3% in Argentina, 3%

in India, 2% in Africa, and 1% in China (Marcopolo, *Annual report*, 2011). In short, Marcopolo buses are mainly for sales in Brazil.

We demonstrate that subsidiaries of "Western MNEs" operating in emerging economies can beat "good enough" products by EMNCs. We do this through a comparative analysis of the Chinese and Japanese motorcycle business in ASEAN countries. We find that the motorcycle subsidiaries of Japanese firms have the innovation and marketing capabilities to develop new LB FSAs and even to transform these LB FSAs into NLB FSAs. Unfortunately, EMNCs in this industry lack such FSAs.

Following the line of arguments by Ramamurti (2009), cheap Chinese motorcycles should have a strong market position in developing countries such as Vietnam, Laos, Cambodia, Thailand, Malaysia, Indonesia, and the Philippines. However, the business reality is that Japanese motorcycles such as Honda, Yamaha, and Suzuki dominate the markets. These are not EMNCs but are more "Western" mature MNEs. In Vietnam, "Honda" is a synonym for a motorcycle. Honda has developed high-quality motorcycles and is well known for its strong engine, reliability, durability, excellent customer care (with its wide network of authorized dealers known as HEADs), and especially fashion style. Suzuki and Yamaha are well known for sport styles. The Vespa scooter of Piaggio (Italy) is perceived as a trendy fashion icon. These Japanese and Italian motorcycle subsidiaries research and develop products that fit local road conditions. They establish strong positions in the local markets and export their products to many countries around the world.

Foreign motorcycle manufacturers invested in Vietnam in the 1990s. The Taiwanese Group ChingFeng was the first foreign investor in motorcycle manufacturing in Vietnam, establishing Vietnam Manufacturing and Export Processing Co. (VMEP), which began production in 1993. ChingFeng originally invested 100 percent equity, while Sanyang Motor Taiwan (SYM) provided management and technical support. VMEP's operational rights were transferred from ChingFeng Group to Sanyang in 2000 (www.sym-global.com). Japanese motorcycle manufacturer Suzuki entered the Vietnamese market in 1996, followed by Honda in 1997 and Yamaha in 1998. The Italian company Piaggio entered the market in 2009 and established a local manufacturing plant. These MNE subsidiaries initially used imported parts, but eventually they increased the localization of components. Many local motorcycle assemblers used Chinese component supplies or imported made-in-China finished motorcycles, which were copies of Japanese motorcycle models (Shintaku and Amano, 2012).

In the period 2000–2005, Chinese motorcycles penetrated the Vietnamese market due to low price. In response, the Japanese motorcycle manufacturers such as Honda, through its R&D center in Thailand, carefully reviewed the motorcycle performance requirements that Vietnamese consumers demanded and developed a new motorcycle model. The Honda subsidiaries in Vietnam and Indonesia, which are two of the fastest-growing markets in the ASEAN region, were the ones responsible for planning and exterior. At the same time, Honda put time and resources into supporting local suppliers that could provide low-cost parts. The company also used functional parts which were already developed and produced at reasonable cost. This allowed Honda to increase its local procurement ratio for parts in Vietnam from 53 percent in 2001 to 76 percent in 2003. In Indonesia, the number of suppliers increased to 130 with Honda's technological assistance. Honda thus reached the cost target in many ways, and could reduce the product price for the new models, Honda Wave in Vietnam and Honda SuperFit in Indonesia, to target price-conscious consumers. Thus, the price differences between the Japanese and Chinese motorcycles were significantly reduced (Shintaku and Amano, 2012). Japanese motorcycle makers quickly gained an increase in sales volume. By the end of 2005, the competition exerted significant pressure on the sales of Chinese motorcycles. Consumers lost faith in Chinese products because of their poor quality and low levels of customer support and after-sales services. Consumers did not want cheap motorcycles; they wanted ones that worked.

While Chinese motorcycles are struggling, the Japanese and Italian motorcycle makers are expanding. Present in Vietnam since 2009, Piaggio manufactures 100,000 products per year, and the localization ratio has reached 70 percent. Despite some warnings about an oversupply, Piaggio Vietnam is very optimistic about its business performance. The demand for high-grade scooters remains very high. Currently, 30 percent of the total annual production of 100,000 units in Vietnam is exported to other ASEAN countries. Meanwhile, Piaggio is developing plans to export to India and Taiwan. Additionally, Piaggio will build a research and development center in Vietnam in the near future (Vietnamnet, March 6, 2012).

Honda Vietnam is the largest motorcycle exporter. In 2011, Honda Vietnam sold 2.1 million products, including 300,000 products exported to the Philippines, Laos, Cambodia, and Afghanistan. After its huge success with the first factory, Honda Vietnam built a second factory in 2012, and its total production capacity reached 2.5 million products per year. Meanwhile, Yamaha Vietnam expects to increase its capacity to 1.5 million products and its total capacity will reach 5 million products per year by 2013, of which 3 million products are for domestic markets and the rest for export (Vietnamnet, March 6, 2012). In short, the high localization ratios, high-quality products and low production costs of Japanese-invested motorcycle subsidiaries in Vietnam are NLB FSAs, which lead to strong exports.

The innovation process of Honda in ASEAN countries is well documented with excellent insights by Shintaku and Amano (2012). These Japanese scholars show the danger of thinking that since income levels are low in emerging economies, cutting price regardless of other considerations makes sense. Price reduction is important as one of the steps toward developing the market, but it fails if the company doesn't also understand the market. In the long-term evolution of local markets, customers gradually learn about products, and their buying behaviors then follow not only their budgets but also their levels of product knowledge. Additionally, Shintaku and Amano (2012) emphasize the need to develop new resources and capabilities in local contexts, which are critical for success. This thinking is consistent with Rugman and Verbeke (2001), Rugman et al. (2011), and Verbeke (2009), with a strong emphasis on creating, deploying, utilizing, and profitably exploiting new SSAs.

Conclusions

The relevant theory to explain the growth and performance of EMNCs needs to be empirically embedded in the nature of EMNC activity. The most surprising finding of this chapter is that analysis based upon a dozen or so superficial case studies of EMNCs has led to misleading theoretical interpretations of EMNCs in the international business literature. The main challenge facing researchers in this area is to better align theories with the empirical evidence.

What is the empirical evidence about EMNCs? It appears that EMNCs need to be very carefully defined. If we take the traditional set of the world's 500 largest firms from the Fortune "Global" 500, there are now 129 firms from emerging economies. However, this exaggerates the number of EMNCs, as the vast majority of the 73 firms from China are purely domestic firms, somewhat handicapped from going international by their administrative heritage as state-owned enterprises (SOEs). There are only five Chinese firms that are truly MNEs. Of the 68 remaining firms from China, we find that most of them build upon their home country CSAs. Such FSA recombinations as take place largely occur with home CSAs. It is extremely rare to find an EMNC that has delegated autonomous strategic decision making to a foreign subsidiary such that SSAs can be achieved through recombinations with complementary assets of the host CSAs. We have also re-examined four "classic" cases of EMNCs, and found that their financial performance is poor and that international expansions via acquisitions tend to yield non-sustainable FSAs.

In short, modern international business theory, with its distinction between FSAs generated by home or host country recombinations, is immensely valuable in explaining EMNCs. These new types of MNEs from emerging markets are perfectly well explained by the international business theory that has been developed to analyze Western-type MNEs. Ultimately, any MNE needs to internalize a knowledge-based FSA. This may be enhanced through technology and efficient managerial resources in the home country, such that a Vernon (1966) product life cycle develops: strong home CSAs recombine with parent MNE FSAs and these are taken to foreign subsidiaries.

Over time, this process of internationalization through wholly owned subsidiaries may lead to development of SSAs, in particular if the subsidiary managers are given autonomy and a mandate for national responsiveness. Such organizational autonomy now needs to be carefully examined in EMNCs as it appears to be a rare phenomenon.

References

Aulakh, P. 2007. Emerging multinationals from developing countries: Motivation, paths, and performance. _Journal of International Management_, 13: 235–240.

Awate, S., Larsen, M. M., and Mudambi, R. 2012. EMNE catch-up strategies in the wind turbine industry: Is there a trade-off between output and innovation capabilities? _Global Strategy Journal_, 2: 168–187.

BAE plc. 2011. *Annual Report.* ara2011.baesystems.com/. Accessed on February 10, 2013.

Birkinshaw, J. M. 2000. *Entrepreneurship in the Global Firm.* London: Sage.

Boeing. 2011. *Annual Report.* www.boeing.com/companyoffices/financial/. Accessed on February 10, 2013.

Bombardier. 2011. *Annual Report.* ir.bombardier.com/en/financial-reports, Accessed on February 10, 2013.

Buckley, P. and Casson, M. 1976. *The Future of the Multinational Enterprise.* London: Macmillan.

Buckley, P. J., Clegg, J. L, Cross, A. R., Liu, X., Voss, H., and Zheng, P. 2007. The determinants of Chinese outward foreign direct investment. *Journal of International Business Studies,* 38: 499–518.

Cuervo-Cazurra, A. 2012. Extending theory by analyzing developing country multinational companies: Solving the Goldilocks debate. *Global Strategy Journal,* 2: 168–187.

Cuervo-Cazurra, A. and Genc, M. 2008. Transforming disadvantages into advantages: Developing country MNEs in the least developed countries. *Journal of International Business Studies,* 39: 957–979.

Datta, K. 2010. Suzlon revival in sight but needs lot more cash just to survive. *The Economic Times,* December 30.

Dunning, J. H. 1958. *American Investment in British Manufacturing Industry.* London: George Allen and Unwin.

1981. Explaining international direct investment position of countries: Towards a dynamic or developmental approach. *Review of World Economics,* 117: 30–64.

1993. *Multinational Enterprises and the Global Economy.* New York: Addison–Wesley.

EADS. 2011. *Annual Report.* www.eads.com/eads/int/en/investor-relations. html. Accessed on February 10, 2013.

Embraer. 2011. *Annual Report.* www.embraer.com. Accessed on February 10, 2013.

Goldstein, A. 2007. *Multinational Companies from Emerging Economies.* New York: Palgrave Macmillan.

Govindarajan, V. and Ramamurti, R. 2012. Reverse innovation, emerging markets, and global strategy. *Global Strategy Journal,* 1: 191–205.

Guillén, M. F. and Garcia-Canal, E. 2010. *The New Multinationals: Spanish Firms in a Global Context.* Cambridge University Press.

Haier. 2009–2012. Annual reports. www.haier.com/en/investor_relations/ 1169/finance_reports.

Hennart, J.-F. 1982. *A Theory of Multinational Enterprise.* Ann Arbor: University of Michigan Press.

2009. Down with MNE centric theories! Market entry and expansion as the bundling of MNE and local assets. *Journal of International Business Studies*, 40: 1432–1454.

2012. Emerging market multinationals and the theory of the multinational enterprise. *Global Strategy Journal*, 2: 168–187.

IBM. 2000–2005. *Annual Report*. www.ibm.com/annualreport/. Accessed on February 10, 2013.

ICRA. 2012. *Indian two-wheeler industry*, February 2012, icra.in/Files/ticker/Indian%202W%20Industry.pdf. Accessed on February 10, 2013.

Kapoor, K. 2012. Tata Nano picks up some speed. *Financial Times*, April 24. Accessed on February 10, 2013.

Karnani, A. 2012. Dubious value of international acquisitions by emerging economy firms. In A. K. Gupta, T. Wakayama, and U. Srinivasa Rangan (eds.), *Global Strategies for Emerging Asia*. San Francisco, CA: Jossey-Bass.

Khanna, T. and Palepu, K. G. 2010. *Winning in Emerging Markets: A Road Map for Strategy and Execution*. Boston, MA: Harvard University Press.

Kumar, N., Mohapatra, P. K., and Chandrasekha, S. 2009. *India's Global Powerhouses: How They Are Taking on the World*. Boston, MA: Harvard Business Press.

Lall, S. 1993. *The New Multinationals*. New York: Wiley.

Lecraw, D. 1977. Direct investment by firms from less developed countries. *Oxford Development Papers*, 29: 445–457.

1993. Outward direct investment by Indonesian firms: Motivation and effects. *Journal of International Business Studies*, 24: 589–600.

Li, P. P. 2007. Toward an integrated theory of multinational evolution: The evidence of Chinese multinational enterprises as latecomers. *Journal of International Management*, 13: 296–318.

Luo, Y. and Tung, R. L. 2007. International expansion of emerging market enterprises: A springboard perspective. *Journal of International Business Studies*, 38: 481–498.

Mahindra & Mahindra SUV (India). 2009–2012. *Annual Report*. www.mahindra.com/Investors/Mahindra-and-Mahindra/Resource. Accessed on February 10, 2013.

Marcopolo. 2011. *Annual Report*. marcopolo.infoinvest.com.br/enu/s-11-enu.html. Accessed on February 10, 2013.

Mathews, J. A. 2006. Dragon multinationals: New players in 21st century globalization. *Asia Pacific Journal of Management*, 23: 5–27.

Mitsubishi. 2011. *Annual Report*. www.mitsubishicorp.com/jp/en/ir/library/ar/. Accessed on February 10, 2013.

Mudambi, R. 2008. Location, control and innovation in knowledge-intensive industries. *Journal of Economic Geography*, 8: 699–725.

Narula, R. 2006. Globalization, new ecologies, new zoologies, and the purported death of the eclectic paradigm. *Asia Pacific Journal of Management*, 23: 143–151.

2012. Do we need different frameworks to explain infant MNEs from developing countries? *Global Strategy Journal*, 2: 41–47.

OneSource. 2013. *Thomson Reuters*.

Peng, M. W. 2012. The global strategy of emerging multinationals from China. *Global Strategy Journal*, 2: 97–107.

Ramamurti, R. 2009. What have we learned about emerging-market MNEs? In R. Ramamurti and J. V. Singh (eds.), *Emerging Multinationals in Emerging Markets*. Cambridge University Press.

2012. What is really different about emerging market multinationals? *Global Strategy Journal*, 2: 41–47.

Ramamurti, R. and Singh, J. V. (eds.). 2009. *Emerging Multinationals from Emerging Markets*. Cambridge University Press.

Rugman, A. M. 1980. *Multinationals in Canada: Theory, Performance and Economic Impact*. Boston: Martinus Nijhoff.

1981. *Inside the Multinationals: The Economics of Internal Market*. New York: Columbia University Press.

2009. Theoretical aspects of MNEs from emerging economies. In R. Ramamurti and J. V. Singh (Eds), *Emerging Multinationals from Emerging Markets*. Cambridge University Press.

Rugman, A. M. and Collinson, S. 2012. *International Business* (6th edition). Harlow, Essex: Pearson Education.

Rugman, A. M. and Doh, J. 2008. *Multinationals and Development*. New Haven and London: Yale University Press.

Rugman, A. M. and Verbeke, A. 1992. A note on the transnational solution and the transaction cost theory of multinational strategic management. *Journal of International Business Studies*, 23: 761–772.

2001. Subsidiary-specific advantages in multinational enterprises. *Strategic Management Journal*, 22: 237–250.

Rugman, A. M., Verbeke, A., and Nguyen, Q. T. K. 2011. Fifty years of international business and beyond. *Management International Review*, 51: 755–786.

Shintaku, J. and Amano, T. 2012. How some Japanese firms have succeeded against low-cost competitors in emerging markets. In A. K. Gupta, T. Wakayama, and U. S. Rangan (eds.), *Global Strategies for Emerging Asia*. San Francisco: Jossey-Bass.

Suzlon. 2008–2012. *Annual Report*. www.suzlon.com. Investor Information. Accessed on February 10, 2013.

Tata Motors. 2012. *Annual Report*. www.tatamotors.com/investors/financials/annual-reports-20F.php. Accessed on February 10, 2013.

Thales. 2011. *Annual Report.* www.thalesgroup.com/Group/Investors/.
    Accessed on February 10, 2013.
Tolentino, P. E. 1993. *Technological Innovation and Third World
    Multinationals.* London: Routledge.
Verbeke, A. 2009. *International Business Strategy* (1st edition). Cambridge
    University Press.
    2013. *International Business Strategy* (2nd edition). Cambridge University
    Press.
Vernon, R. 1966. International investment and international trade in the
    product cycle. *Quarterly Journal of Economics*, 80: 190–207.
Vietnamnet. 2012. Vietnam to become Asian leading motorbike production
    base? *Vietnamnet*, March 6. http://english.vietnamnet.vn/en/business
    /19548/vietnam-to-become-asian-leading-motorbike-production-base-.
    html. Accessed on February 10, 2013.
Wells, L. T. Jr. 1983. *Third World Multinationals: The Rise of Foreign
    Investment from Developing Countries.* Cambridge, MA: The MIT
    Press.
Yin, R. K. 2003. *Case Study Research: Design and Methods* (3rd edition).
    London: Sage.
Zeng, M. and Williamson, P. J. 2007. *Dragons at Your Door: How Chinese
    Cost Innovation Is Disrupting Global Competition.* Boston: Harvard
    Business School Press.

5 The limits of 'new' multinational enterprises: institutions, systems, and 'members-only' location advantages

RAJNEESH NARULA

Introduction

In this chapter I analyse the role of locations in shaping the mobility (or lack thereof) of multinational companies (MNCs) (and in particular emerging country multinational companies (EMNCs)) in a globalizing world. I am of the opinion that emerging country MNCs are not vastly different from 'adolescent' MNCs from other home countries, in terms of the principles by which they internationalize (Narula, 2010, 2012). I use the term 'adolescent' in the sense proposed by Ramamurti (2008) to describe an MNC that is not 'mature' in the extent to which it has developed firm-specific assets to manage and coordinate complex cross-border transactions. I am also of the opinion – despite the impression in some of the academic literature, as well as the popular press – that EMNCs as a phenomenon will not continue to demonstrate the consistently rapid growth rates that have fascinated commentators on globalization. As such, my discussion here is relevant to all adolescent MNCs, of which EMNCs are a subset. I will argue that there are two seemingly apposite explanations for their limited growth in the future. First, given that EMNC activities abroad are a function of their home country activities, the challenges of their home countries to fully adapt to the challenges of global interdependencies will impede growth. Second, the ability of EMNCs to fully exploit the opportunities available to them in developed country host locations is also affected by the weaknesses of their home country milieu, and the challenges of integrating into their host countries.

As I intend to explain, firms are not floating islands of economic activity, but are bound to locations because they are embedded (or insufficiently embedded, as the case may be), and this determines their success or failure, perhaps just as much as does their ownership of firm-specific assets. These firm-specific advantages (FSAs) are themselves a function of these relationships.

To step back just a bit: globalization as used here is taken to mean the increasing interdependence of firms, countries, and markets for goods, services, and capital (Narula, 2003). Generally speaking, globalization has not made firms (of which a subset are MNCs) necessarily more mobile. This reflects misunderstandings about the nature of globalization and how it affects locations, especially the nation-state. The nation-state still matters as a unit of analysis. Borders may have become fuzzy, but sovereignty still matters because governments still matter. As I will highlight here, emerging countries (like all countries) are complex organisms, of which firms are a relatively small subset of actors. The way these various actors relate to each other is also an important factor in shaping their location (L) advantages. It is for this reason I wish to emphasize the importance of taking a systems view of an economy.

Globalization means that the milieu within which economic activity takes place has been considerably altered, such that the way in which most economic actors organize themselves, as well as their interactions with other actors, has fundamentally changed. This means that institutions and actors that are geographically distant from the location under analysis play a non-negligible role in influencing the dynamics within the system.

It is worth emphasizing that I take as a starting point that the location-specific assets of the home country determine to a significant degree the firm-specific assets of its firms and MNCs. It is important to understand why this strong bond continues to persist despite globalization, and why this is likely to remain so. This requires an understanding of the interdependence between actors within a system, and the role of institutions. I seek in this chapter to highlight the importance of institutions, but not in the somewhat generic way that they are utilized in the international business (IB) literature, which tends to examine institutions as a black box of efficient and inefficient rules within countries that exogenously impinge on the actions of MNCs. Institutions matter because they are an invisible mesh that envelop, shape, and constrain the actions of actors in a given milieu, and these actors are themselves – sometimes collectively and occasionally individually – responsible for the nature of institutions. Economic actors – by their very presence in a specific locale – affect institutions, both singly and collectively.

I intend to use this framework to help highlight that location advantages are not always freely available to all actors in a given location. Especially for more knowledge-intensive activities, there are important location advantages that are 'members-only' and for which access is restricted to incumbents, and that do not have a public-good nature implied in some of the IB literature (Narula and Santangelo, 2012). This lies at the heart of the inertia of firms, and the difficulties of successfully leveraging location-bound assets in other countries, as well as the challenges of 'leaving home', since they may forfeit domestic 'membership' to do so. MNEs do not easily embed in a new location, and this requires considerable firm-specific assets associated with recombinant advantages, which are hard to acquire except through experience. There is also a specific set of issues relating to EMNCs, and these relate to the weakness of their home country L advantages. Home country L assets play a large part in defining EMNCs' FSAs, and where governments are unable to upgrade these (*inter alia* due to government failure or regulatory capture) it weakens the building block upon which sustainable outward FDI is possible.

The MNC as part of a 'system' and the role of globalization

Economic globalization is essentially about structural changes in the world economy that have resulted in: (1) an increasing number and range of both national (and collocated) and non-national (and not-collocated) actors that impinge on the activity of any given actor; and (2) an alteration in the nature and variety (both in terms of intensity and extensiveness) of the interactions due to this increased number of actors. Globalization means that the milieu within which economic activity takes place has been considerably altered, such that both the way in which most economic actors organize themselves and the way in which they interact with other actors has fundamentally changed. This means that institutions and actors that are physically 'elsewhere' from the location under analysis now play a non-negligible role in influencing the dynamics within the system.

It is important to acknowledge that globalization is a process. This growing interdependency between economic actors has been ongoing for a long period of time, and different locations have achieved different levels of cross-border interdependencies. Of course, there is huge variation between and among countries, and this is especially so in the case of developing countries. My main concern in this instance is to highlight that developing countries have been thrust into an accelerated and much more compressed version of what has been happening more gradually and over a longer period of time in most developed economies. In order to appreciate the challenges and opportunities that this compressed process represents, we need to see the economy as a 'system'.

I have used the term 'economic actors' deliberately, to include here not only MNCs, but all formally and systematically organized entities, each functioning (however imperfectly) as a clearly delineated single organization for the generation of a specific set of outcomes or goals defined by their stakeholders. 'Stakeholders' and 'goals' differ among these actors. For firms, the goal tends to be optimizing profits, and the stakeholders are its shareholders. The motives of governmental and non-governmental organizations (which I will refer to here as 'non-firms') are not profit-based, so the improved welfare of a certain section of society is often a primary outcome or goal. By referring to economic actors I am able therefore to account for very small actors (such as individual entrepreneurs), or very large ones (such as a nation-state, which itself consists of individuals). They are – at least all that wish to be successful – engaged in generating outputs by means of marshalling the resources of their organization in the most efficient way possible. I use the term 'efficient' to mean the basic principle of outputs generated per unit of input. The logic of how each economic actor interacts with others is based on similar principles, regardless of its size or the nature of its intended goal.

Interactions between the various actors are shaped by institutions, and by institutions I mean 'routines, habits, and procedures' that regulate the interaction between economic actors (Edquist and Johnson, 1997). These may be codified, formally acknowledged and established through laws, regulations, and other codified protocols, or may be more informal in nature, and in that case often uncodified.

There is a strong neo-classical economics bias to the IB and management literature that implies that firms are free agents, and because knowledge is in principle available freely to all, entrepreneurs are able to determine their outputs based largely on firm-specific resources and profit-maximizing motives. This is not entirely true, however, because firms are also constrained by other actors within their milieu, which we refer to here as a 'system'. Firms are embedded through historical, social, political, and economic ties to other actors within this system. Governments may restrict entry into certain sectors, for instance.

Complementary assets from support and related industries are also essential. To set up an airline requires the availability of jet fuel, maintenance service providers, caterers, airports, airport facilities, etc. It also requires a government policy that permits private firms to engage in this industry, and regulations (and agencies to implement them) on safety, pollution, air traffic control systems, etc.

A variety of academic perspectives incorporate a systems approach: for instance, the innovation systems concept (e.g. Lundvall, 1992; Edquist, 1997; Narula, 2003) and network theory (Gulati, 1998). A number of these approaches have delineated their analysis by taking the nation-state as the boundary of their analysis. It is also possible to think of a national system as imperfectly analogous to Porter's (1990) diamond of national competitive advantage.

As with Porter's diamond, however, few economies are stand-alone, and most have a distinctive international aspect to them (Dunning, 1992; Rugman and D'Cruz, 1993). However, depending upon the degree to which economies are internationalized, it may be unreasonable to consider highly internationalized economies purely from a national perspective, as emphasized by Rugman and associates in the double diamond approach (Rugman and D'Cruz, 1993; Moon et al., 1995).

Likewise, similar comments have been made about the national system of innovation approach. While such an approach made considerable sense in a pre-globalization era, by the twenty-first century few countries have truly 'national' systems. By and large, most economic actors within a system have a growing interdependence on actors outside their national boundaries (Narula, 2003). Of course, the degree to which non-national actors affect domestic activity varies considerably.

The pre-globalization era and the internationalization of emerging market firms

It is safe to say that prior to the 1990s – which I will refer to as the *pre-globalization era* – most developing economies[1] were closed systems,

---

[1] It is worth noting that most of the communist economies of Central and Eastern Europe (referred to here as the 'transition' economies) were even more closed. However, through the process of economic transition over the last two decades, most of these economies may now be thought of as developing economies, with few artefacts of the non-capitalist era remaining. Of course, significant exceptions exist, but even so, growing cross-border trade and investment has meant that few have purely national systems (Narula and Jormanainen, 2008).

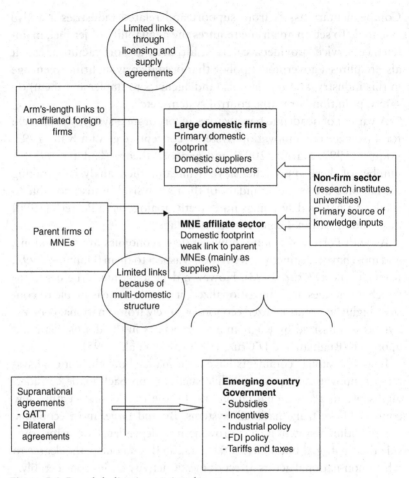

Figure 5.1 Pre-globalization national systems.

with a policy orientation best described as import-substituting and inward-looking, with only sporadic external linkages (Figure 5.1). Most developed economies and a handful of emerging economies (notably the newly industrialized Asian countries: Singapore, Hong Kong, Taiwan, and Korea) had an outward-looking, export-oriented economic system with cross-border linkages.[2] In the pre-globalization era, however, these non-national links were typically shallow, either

---

[2] Even among these four Asian NICS there was considerable variation between countries (Lall, 1992, 1996).

through trade or occasionally FDI; inward FDI accounted for less (usually much less) than 5 per cent of value adding of these economies. As such, even these economies could usefully be modelled as primarily 'national' systems (Narula and Dunning, 2010).

Figure 5.1 gives a general idea of the primary influences on economic actors in pre-liberalized, import-substituting economies circa 1980s. As Figure 5.1 illustrates, domestic firms in developing countries tended to have limited and sporadic international links, being largely dependent upon domestic suppliers and customers. Limited linkages to foreign companies existed through arm's-length agreements such as technology licensing, turnkey contracts, and capital equipment imports. Likewise, MNC affiliates in the local economy were 'detached' from their parent MNCs, as most MNCs tended to organize their emerging economy activity on a multi-domestic basis, concentrating on meeting local markets. The domestic non-firm sector was the primary source of employees and scientific and technological infrastructural support, and its link to international sectors was also limited and indirect.

The limited links were not just a result of the policy frameworks and the political economy of these developing countries, but were to some extent structural to the world economy at large. The impact of major technological changes such as in information and communication technologies (ICTs) and improvements in transportation have allowed firms to engage more directly in cross-border activities across the board, and also to coordinate and integrate these activities since the 1980s (Cuervo-Cazurra, 2012).

Emerging economy government policies played a primary role in the activities of the domestic system, creating a variety of incentives and restrictions to promote their industrial and development policies. Policy was largely shaped by domestic priorities, with a relatively small influence due to various supranational agreements such as GATT, and bilateral treaties.

Even in the developed countries, it was still the case in the 1960s and 1970s that economies were largely 'national'. Nonetheless, assisted by *de facto* and *de jure* economic integration, coupled with social and political ties that have evolved over a long period, developed countries have traditionally had a greater degree of cross-border interdependence (albeit between geographically proximate countries

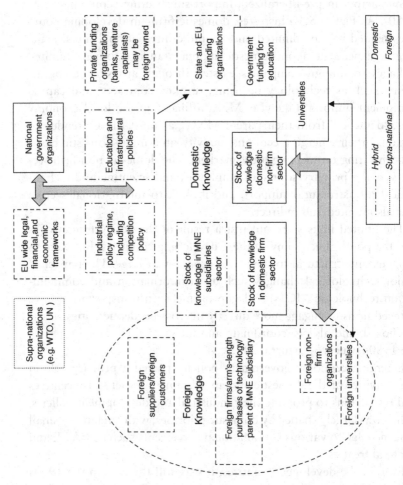

Figure 5.2 Interrelationships within the system of a typical EU country.

within the same region). With globalization, this interdependence has increased even further. Figure 5.2 gives a sense of a 'typical' system for an EU country post-1992 (i.e. after the single market was established). Similar but less intense linkages will be seen between Canada and the US.

Figure 5.1 and Figure 5.2 are obviously stylized expressions of two different types of economies, but together they help to contrast and highlight the degree to which developing countries and advanced economies had non-national influences within their economic system. They help to illustrate the 'gap' between the two systems and the degree to which domestic firms were dependent upon external actors.

The globalization era and the internationalization of emerging market firms

The *globalization era has* seen a fundamental change in the economic structure of emerging economies, from a closed system towards a more outward-oriented and internationally interdependent system. This 'structural adjustment' implied that developing economies began to shift their close systems (Figure 5.1) towards a more intertwined 'global' system as depicted in Figure 5.2. Specifically, this occurred through a concatenated series of changes. This is a process that is idiosyncratic to each individual economy and is still ongoing, but broadly speaking all developing economies are experiencing a similar set of profound changes.

First, the competitive pressures on domestic firms increased in almost every country, due to inward FDI. Furthermore, there have been increasing numbers of domestic firms that are formally or informally linked to networks of firms abroad, in addition to once purely domestic firms that have become MNCs. Customers are not limited to domestic suppliers, and there is keen pressure on prices and quality.

Second, the economic structure of the domestic market has also changed. State-owned enterprises (SOEs) and powerful large private enterprises (which have tended also to enjoy privileged status within the domestic milieu, as national champions) have been able to expand abroad financed in part by monopoly profits from closed, protected markets generated over the pre-globalization era. WIPRO, a large Indian software company, for instance, began life as India's largest manufacturer of vegetable and cooking oils, expanding into ICTs only after liberalization. At the same time, the liberalization of the domestic economy has acted as a catalyst for a new generation of domestic actors, which are typically small but able to exploit the new opportunities that derive from more open markets.

Third, new sources of inputs – either in the form of services and support industries, or in the form of suppliers within the same value chain – from abroad have also become available. For example, foreign-owned banks and other financial service providers have increased the competition in a sector that typically in most developing countries has been dominated by a few large, inefficient domestic (state-owned) players.

Fourth, firms are affected by extra-national regulation. As their customer and supplier bases are increasingly located abroad, they must comply with and react to government policies and regulations in multiple locations.

Figure 5.3 illustrates how internationalization in the scope of the system of emerging economies has evolved over the last 20 years. Some domestic firms have established foreign activities, and the domestic system is now indirectly influenced by knowledge sources through the activities of their foreign affiliates. MNC affiliates have become more integrated with their parent firms, as MNCs have sought to reassert control and exploit economies of scale and scope from a wider MNC network. At the same time, firms – of all nationalities – have become dependent upon a broader geographical clientele as well as more diverse networks of suppliers, both domestic and foreign.

Firms in the domestic milieu are no longer as reliant upon the domestic non-firm sector. Either indirectly via links through their foreign-located affiliates, or directly, they are engaged with foreign-located universities, research institutes, and non-governmental organizations.

Indeed, many of the advanced economy universities and research institutes have also internationalized their operations, setting up campuses and facilities in developing countries. Fraunhofer, a German private (but state-supported) research organization, has actively begun to established research facilities in South America and Asia. Most universities – regardless of nationality – have active research links with other universities in a broad swath of countries, which include staff exchanges and joint research laboratories.

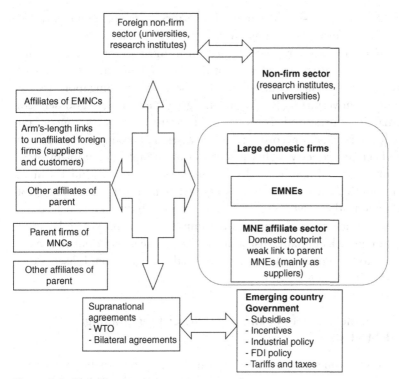

Figure 5.3 Globalization-era system.

Emerging economy governments now – in this new global milieu – have limited policy space due to World Trade Organization (WTO) agreements which restrict domestic policies on subsidies, incentives, national champions, tariffs, barriers to entry, and preferential treatment. In addition, domestic firms are also affected directly by the governments of other countries. As they have operations in multiple locations, they are affected by policies of the various host governments. In addition, they interact with customers and suppliers in multiple locations, and must abide by their regulatory requirements.

It is important to highlight that while there is indeed a more complex milieu in terms of the types of actors engaged in the globalization-era system, the degree of embeddedness between these various actors is still in flux. Comparing Figure 5.2 with Figure 5.3, the cross-border aspect of the new developing country system is still shallow compared to the developed country system. This is especially so because a number of newer players – such as inward investors – are not fully embedded within the formerly national system. MNCs – despite treaties within the WTO requiring national treatment in most sectors – are still not accorded equal treatment in most developing countries. A variety of issues still remain outstanding, with the so-called 'Singapore issues' covering government procurement, agriculture, health, and services remaining unresolved. National policies are not always concordant with international accords. In other cases, national policies such as intellectual property rights protection are simply not implemented, or implemented half-heartedly, in countries as varied as India, China, and South Africa. Governments and other non-firm actors have not adapted to their new roles, and have often not fully acknowledged the new realities of regulation and the importance of providing location advantages. Essentially, institutions (both formal and informal) have failed to keep pace with the new national configuration. I discuss this further in the next section.

The inefficiency of systems as a barrier to upgrading in EMNCs

The discussion in the previous section about the new reality of a larger number of actors is a stylized one. Nonetheless, there is considerable variation in the degree to which actors have responded to opportunities – both potential and immediate – to embed across borders, and to exploit cross-border interdependencies.

In addition, liberalization has not always led to a growth in the domestic firm sector. The influx of foreign-owned and controlled MNCs has increased the competition levels faced by domestic firms. Crowding-out affects firms that have weaker FSAs (Beaudry and Breschi, 2003). Crowded-out domestic firms simply do not have the FSAs to compete against large foreign MNCs, which have scale economies as well as greater efficiencies that derive from being multinational. At a broader level, the failure of domestic firms in developing countries to overcome increased competition reflects the weaknesses of the system, which has not been able to respond to the challenges of liberalization because the necessary location assets did not exist, in terms of technological and absorptive capacity. This may reflect a weak non-firm sector that is unable to assist domestic actors in upgrading their assets. It may also reflect a failure to link up development and industrial policies with

FDI policies. Upgrading of domestic actors through spillovers and linkages from inward FDI is not an automatic process, and requires a certain threshold level of absorptive capacity (Narula and Dunning, 2010; Morrissey, 2011). Spillovers are externalities that accrue from one firm to another, and imply a process of learning by the recipient firm because of some formal or informal association between the firms in question (Morrissey, 2011). MNC-assisted development presumes that inward investors will create linkages with local firms, but where these firms do not have the requisite skills, such linkages will be established with suppliers located abroad, with whom the MNC already has associations in its other operations. Even where linkages are indeed established, this does not imply that spillovers will occur (Narula and Driffield, 2011).

The point is that moving from pre-globalization (as in Figure 5.1) to a globalization era structure (as in Figure 5.3) does not happen automatically. Actors in any system tend to change their existing patterns of cooperation and interdependency grudgingly. This is known as 'inertia', and reflects the tendency of actors to replicate their previous actions, and a reluctance to implement change or modify routines. Inertia by itself is a natural phenomenon, and is neither 'good' nor 'bad'. Inertia can be positive when actors develop inertia around routines that have historically generated a positive outcome. A fundamental shift from one political and/or economic regime or policy stance can also represent a discontinuity or 'shock', which requires a modification of existing routines. Inertia is not the same thing as an inability to upgrade. At the country level, there is often a strong institutional inertia to overcome; whether the discontinuity is as fundamental as the one experienced by the former centrally planned economies during their transition, or is from an import-substituting stance to a more open, export-oriented one, as experienced by many developing countries, the difference is only one of degree (Neuber, 1993; Narula and Jormanainen, 2008).

Inertia can be a pervasive phenomenon at the level of a whole economy, because often there is a self-reinforcing interaction between industrial enterprises; the infrastructure and politics which perpetuates the use of specific technologies, production of specific products, and/or through specific processes; and specific customer-supplier associations. Institutional restructuring is not an instantaneous or costless process, and results in inefficient outcomes because actors in the system are obliged to alter their *raison d'être*. Institutions developed for, or specialized around, a particular economic system are not efficient in responding to the needs of another system. In the case of the import-substituting countries, institutional inertia was often associated with selected industries built around national champions. Institutional inertia in most cases has meant that aspects of import-substitution policies continue to shape the 'flavour' of current policies, particularly those to do with national champions and interest groups, who continue to heavily influence policy (Narula, 2002).

Actors in that system can become locked-in to specific industries and specific technologies. Therefore, it is not uncommon that the technological specialization of both firms and locations changes relatively slowly over time (Cantwell, 1989; Cantwell and Iammarino, 2003). Over-specialization of knowledge infrastructure to meet the specific needs of specific sectors and industries can also lead to *ex post* inefficiencies. Firm-infrastructure relations can be so closely interdependent that the boundaries and functions of firms and the various components of the knowledge infrastructure are unclear, and *de facto* operate as one large unit (Grabher, 1993). Rigidities due to the inertia of institutions and the knowledge infrastructure can seriously affect the ability of an economy and its actors to adapt to new technologies, and/or the entry of new actors into the system. If inertia persists over a long period, domestic actors will not survive unless non-firm actors (typically government policy-determined organizations) or firms themselves seek to address these constraints and are able to overcome the lock-in. However, the external agencies themselves often suffer from cognitive inertia, or are constrained by politics from radically modifying the system.

The non-firm sector is important as an agent of change when major exogenous shocks occur, because it has the potential to minimize the disturbances from the environment. By establishing standards, subsidizing basic research, providing incentives to sunset industries to restructure, and improving the available human resources needed for new sectors, the non-firm sector can help overcome structural problems due to liberalization. For instance, this sector can help to retrain workers in new skills and sectors, or change the university curricula, etc. It can create incentives for the adoption of new technologies, or improve the access to these technologies by making them available more cheaply. However, government intervention is conditional on available resources. Developing country governments and firms often do not have the resources – or the expertise – to invest in reducing the shock of exogenous changes. There is also the somewhat larger problem of an inefficient non-firm sector, and an unresponsive government (government failure being a widespread problem in developing countries). As such, the knowledge infrastructure may be unable to overcome lock-in as rapidly as firms need.

Firms also suffer from inertia, and ultimately institutional inertia (where governments do not respond) has to be addressed by firms who have an incentive to respond to environmental changes (Hannan and Freeman, 1984). They may respond to these challenges by replacing the inefficiencies of the state by creating internal alternatives to knowledge infrastructure. This may be through creating firm-specific training facilities (for example, Indian conglomerates Tata and Infosys have their own universities). Others overcome limitations in local capital markets by relying on intra-conglomerate loans. Limitations in IPR protection are overcome by a greater degree of vertical integration. These solutions, however, depend upon being large in terms of size, and being able to cross-subsidize, which also means generating larger than normal profits to cover these costs (which in turn, implies remaining in protected markets). Internalizing functions that are traditionally location advantages (in principle available to all) also means that new entrants must resort to internalizing such activity, acting as a barrier to entry and a limit to being embedded locally.

This also implies that domestic firms from developing countries may find it cheaper to move their activities abroad to access more efficient knowledge infrastructures, rather than developing their own solutions to the weaknesses of the home system. In other words, firms may choose an exit strategy, seeking to re-locate all or parts of their innovative activity to exploit a more optimal SI elsewhere.

Most countries do not have an 'ideal' system, with most countries' systems being 'incomplete' or 'unbalanced' because some aspects of the systems are inefficient or simply non-existent. This is especially so in developing countries. Even where an efficient, complete, and balanced system exists, exogenous shocks are likely to create inefficiencies. Institutions are the 'glue' that bind the various actors together, and determine the efficacy of their interaction (or lack thereof). Formal institutions are codified and administered by state-administered organizations which are themselves formal institutions, since they are formally defined by law, and their structures are designed to create and implement new and existing formal institutions. Indeed, the political and economic spheres are rarely independent, and this is all the more so in a pre-globalization era, in developing countries that had implemented import substitution programmes, or in the former centrally planned economies. In general, the policy environment in which economic actors function has a high degree of interdependency between the economic and political spheres. Informal institutions represent routines which are essential to the implementation of formal institutions. One of the most important aspects of informal institutions is that they cannot be easily established, and once established, cannot be easily modified.

The point I am trying to make here is that you may have all the 'building blocks' of a 'globalized' economic system, but they may still not work together efficiently, because institutions do not always adjust themselves as rapidly as necessary to the new realities of the globalization. Emerging economies have moved towards an open system structure similar to that of the developed economies, but because of structural and institutional inertia, or simply due to a resource constraint, they may not function efficiently.

Domestic firms may respond to poor domestic systems by relocating themselves (or part of their activities) to another country through FDI. Nonetheless, this option is not as straightforward as it may seem – entering a new country with the goal of accessing an innovation system in the host economy is not costless. Embeddedness takes time to achieve, again, because the knowledge of institutions takes time to acquire. Furthermore, not all location advantages are public goods, especially those associated with knowledge-intensive sectors. As I discuss in the next section, some location advantages are 'members-only'. This has consequences for embedding foreign MNCs in developing countries (thereby affecting these countries from linkages due to inward FDI), and the abilities of emerging country MNCs to embed themselves abroad (and therefore attenuating the possibility of their home countries benefitting from reverse knowledge transfer).

Location stickiness, 'members-only' access, and EMNC internationalization

Earlier interpretations of the eclectic paradigm suggest that Location (L) advantages are a set of characteristics associated with a location that are in principle equally accessible and applicable to all firms that are physically or legally established in that location. L advantages are about relevant complementary assets outside the boundaries of the MNC (or other firm actor) that are location-bound (Narula and Santangelo, 2012). However, in this chapter we take the view that not all L advantages are in fact freely available to all. In essence, location advantages are 'public' goods because they are not private goods, but not always in the sense of being 'public goods', because they may not be used by others without (some) detriment to their value.

The key to appreciating L characteristics is that universal accessibility can be 'in principle'. They are 'in principle' available to all, but some are more public than others; this is the central point I want to make. I want to distinguish between two types of L advantages. First those that resemble the classical view of L advantages: 'public good' L advantages, which are available at marginal (and similar) cost to all economic actors in a given location. They remain macro and 'generic', and are available to all firms regardless of size, nationality, industry, or geographical unit of analysis. Some are exogenous, and are the natural assets of the location, such as population, climate, accessibility, etc. Some are independent of economic stage of development (such as the presence of natural resources), while others are stage-dependent and endogenous, in the sense that the various actors within a system contribute to their development. Examples include skilled and unskilled human capital, health care, utilities, telecoms, ports, security, efficient bureaucracy, public transport, etc. Others are sociological or anthropological, such as culture, norms, religion, and political stability (Narula and Santangelo, 2012).

The second type of L advantages are quasi-public goods, whose access is a function of membership in a system or network of actors. I will call these 'members-only' L advantages; elsewhere I have also referred to them as 'collocation' L advantages (Narula and Santangelo, 2012), although they are not in fact the same thing. The difference between the two types is that collocation advantages do not have to be restricted to 'members only'. Collocation L advantages derive from the proximity of other actors, may be externalities, and are in principle available to all collocated firms. For instance, where firms in the same industry are collocated, there is an opportunity to get appropriately skilled and experienced workers and the possibility of knowledge spillovers through mobile employees.

'Members only' L advantages are associated with 'clubs'. To para-
phrase the American Express marketing department: 'membership
should have its privileges'. Just as in any respectable club, the value of
membership derives from the value of the goods and services that it
provides members, and the exclusivity of access to these goods and services. The exclusivity implies barriers to entry, such as fees. However,
not all clubs arise by creating exclusivity – it can be the exclusivity that
causes clubs. When a certain set of assets is in limited supply, those
with access to them do not wish to compete with others through markets for this access. Creating restrictions to new entrants and establishing quasi-internal markets for scarce resources then becomes a viable
strategy.

A systems view is crucial to understanding 'members-only' L
advantages for two reasons. First, the effect of interactions is central
to understanding the actions of firms, including their choice of location. It is not just the presence of suppliers, customers, competitors,
or regulators. Each on its own plays a role, but the synergetic effects
are a function of the sum total of the presence of all these factors.
These are economies of agglomeration, and it is this that determines
the 'stickiness of locations' (or its absence). Indeed, spillovers tend to
be more intense between parties that are located close to each other
in space (e.g. Jaffe and Trajtenberg, 1996, 1998; Jaffe et al., 1993;
Maurseth and Verspagen, 2002). The marginal cost of transmitting
codified knowledge across geographic space does not depend on distance, but the marginal cost of transmitting *tacit* knowledge increases
with distance (Criscuolo and Verspagen, 2008). The spatial aspect has
also been evaluated in terms of the compatibility of organizational
cultures and social networks that reflect the culture of the location,
and these themselves are shaped by the nature of the polity, and the
social and economic institutions of that location (Granovetter, 1985).
The systems perspective helps us to understand these various stimuli
as a 'package', rather than a collection of discrete components. It also
helps us to link to the idea that there are certain kinds of knowledge
that are only available to members with a particular location-specific
absorptive capacity by virtue of their constant interaction. Firms are
embedded in different and unique external local networks of suppliers,
customers, competitors, institutions, authorities, and associations
(Granovetter, 1985; Zaheer and McEvily, 1999). It is well known that
trust between network members lowers the costs of negotiation and

resolves conflict (Zaheer et al., 1998). In particular, network membership reduces opportunistic behaviour and improves knowledge transfer, because network members have a greater awareness of the informal institutions that govern their interaction (Gulati, 1998: 304).

Second, understanding agglomerations by considering a systems view allows for the emphasis of institutions, and helps us to come to grips with the well-known but terribly imprecise concept of something that is 'in the air' (Marshall, 1920). Embeddedness in a location provides membership in a 'club' of complex relationships with suppliers, customers, and knowledge infrastructure through formal and informal institutions. These are 'goods' associated with the networks that are only available to those that are collocated, because they have evolved under the same informal institutions. Thus they are quasi-public goods, which firms located there have invested in to acquire knowledge of these institutions (Iammarino and McCann, 2006; Narula and Santangelo, 2009).

Members-only L advantages have a lot to do with informal institutions. In particular, and sometimes most fundamental, is the 'know-who' (Narula, 2002). Building up links with various actors (in the IB literature, this is analogous with 'trust' and 'relationship capital'), is time-consuming and expensive, but once created, these links have a low marginal cost of maintenance.

For an outsider, the high costs of becoming familiar with, and integrating into, a new system may be prohibitive (Narula, 2003). These are the liabilities of outsidership. For an insider, however, such membership comes with privileges which provide opportunities for rent generation. Indeed, more recent work on informal institutions – which are notoriously difficult to quantify – points to the absence or inefficiency of institutions as a primary force inhibiting economic development (e.g. Rodrik, 1999; Rodrik et al., 2004; Asiedu, 2006).

The concept of location is a generic one, allowing us to speak of different units of analysis, even though the assumption remains that the default unit of analysis is the country. However, even within countries, sub-national regions have different sets of L advantages (Narula and Santangelo, 2012). Supra-national regions, such as the European Union (EU), that function as a single administrative unit also need to be considered in certain cases, because they provide an additional layer of policies, regulations, and laws. An MNC may engage with all three levels of location.

When location-bound assets are in the private domain (i.e. they are internalized by specific economic actors), they are no longer L advantages but constitute firm-specific assets, since they assist rent generation/market share retention by specific actors to the exclusion of other economic actors. That the primary difference between FSAs and location advantages is a matter of internalization is an important point. It is therefore not especially surprising that FSAs can be location-bound and 'sticky': that is, they are most effectively utilized in specific locations and firms have difficulty exploiting them in other locations.

That firms' FSAs can be 'sticky' and location-bound should not come as a big surprise. Until about the 1960s, economic activity was presumed to be largely immobile, because both capital and labour were seen to be location-bound, and self-evidently there was little propensity to mobility. The field of IB has largely revolved around explaining the rapid growth of MNCs in these 50 years, and it is a recent phenomenon that scholars have begun to presume the exact opposite, i.e. that all assets and firms are largely mobile.

One of the constants – despite the structural changes in the world economy, and a move from location-bound firms to MNCs – is that it is still largely true that the competitiveness of firms is primarily shaped by the attributes of the location, and as locations have evolved in the nature of their inherent strengths and weaknesses, the kind of economic activity based there has also fluctuated. This had obvious ramifications for the nature and extent of trade, and the conditions that permitted one region or country to be more successful than others.

Nonetheless, the modern MNC has gradually decoupled the relatively straightforward relationship between the competitiveness of firms in a given location and the competitiveness of the location itself. Conventional wisdom in a pre-globalization era held that the competitiveness of countries explained the competitiveness of firms located there, and while this is still true, it is less so than it was a few decades ago. The 'typical' firm in the 1950s was neither multinational nor multi-plant. It was also organizationally and geographically associated primarily with one or a few locations, and with one or a few countries. Economic studies were able to work under the realistic assumption that firms could be viewed as generic (Beugelsdijk et al., 2010). The more spatially and organizationally complex the MNC has become, the greater has become its interdependence upon multiple locations, each with varying degrees of embeddedness (Meyer et al., 2011). In the globalization era, the MNC has the potential to shape the characteristics of its location as much as it is itself shaped by its milieu, given that it is embedded in several locations. However, fully globalized and 'transnational' MNCs for whom the home country plays a marginal role are still the exception and not the rule: home countries and regions continue to account for the lion's share of MNC activity. This is certainly true for emerging country MNCs.

As such, location plays a central role in understanding the nature, extent, and rate of internationalization of firms and the evolution of the 'typical' MNC. It also helps to underline that locations matter not in a generic sense of countries, but in the sense that locations are about the agglomeration of a variety of activities by a large number of actors who happen to be collocated.

Closing remarks: the limits of EMNC mobility and implications for home country policy

The beginning of the third millennium has largely been marked by a celebration of the highlights and dubious outcomes of globalization, which is inextricably linked to a discussion of the role of capitalism. The 'sudden' appearance of certain emerging economies as active and significant players in the world economy is one of the recurring themes of this current epoch. The arrival of certain emerging economies as important home and host countries for outward FDI, and their rapid growth over the last two decades, has been taken as a sign that they have adapted well to the opportunities of globalization.

This line of thought has some fundamental flaws. Globalization has wrought some fundamental changes to the structure of the emerging economies. In no small part, this is due to economic and political liberalization, but the necessary systematic transformation of these economies is still far from complete. There is a high degree of endogeneity and interaction among and between institutions, science and technology infrastructure, the competitiveness of industrial enterprises, and the endowments of any given economy. The sudden exposure of these economies to the vagaries of international competition has not necessarily facilitated their institutional restructuring. Liberalization in developing countries did not always take place gradually, as was the case in most developed countries. Even the success stories like Brazil, India, and China have not been able to shift easily to taking a multilateral view towards hitherto-domestic issues. Institutional inertia in most cases has meant that developing countries have been quick to see the costs of globalization (principally the erosion of economic (and political) sovereignty and the sterility of policies and attitudes associated with import substitution) as outweighing the benefits associated with it. Although by the mid-2000s, many developing countries had largely overcome institutional inertia due to the shift towards open economies, it continues to shape the 'flavour' of policies. National champions and interest groups dominant in the IS era continue to hold sway; a suspicion of MNCs continues to limit access in certain sectors. This means that new inward FDI to emerging economies still struggles to embed itself in these economies, limiting the opportunities for spillovers to the domestic sector. With the arrival of a wide variety of new actors, and the growth of outward activity, the equilibrium within many countries has been lost, and they are still adjusting to a wide variety of new formal and informal institutions. This has significant implications for EMNCs, who have moved abroad in some cases as a reaction to the institutional instability at home (Khanna and Palepu, 2006; Witt and Lewin, 2007). They have also relocated in response to the limited learning opportunities in the domestic economy, given the inability of the state to provide world-class knowledge infrastructure. Where the local system does not meet the needs of firms, they can respond by exiting, so as to acquire these inputs from systems which are able to provide them (Narula, 2002).

It is true that liberalization has helped correct many inefficiencies, *inter alia*, improving important macro-economic fundamentals, and reduced the excessive role of the state in domestic industrial activity. On the other hand, it has also led to a rapid and overzealous reduction in the state's involvement in the provision of public goods and location advantages which are necessary conditions for industrial development (Katz, 2001). It is worth noting that another important feature of globalization – rapid technological change, and a growing share of knowledge-intensive activities within traditional labour intensive fields – requires new kinds of L advantages from countries that have difficulty providing the most basic infrastructure.

It is also true that a certain group of EMNCs are internationalizing from a position of strength, and engaging in market-seeking investments abroad. However, a number of these firms are only now beginning to realize that internationalization requires more than having superior products and services. Firms also need transaction-type O advantages which include the ability to organize and manage complex cross-border hierarchies (Narula, 2012). These are not easily acquired. As research on intra-firm knowledge flows has shown, moving knowledge between affiliates is a challenging task (Monteiro et al., 2008).

EMNCs (like all MNCs) hope to be able to integrate themselves into their foreign locations to exploit location-specific assets in combination with their O advantages. However, this requires recombinant 'bundling' advantages. Determining how to most efficiently integrate O and L advantages together is not an easily acquired capability (Verbeke, 2009; Narula, 2012). This brings up the challenges of reverse knowledge transfer. Firms seeking to transfer knowledge assets acquired in one location to others (and in particular to their parent firm in the home country) are faced not just with the challenges of intra-firm knowledge transfer, but also the challenge to integrate and transfer these assets to its affiliated suppliers and related firms (Rabbiosi, 2011). At a broader level, we do not know how MNCs transfer knowledge effectively between different organizational units, and more importantly, why some firms are more successful in leveraging knowledge created elsewhere. Indeed, this is a significant issue for EMNCs.

In addition, however, EMNCs need to acquire access to specific L advantages which may not be 'public good' type L advantages, but rather 'members-only' L advantages. Becoming integrated within a specific national or regional system is a time-consuming process, because becoming an insider is not a straightforward process. Such knowledge is hard to acquire or exchange through markets.

Although I have not dwelled on the matter, this chapter provides a precursor to explain the location-boundedness of the FSAs of firms. It is now well recognized that not all FSAs are easily portable, as Rugman and Verbeke (2001) highlighted, which naturally raises the question of subsidiary-specific advantages that are not necessarily available to the MNC at large. These require us to revisit the nature of FSAs.

References

Asiedu, E. 2006. Foreign Direct Investment in Africa: The role of natural resources, market size, government policy, institutions and political instability. *World Economy*, 29: 63–77.

Beaudry, C. and Breschi, S. 2003. Are firms in clusters really more innovative? *Economics of Innovation and New Technology*, 12(4): 325–42.

Beugelsdijk, S., McCann, P., and Mudambi, R. 2010. Introduction: Place, space and organization, economic geography and the multinational enterprise. *Journal of Economic Geography*, 10: 485–93.

Cantwell, J. A. 1989. *Technological Innovation and Multinational Corporations*. Oxford: Basil Blackwell.

Cantwell, J. and Iammarino, S. 2003. *Multinational Corporations and European Regional Systems of Innovation*. London: Routledge.

Criscuolo, P. and Verspagen, B. 2008. Does it matter where patent citations come from? Inventor versus examiner citations in European patents. *Research Policy*, 37: 1892–908.

Cuervo-Cazurra, A. 2012. How the analysis of developing country multinational companies helps advance theory: Solving the Goldilocks debate. *Global Strategy Journal*, 2: 153–67.

Dunning, J. H. 1992. The competitive advantage of countries and the activities of transnational corporations. *Transnational Corporations*, 1: 135–68.

Edquist, C. 1997. *Systems of Innovation*. London: Pinter/Cassell Academic.

Edquist, C. and Johnson, B. 1997. Institutions and organisations in systems of innovation. In C. Edquist (ed.), *Systems of Innovation: Technologies, Institutions and Organizations*. London: Pinter/Cassell Academic.

Grabher, G. (ed.). 1993. *The Embedded Firm*. London: Routledge.

Granovetter, M. 1985. Economic action and social structure: The problem of embeddedness. *American Journal of Sociology*, 91: 481–510.

Gulati, R. 1998. Alliances and networks. *Strategic Management Journal*, 19: 293–317.

Hannan, M. and Freeman, J. 1984. Structural inertia and organizational change. *American Sociological Review*, 49: 149–64.

Iammarino, S. and McCann, P. 2006. The structure and evolution of industrial clusters: Transactions, technology and knowledge spillovers. *Research Policy*, 35: 1018–36.

Jaffe, A. and Trajtenberg, M. 1996. Flows of knowledge from universities and federal labs: Modelling the flow of patent citations over time and across institutional and geographic boundaries. *NBER Working Paper*. www.nber.org/papers/w5712. Cambridge, MA: National Bureau of Economic Research.

1998. International knowledge flows: Evidence from patent citations. *NBER Working Paper*. www.nber.org/papers/w6507. Cambridge, MA: National Bureau of Economic Research.

Jaffe, A., Trajtenberg, M., and Henderson, R. 1993. Geographical localisation of knowledge spillovers, as evidenced by patent citations. *Quarterly Journal of Economics*. 58: 577–98.

Katz, J. 2001. Structural reforms and technological behaviour. The sources and nature of technological change in Latin America in the 1990s, *Research Policy*, 30: 1–19.

Khanna, T. and Palepu, K. 2006. Emerging giants. *Harvard Business Review*, 84(10): 60–9.

Lall, S. 1992. Technological capabilities and industrialization. *World Development*, 2: 165–86.

1996. *Learning from the Asian Tigers*. Basingstoke: Macmillan.

Lundvall, B.-Å. 1992. *National Systems of Innovation: Towards a Theory of Innovation and Interactive Learning*. London: Pinter.

Marshall, A. 1920. *Principles of Economics*. London: Macmillan.

Maurseth, P. and Verspagen, B. 2002. Knowledge spillovers in Europe: A patent citations analysis. *Scandinavian Journal of Economics*, 104: 531–45.

Meyer, K. E., Mudambi, R., and Narula, R. 2011. Multinational enterprises and local contexts: The opportunities and challenges of multiple embeddedness. *Journal of Management Studies*, 48: 235–52.

Monteiro, F. L., Arvidsson, N., and Birkinshaw, J., 2008. Knowledge flows within multinational corporations: Explaining subsidiary isolation and its performance implications. *Organization Science*, 19: 90–107.

Moon, H. C., Rugman, A. M., and Verbeke, A. 1995. The generalized double diamond approach to international competitiveness. In A. Rugman, J. Van Den Broeck, and A. Verbeke (eds.), *Research in Global Strategic Management. Volume 5: Beyond the Diamond*: 97–114. Greenwich, CT: JAI Press.

Morrissey, O. 2011. FDI in Sub-Saharan Africa: Few linkages, fewer spillovers. *European Journal of Development Research*, 24: 26–31.

Narula, R. 2002. Innovation systems and 'inertia' in R&D location: Norwegian firms and the role of systemic lock-in. *Research Policy*, 31: 795–816.

2003. *Globalisation and Technology: Interdependence, Innovation Systems and Industrial Policy*. Cambridge: Polity Press.

2010. Keeping the eclectic paradigm simple. *Multinational Business Review*, 18: 35–50.

2012. Do we need different frameworks to explain infant MNEs from developing countries? *Global Strategy Journal*, 2: 188–204.

Narula, R. and Driffield, N. 2011. Does FDI cause development: The ambiguity of the evidence and why it matters. *European Journal of Development Research*, 24(1): 1–7.

Narula, R. and Dunning, J. H. 2010. Multinational enterprises, development and globalization: Some clarifications and a research agenda. *Oxford Development Studies*, 38: 263–87.

Narula, R. and Jormanainen, I. 2008. When a good science base is not enough to create competitive industries: Lock-in and inertia in Russian systems of innovation. MERIT-UNU Working Papers, 2008–059. Maastricht, Netherlands: United Nations University, Maastricht Economic and Social Research and Training Centre on Innovation and Technology.

Narula, R. and Santangelo, G. D. 2009. Location, collocation and R&D alliances in the European ICT industry. *Research Policy*, 38(2): 393–403.

2012. New insights on the role of location advantages in international innovation. In A. Verbeke and H. Merchant (eds.), *Handbook of Research on International Strategic Management*: 291–309. Cheltenham: Edwards Elgar.

Neuber, A. 1993. Towards a political economy of transition in Eastern Europe. *Journal of International Development*, 5: 511–30.

Porter, M. E. 1990. *The Competitive Advantage of the Nations*. New York: Free Press.

Rabbiosi, L. 2011. Subsidiary roles and reverse knowledge transfer: An investigation of the effects of coordination mechanisms. *Journal of International Management*, 17: 97–113.

Ramamurti, R. 2008. What have we learned about emerging MNEs? In R. Ramamurti and J. Singh (eds.), *Emerging Multinationals from Emerging Markets*, Cambridge University Press.

Rodrik, D. 1999. The new global economy and developing countries: Making openness work. Policy Essay 24, Overseas Development Council. Washington, DC: John Hopkins University Press.

Rodrik, D., Subramanian, A., and Trebbi, F. 2004. Institutions rule: The primacy of institutions over geography and integration in economic development. *Journal of Economic Growth*, 9: 131–65.

Rugman, A. M. and D'Cruz, J. R. 1993. The double diamond model of international competitiveness: Canada's experience. *Management International Review*, 33: 17–39.

Rugman, A. M. and Verbeke, A. 2001. Subsidiary-specific advantages in multinational enterprises. *Strategic Management Journal*, 22: 237–50.

Verbeke, A. 2009. *International Business Strategy: Rethinking the Foundations of Global Corporate Success*. Cambridge University Press.

Witt, M. and Lewin, A. 2007. Outward foreign direct investment as escape response to home country institutional constraints. *Journal of International Business Studies*, 38: 579–94.

Zaheer, A. and McEvily, B. 1999. Bridging ties: A source of firm heterogeneity in competitive capabilities. *Strategic Management Journal*, 20(12): 1133–56.

Zaheer, A., McEvily, B., and Perrone, V. 1998. Does trust matter? Exploring the effects of interorganizational and interpersonal trust on performance. *Organization Science*, 9(2): 141–59.

6 | The evolution of EMNCs and EMNC thinking: a capabilities perspective

DONALD LESSARD

Introduction

After describing three parallel evolutions in international business – the phenomenon, the context, and the way we understand the phenomenon – this chapter explores what is special about emerging market multinational companies (EMNCs), including the emergence of a new class of internationally active firms – global value chain enterprises (GVCEs). It then addresses the question of whether EMNCs possess ownership advantages by applying the lens of the RAT-CAT capabilities framework to a set of EMNCs. It concludes with a set of propositions regarding EMNC and GVCE firm-specific advantages.

The three evolutions

International business (IB) is undergoing three parallel evolutions: the phenomenon, the context, and how we as IB scholars see both of these. As applied scholars, the evolution of the phenomenon is the one that should matter most. More and more companies are conceived of and driven from emerging economies, and they are interesting. Further, the context in which they operate is radically different from the one that spawned advanced economy-based multinational companies (AMNCs) and gave rise to our current conception of the MNC. Finally, the way we view MNCs in general and emerging market multinational companies (EMNCs) in particular lags changes in both what they are and the context that gives rise to them.

The evolution of EM-based companies that are internationally active

Many emerging market firms now competing internationally have been around for a long time. In the case of the so-called *multilatinas*, many are the same names I was following in my dissertation (Lessard, 1970, 1973). Of course, there are many new names, but the more interesting phenomenon is how much more internationally active most of these firms are now.

Not all EM-based firms that are internationally active fit the traditional definition of an EMNC. Being internationally active can take the form of traditional market-seeking "horizontal" FDI, essentially replicating the home country business model in other counties, or traditional resource-seeking vertical MNCs like mining or oil firms. In either case, being internationally active involves foreign direct investment (FDI) as the firm engages in activities outside its home country that it governs through ownership. However, in today's global world, being internationally active can take the form of insertion into a global value chain, either within or outside of the firm's home country, which is just as likely to be governed by relational arrangements as by ownership, and thus may not represent FDI. I take the view that the purview of IB should be all internationally active firms, not just the ones that engage in FDI.

The definition of internationally active global value chain enterprises (GVCEs) is an open question, but in my judgment it should include firms that are active in design and aggregation, including original design manufacturers (ODMs) and major original equipment manufacturers (OEMs), but not relatively passive suppliers of standard components or products. By this definition, for example, Quanta and Foxconn in the electronics supply chain would both be GVCEs, but most suppliers in the apparel supply chain would not. However, supply chain orchestration firms such as Li and Fung would fall into this category (see Buckley, 2009, for an insightful discussion of emerging global production networks).

Firms become internationally active for a variety of reasons. A common first reason is to protect market power at home. This was the case for the Mexican construction materials firm CEMEX, a company that I draw on extensively for insights. Its initial internationalization, the acquisition of two locally focused cement companies in Spain, was motivated by a desire to protect its market position in Mexico and its independence in a globalizing industry. It is a matter of historical record that it had hired BCG to work with it to prepare a strategic reaction to the possible entry by European cement companies in its domestic oligopoly.

Another reason to become internationally active is to build on success at home. Many EMNCs have followed the classic pattern of building market positions and capabilities at home, and then projecting them into other markets, just like traditional AMNCs.

Yet another reason arises out of the offshoring/global supply chain revolution of the 1980s. Many EM-based firms became specialists in a particular stage of the supply chain and subsequently sought to integrate forward or backward to expand their options and/or to limit the commoditization of their existing positions. In today's world, where supply chains are open, roughly half of all traded goods are intermediate products. Most of these are not traded at arm's length, but are orchestrated. We in IB need to pay more attention to firms that orchestrate and control international transactions and extend our purview beyond EMNCs that control transactions through ownership.

Finally, a few EM-based firms have begun to create new metanational value propositions (Doz et al., 2002), combining inputs, stimuli, and resources from various countries to do something that could not have come from any one. Whether this metanationality is more prevalent among EMNCs or AMNCs is an interesting question, though I expect that metanationality will become more prevalent among EMNCs, as argued by Santos (2007).

Though perhaps in a slightly different order, this is a fairly classical set of motivations for becoming internationally active. Even GVCEs have their counterpart in the extractive MNCs that in many cases predated the home-based projectors.

The evolution of the EMNC context

The evolution of EMNCs closely parallels the evolution of the context for international business, including manufacturing technology, information-communication-transport, international regimes, markets, and international finance. A timeline of major changes over the last century is illustrated in Figure 6.1.

The figure begins with the technological context of manufacturing, which begins with the revolution brought by Ford's assembly line in the early 1900s, followed by the Toyota production system in the 1950s and the rise of offshoring and outsourcing in the 1990s. Interestingly, these are more about the organization of manufacturing than the specific technologies involved.

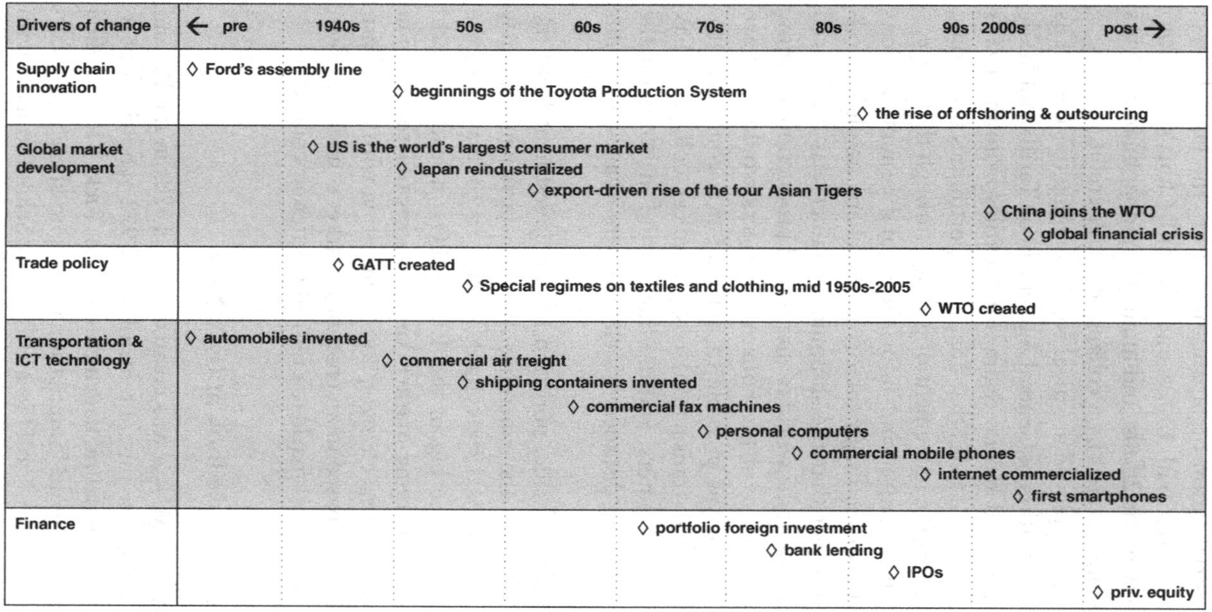

Drivers of change	pre	1940s	50s	60s	70s	80s	90s	2000s	post →
Supply chain innovation	◇ Ford's assembly line	◇ beginnings of the Toyota Production System				◇ the rise of offshoring & outsourcing			
Global market development		◇ US is the world's largest consumer market	◇ Japan reindustrialized	◇ export-driven rise of the four Asian Tigers				◇ China joins the WTO	◇ global financial crisis
Trade policy		◇ GATT created		◇ Special regimes on textiles and clothing, mid 1950s-2005			◇ WTO created		
Transportation & ICT technology	◇ automobiles invented		◇ commercial air freight / ◇ shipping containers invented	◇ commercial fax machines	◇ personal computers	◇ commercial mobile phones	◇ internet commercialized	◇ first smartphones	
Finance					◇ portfolio foreign investment	◇ bank lending / ◇ IPOs			◇ priv. equity

Figure 6.1 Evolution of EMNC context.
Source: Fung Global Institute, finance line by author.

The next line traces global market developments beginning with the dominant demand position of the US in the early post-World War II era, the reindustrialization of Japan, the rise of "the Four Tigers" (Hong Kong, Singapore, South Korea, and Taiwan), China's entry into the global economy in the 2000s, and finally the global financial crisis of 2008 that was precipitated by a collapse of trade credit.

Trade policy regimes played a critical role in shaping this context as well. Following the creation of General Agreement on Tariffs and Trade (GATT) in 1947, we had special regimes for textiles from the 1950s through 2005 – a maze of rules that created opportunities for adding value by orchestrating the movement of product through that maze.

Changes in transportation and information and communications technology (ICT) also are major factors in the changing global context. It is easy to forget that the shipping container was introduced only in 1955. Without it, the world of distributed production we know and the export-driven rise of the Four Asian Tigers would not have been possible. Once it was possible to put stuff in a container at a relatively low handling (transaction) cost, distances collapsed. Fax machines, personal computers, and the Internet did the same for the ability to coordinate at a distance. It's clear we are in a radically different world now.

Finally, on the finance side, portfolio foreign investment from the advanced countries into the emerging markets started in the early 1970s, but took off in the 1990s. Bank lending to companies in the emerging markets became big in the 1980s. IPOs in leading world financial markets of emerging market companies became the norm in the 1990s. With all of these changes, and culminating with global private equity, a company based in an emerging market is no longer hostage to its domestic capital market, a radically different context.

The evolution of how we look at (E)MNCs

Our current theory of MNCs was created in the 1970s in the US and other key FDI bases of the time. I remember in 1972 venturing out to teach my first international management class at Tuck. I had studied at Stanford, where the word "international" was nowhere in our curriculum, and came "down" to Harvard Business School to meet with Ray Vernon and learn about his multinational enterprise study with its "fantastic" database of 187 companies, all US-based multinationals

(Vernon, 1971). The US was on top and was the world's lead market. Of course, others were following the phenomenon as well. John Dunning was beginning to chronicle the growth and development of the MNC (Dunning, 1973, 1981) and the Scandinavians Jan Johanson and Eric Vahlne were at work with their own process perspective (Johanson and Vahlne, 1977).

In this context, and for many years, the focus on EMNCs was largely about what was strange or different about them: "Isn't it interesting that firms from strange places can actually compete internationally?" There were exceptions of course, such as Wells' book showing that many of the same arguments made to explain AMNCs also applied to EMNCs (Wells, 1983).

As the phenomenon became more visible, the question increasingly became one of "how do I have to adjust my lenses to explain, understand, and advise this strange phenomenon?" I hope we are long past that stage, and well into a second one of "how do I integrate EMNCs into the general phenomenon?" Now that there is no question that EMNCs are a part of the global economic fabric, I envision a third question: "How do I explain the heterogeneity of internationally active firms and forms, and what general insights can I gain by exploiting this heterogeneity?" It's not about research on EMNCs. It's about research that uses the heterogeneity in forms, types, and origins of firms that are internationally active to truly understand what's going on in the changing global organization of business.

A key distinction of EMNCs relative to AMNCs is that they are latecomers (for an excellent review of what distinguishes EMNCs from MNCs in general, see Ramamurti, 2012). Further, they come from relatively low-cost bases, often from countries with "weak institutions" and "incomplete diamonds" (Porter, 1990, 2000). Being a "latecomer," most importantly, means that these firms can learn cross-sectionally from the experience of others. Contrast this with Vernon's original product lifecycle (Vernon, 1966) where firms had to learn on their own, longitudinally. Nowadays, EMNCs can look over AMNCs' shoulders. They still have to learn by doing, but they also can learn by observing (Vernon, 1979).

Of course, many EMNCs are not new. Some were born at the turn of the twentieth century, and many were born 30 or 40 years ago, but a lot of them are only now coming to life as internationally active companies in this era of broadband communication and relatively open trade, finance, and IP. There is a much more diverse set of market dynamics, and a much more dispersed and diverse base for innovation.

The presence of these latecomers has brought back an earlier phase of IB scholarship. By the 1990s, IB as taught in the US had by and large forgotten about internationalization and had refocused on global strategy, since most Western multinationals had internationalized long ago and their problems were function, geography, business, coordination, and transnational or metanational integration and innovation, as opposed to deciding where to go for what purpose. With the emergence of EMNCs, internationalization came alive again.

EMNCs typically have relatively low-cost home bases, but this is not a new phenomenon. US firms became international when their costs were high compared to their markets, so they favored direct foreign investment. Japanese companies, in contrast, became international when they had relatively low costs compared to the dominant competitors. As a result, they began with exports, then gradually internalized their sales and branding, and eventually moved to local manufacturing of (some) products. Korean firms and now Chinese firms are following a similar pattern.

That EMNCs come from countries with relatively low-income home bases has important implications for product mix as well. Such firms are quite likely to have developed products with different price points and different value propositions, in fast-growing home bases. As a result, they might not be relevant to the most advanced markets, but as we shall see shortly, they may be more relevant to other emerging markets than the products and value propositions of firms from the most "advanced" countries.

The fact that EMNCs emanate from less institutionalized home bases has been a key theme in the emerging markets literature (Khanna and Ishay, 2007), although rather than "less" I prefer "differently." Sudan may be under-institutionalized, but a typical Latin American country is not. It may in fact have deeper institutional roots than the US. It may or may not be as functional, but that's not to say that it's not institutionalized.

Equally important is the fact that some, but not all, EMNCs have less-than-complete "home-based diamonds." However, if they don't have some element in that diamond that stands out, I doubt they can compete internationally. To the extent that their diamonds are not complete, they will see internationalization as a way to complete themselves, as well as to exploit the advantages they have.

EMNCS have O(wnership) advantages?

A key motivation for this volume is the statement by Ramamurti: "... a bedrock principle of international business (IB) theory is that to become an MNE, a company must possess significant 'ownership advantages' that can offset its disadvantages in competing abroad (citing Dunning, 1988). Yet, on the surface, EMNCs seem to lack the technology, brand, or management advantages of DMNEs ..." (Ramamurti, 2012). My first reaction to the thought that EMNCs do not possess an "O-advantage" – some form of firm-specific core competence or capability that travels – is that it is very unlikely[1]. Do these companies just stumble into the world economy on the basis of some generalized home country conditions or, worse yet, in response to some set of institutional voids at home? I concur with Ramamurti, and believe that in general they do. In this context, understanding the origins of these advantages and why and how they travel should be a core element of EMNC (and GVCE) research.

One possible source of a view that EMNCs lack O-advantages is pure ethnocentrism: "My god, these companies come from poor, backwards countries with weak institutions and so on, so how can they possibly have an O?" This gap may also be related to a shortcoming of the typical OLI and transaction cost narrative of FDI: that O, competitive advantage, just falls from the sky and the key competitive task is to minimize the transaction costs of exploiting it. What a strange way to conceive of business strategy! Business strategy is at least as much about figuring out what a firm can do well that creates value for customers and that others cannot readily replicate, as it is about how to minimize the cost of doing so.

Finally, it is likely that the view that EMNCs do not have an O is due to a fundamental confusion between "most advanced" and "most relevant" countries in terms of products, technologies, business models, or

---

[1] O-advantages refer to "ownership specific advantages" of the firm – specific assets, resources, and core capabilities of the firm. These are part of Dunning's trilogy of O (Ownership), L (Location), and I (Internalization) that explains why cross-border activities are conducted within multinational firms rather than through arms-length trade or partnering relationships.

management practices. In a globalized world where most economies are emerging, firms based in emerging economies will in many cases possess capabilities that are more relevant to the markets (or supply chains) they face than firms from the most advanced countries.

This is not to say that EMNCs (and GVCEs) do not have to overcome disadvantages. But there's more here than "adversity breeds success." EMNCs must have some O-advantages that overcome their liability of foreignness, or the idea that firms that cross borders lack the knowledge, legitimacy, and relationships possessed by home country firms (Hymer, 1976; Zaheer, 1995); the cost of complexity associated with internationalization, or the idea that doing business internationally involves more elements and interactions than would be the case within a single country; and the costs (relative to AMNCs) of overcoming some gaps in their own home institutions.

EMNC capabilities

I take a capabilities view, wherein internationalization (and international integration) is a process of exploiting and enhancing capabilities (Lessard and Lucea, 2009; Lessard et al., 2012).[2] For me, it relates closely to what I refer to as creating a virtual diamond (Lessard, 2003). A firm creates a virtual diamond when it adds demand or factor conditions from various host countries to those of the home country to underpin its overall strategic capabilities. Many firms, but especially emerging market firms, draw on conditions from other regions as well as their home base for competitive advantage, in essence creating virtual diamonds.

The following are three cases that exemplify EMNCs' (initially home-based) O-advantages.

Acer, a Taiwan-based manufacturer and branded seller of laptop computers, was an early EMNC that emerged in the 1980s and is still a very successful company. Like many other Taiwan-based electronic firms of the era, it had capabilities in manufacturing and design for manufacturing, but it is not clear to what extent these resulted in competitive advantage given that many other firms possessed them as

[2] My RAT/CAT capabilities model builds on the work of many authors including Prahalad and Hamel (1990), Kogut and Zander (1993), Teece (1997, 2006), and Barney and Clark (2007).

well. What distinguished Acer from many other Taiwan-based firms at the time, and from MNCs based elsewhere, was the ownership and organizational structure it developed that allowed it to establish its brand and deep customer relationships in a large number of countries. Acer came from a country with weak capital markets and no bilateral investment treaties, among other things, which would appear to make it a disadvantaged home base for a multinational company. It overcame these disadvantages by creating JVs with local co-investors in many countries, which allowed it to retain control without the 100 percent ownership typical of MNCs (St. George and Bartlett, 1998; author interviews with Stan Shih). As a result, Acer's O-advantage was that it could partner more easily than others with local complementors, who began as distributors but became co-owners of locally facing sales units, while still exercising control in order to obtain centrally based economies of scale and scope.

CEMEX, the Mexican-based leader in cement and concrete that became one of the top three firms worldwide by 2007, only to fall with its disastrous acquisition of Rinker, had (and perhaps still has) an O-advantage in post-merger integration (PMI) that it developed initially in its home base. Mexico was a regionalized country that had been consolidating internally for 50 years. This competence in turn was highly relevant in a consolidating global industry (Podolny and Roberts, 1999; Ghemawat and Matthews, 2006; Lessard and Reavis, 2009). CEMEX was also very good in IT-based operating excellence (Chung et al., 2005). Where did they get it? By developing and attracting world-class industrial engineers to Monterrey. This could be deemed in part a country-specific advantage (CSA), but the active involvement of CEMEX in the development of Monterrey Tech and its superior ability to attract the top graduates made it a firm-specific advantage (FSA; Rugman, 1981; Rugman and Verbeke, 2001). The company also developed from the home base a capability to sell cement as a consumer product (Lee and Hoyt, 2005), as Mexico had a very high proportion of "self-builders," and this capability turned out to be highly relevant in many other emerging countries with similar demand patterns.

Finally, there is ABInbev, the world's leading beer company. Why are the Brazilians leading the world beer industry? There are many reasons, but the main ones seem to be their mastery of the capabilities required to capture value in highly concentrated markets, a laser-like focus on efficiency, and the application of investment-banking-style high-powered incentives for high-performing managers in what had hitherto been a relatively sleepy industry (Neto, 2008; Teixeira et al., 2009; author interviews with Gustavo Pierini, Principal in Gradus Consultoria). These advantages can be traced to the initial 1992 merger between Brahma and Antarctica, which gave the newly combined company control of nearly 60 percent of the beer market in Brazil. The new company reduced costs by streamlining distribution (going from 750 to 250 distributors, among other things) and consolidating plants, but it also pulled a lot of margin from distributors by renegotiating terms and from customers through market power and effective use of customer information to extract the optimal price in different demographic, geographic, and seasonal market segments. The Brazilians (who retain important leadership roles in the whole company, but whose Ambev name has been submerged under the In of Interbrau and the AB of Anheuser Busch) learned how to capture value in mature, consolidated markets and were able to take this knowledge to other countries where it could be applied.

Importantly, each of these successful EMNCs not only exploits home-based O-advantages, but some also reach out to other locations in order to enhance these advantages. Lessard et al. (2012) formalize this process in terms of RAT and CAT, two tests that determine whether or not a firm possesses capabilities that can be exploited via internalization and whether or not it can tap other locations to develop and capture new capabilities that become part of its core competence.

Quoting Lessard et al., "Two crucial questions every strategist must ask are how well the company's capabilities will travel and where they might best be replicated. One way to answer these questions is to use what we call the 'RAT Test'; RAT stands for *relevant, appropriable and transferable*. The RAT Test helps identify whether a particular market is suitable for the successful deployment of one of a company's home-market businesses" (2012: 63).

The RAT Test questions are:

1. Are the capabilities developed in the home market *relevant* in the target market to create value by increasing customers' willingness to pay and/or lowering costs?
2. If deployed in a foreign target market, would these capabilities be *appropriable*? In other words, do they allow for the capture

of (some of) the value they create? Are there sufficient barriers to imitation and innovation to prevent competitors from matching the capabilities or finding alternative solutions? Are the necessary complementors (value chain partners) each present and without undue market power?

3. Are these capabilities *transferable*? Can the company deploy its capabilities effectively in the target foreign location without sacrificing too much value creation and capture potential?

Again quoting Lessard et al., "Companies also expand internationally to gain access to strategic assets or to develop new capabilities. In these cases, it is critical for strategists to determine whether the new additions will actually result in an *overall* enhancement of the company's capabilities and, as a result, of its global competitive position" (2012: 64). This can be determined by the CAT Test, whose questions are:

1. Are the new assets and capabilities that we will develop/acquire in the new market *complementary* to the existing capabilities that constitute the base of the company's competitive advantage?
2. Are they *appropriable*? Can the company appropriate enough of the value of these new capabilities, or will other companies extract the value of the capabilities/resources that they supply?
3. Are they *transferable*? Can the company effectively bring them back from the source location and integrate them into its capability set without sacrificing their value?

Looking back at Acer, we can see that its manufacturing capabilities and governance procedures were RAT, though undoubtedly it also acquired some CATs over the years as well.

CEMEX had a clear set of RAT capabilities in operations and PMI, but also an active learning system that allowed it to capture numerous CAT capabilities that increased its "O" well beyond those that originated in its home base. This is illustrated in Figure 6.2 for CEMEX for the three stages of internationalization as described by Lessard and Lucea (2009). In the first phase, CEMEX took its RAT capabilities of operational excellence and acquisition experience, which it had developed in Mexico, and found that they added significant value in Spain. However, it immediately brought back several CATs as well – petroleum coke (and a lower cost alternative fuel capability in general) and

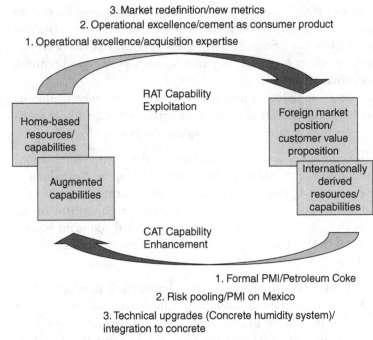

3. Market redefinition/new metrics
2. Operational excellence/cement as consumer product
1. Operational excellence/acquisition expertise

RAT Capability
Exploitation

Home-based
resources/
capabilities

Foreign market
position/
customer value
proposition

Augmented
capabilities

Internationally
derived
resources/
capabilities

CAT Capability
Enhancement

1. Formal PMI/Petroleum Coke

2. Risk pooling/PMI on Mexico

3. Technical upgrades (Concrete humidity system)/
integration to concrete

Figure 6.2 The RAT CAT cycle of capability exploitation and enhancement.

a formalized post-merger integration (PMI) process – codifying what it had developed at home but never formalized to the same extent. In the second phase it continued to bring (upgraded) operational excellence and PMI and a new set of capabilities it was developing to sell cement as a consumer product to its expansion throughout Latin America. The company brought back a capability (both physical and organizational) to pool risk among its various units. In the third and final phase it brought all of these, plus a new business model incorporating both new market definitions and metrics, to two multinational acquisitions, and brought back a number of enhanced technical capabilities.

ABInbev's RAT appears to have more to do with capturing value in mature, concentrated markets. Whether this is an R(elevant) or an A(ppropriable) advantage in other markets is ambiguous. The limits on its transferability result from the fact that by law and by virtue of the configuration of existing assets, it cannot fully exercise its abilities to cut costs and capture margin. By and large the capabilities that allow it to extend its competitive advantage internationally are relevant – it makes, distributes, and markets beer in ways that are relevant. This is despite the fact that it does not appear to introduce many innovations in products or services that increase customer satisfaction, but rather it focuses on cost and value extraction. It has capabilities to capture a very large share of the margin pool through consolidation, expert use of data, and hardball tactics. These capabilities are R and A where they can dominate the chain. They are T(ransferable) when similar management methods and incentives are compatible with local values (for an excellent analysis of the transferability of management methods, see Siegel and Larson, 2009). ABInbev's use of CAT capabilities, in contrast, appears to be limited. Ambev, the initial Brazilian firm, did learn a great deal from international benchmarking, but did so largely from Brazil through multinational firms that it was working with there.

Another interesting case is Haier, with its cost innovation capability (Khanna et al., 2012; Williamson and Yin, 2013). The appropriability of the value created by this capability, of course, depends on the strength of retailers compared to brand owners and OEMs, but in the US and many other countries, Haier seems to have been able to capture margin. Transferring this capability requires blending home-based cost engineering with local opportunities to add features, and it appears that there is some debate within Haier over the T(ransferability) of this capability.

The resulting dynamic, of course, is that as a firm goes from a home footprint to a global footprint, it may also extend its resource or capability basis from home-based to home-based plus, or even to metanational, as illustrated in Figure 6.3. Initially, all of its capabilities are home-based in origin. As it learns from other locations it gradually moves its capabilities base to home-based plus or metanational. Some firms achieve a substantial global footprint with only a home-based set of capabilities (e.g., IKEA), whereas others begin changing with their first steps outside of the home country (e.g., CEMEX).

Companies based in countries with "ideal diamonds" will have strong RATs and, as a result, continue to rely on home-based capabilities. EMNCs with incomplete home bases, in contrast, are more likely to complement their home-based RAT capabilities with CAT capabilities that they access or develop elsewhere. It should be noted, however, that at least some of the home-based conditions of EMNCs are highly R(elevant) for exploitation in most of the world, which is comprised of emerging economies.

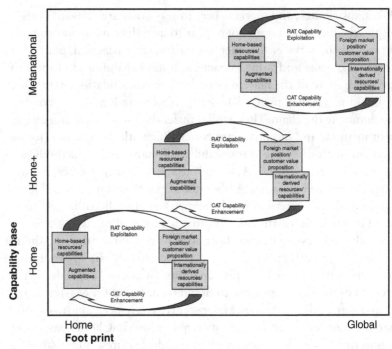

Figure 6.3 The RAT CAT dynamic.

These examples are meant to be illustrative rather than definitive. They all are established firms in mature industries whose scale, scope, and systematic management are key. Undoubtedly a group of newer firms in more dynamic industries would display a different set of capabilities, but I am confident that the RAT-CAT framework would remain relevant.

GVCE capabilities

Turning to GVCEs, we see a similar pattern. For example, the Indian-based software firm Infosys began as many others, arbitraging the cost of Indian and developed country software engineers, both through "body shopping" and servicing MNCs that had moved some of their IT operations to India. It soon developed ways to embed itself in the Indian talent market that were superior to other Indian firms or AMNCs, as well to begin matching AMNCs in the ability to connect with Western customers. It also evolved a series of practices to facilitate and lower the integration cost of its Indian back-end with its US (and later other industrialized country) front-end (Pahwa et al., 2008). This "dually embedded cross-border integration" is a key O-advantage relative to both other Indian firms and MNCs that have access to the same CSAs. Infosys does fit the standard definition of an MNC as a firm with activities in multiple countries governed by ownership (internalization), though it would leave only a faint trace on an FDI map.

Another interesting set of GVCEs is the group of SMEs located in Malaysia's Penang Peninsula (Samel, 2012) that specialize in providing "flexibility" in the electronics supply chain. These firms are located at the bottom of the "smile curve" (Figure 6.4 below), introduced by Stan Shih of Acer to show that electronics assembly, with its requirement for relatively simple capabilities and hence low barriers to entry, would easily become commoditized and therefore be less profitable than the two "ends" of the curve that are anchored in technological capabilities and IP at the "upstream" end and brand name and/or other forms of sticky customer-facing capabilities at the "downstream" end (Lundquist, 2007). The Penang firms are located in what should be the "low profitability center" of the curve, but have a differentiated position due to the relevance and difficulty of providing flexible capacity. By specializing in bearing volatility in product demand, Penang's assemblers in the electronics supply chain have succeeded in commanding both relatively high wages for their workers and relatively high margins for themselves.

They do so on the basis of accommodating labor regulations and institutions (including an ample pool of immigrant labor), a broad set of relationships with design and end-product firms that allow them to pool product fluctuations, and relatively simple technologies that can be reconfigured quickly (e.g., changing the number of assembly lines). The volatilities of orders for each product/relationship act as a barrier to entry, since it is costly for new entrants to match the scale and organizational and managerial capabilities required for pooling and pliability. This bundle, then, is the O-advantage of this group of firms, a capacity that is relevant and appropriable, but does not need to be "transferable" since its internationalization involves insertion into global value chains from Malaysia. This means it is not an MNC in classic terms, but it clearly is active internationally.

Foxconn, which is now a regular fixture in the press given its important role in manufacturing Apple's products and its embeddedness in

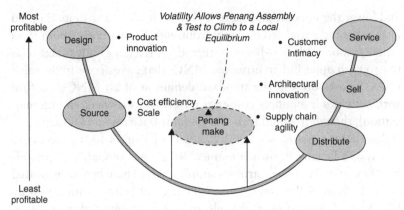

Figure 6.4 Risk specialization in the value chain profit curve.
Source: Samel (2012).

a country with dodgy labor practices (a CSA?), is becoming a classic MNC now that it is following Selectron and other contract manufacturers in having facilities in multiple countries. Its unique value proposition, however, is being able to quickly mobilize an army of workers to address the pulsed demand of winner-take-all products such as the iPhone. The sheer scale required is the barrier to entry, and the players must be located in countries/regions with an enormous labor pool, compliant labor relations, a cluster that is large enough to attract the co-specialist suppliers that are required to support just in time (JIT) assembly of these products, and the housing and transport infrastructure to match. All these could be deemed CSAs (country and/or cluster-based advantages), but the ability of the firm to marshal and orchestrate actively at this scope is quite unique. This is its O.

These observations can be summarized in three statements regarding the O-advantages of EMNCs and GVCEs:

1. Successful horizontal EMNCs possess O-advantages that initially were developed in the home market.
2. Successful vertical EMNCs (GVCEs) possess O-advantages in the cross-border home-to-GVC integration of activities that initially exploit the comparative (country-based) advantage of their home base.
3. Successful EMNCs and AMNCs develop further O-advantages based on their international experience.

Horizontal (classic) EMNCs typically internationalize on the basis of capabilities that they have developed over a number of years in their home market and that are RAT for other markets. Increasingly, these others markets are rapidly growing emerging markets where the home country-based capabilities are even more directly relevant. Vertical GVCEs follow a similar pattern, though their initial "niche" is to connect their home country to a global value chain, a boundary-spanning capability to begin with. In a number of documented cases, though, companies began this boundary spanning by serving multinational buyers at home.

Over time, both classic EMNCs and GVCEs acquire or develop new skills from operating in foreign locations (or from deepening their reach into global value chains), and many of them succeed in incorporating this new set of capabilities into their core. Although not tested, my view is that they typically do this even faster than AMNCs that are based in seemingly more beneficent environments.

Conclusions

EMNCs are here to stay. They are no more strange or exotic than the home-based "projection strategy" Western firms that grew up in the 1970s. GVCEs are more novel, though their antecedents go back a long way as well. EMNC-based innovation and enterprise development is a reverse only in the eye of the beholder. Early US inventors such as John Deere and Elias Howe were reverse from the perspective of the UK. Innovation is increasingly distributed across the world, and since many of the innovations of EMNCs or GVCEs will never pass through advanced countries, the notion of reverse loses its meaning.

The heterogeneity of multinational firm types and firm origins that we observe is a great asset for research. Many early questions regarding the role of CSAs and FSAs can be revisited in this new context. In doing so, it is important to distinguish between horizontal and vertical DFI and to keep one's eye on the capabilities that drive the creation of value as well as the resulting market positions that allow its extraction. This is not only about EMNCs and GVCEs, but also about new firms and forms that are emerging from advanced countries as well, as both RAT and CAT capabilities come into play.

References

Barney, J. and Clark, E. 2007. *Resource-based theory: Creating and sustaining competitive advantage.* Oxford University Press.

Buckley, P. J. 2009. The impact of the global factory on economic development. *Journal of World Business,* 44(2): 131–143.

Chung, R., Marchand, D., and Kettinger, W. 2005. The CEMEX WAY: The right balance between local business flexibility and global standardization. Lausanne, Switzerland: IMD. Case no. IMD284.

Doz, Y., Santos, J., and Williamson, P. 2002. *From global to metanational: How companies win in the knowledge economy.* Boston: Harvard Business School Press.

Dunning, J. H. 1973. The determinants of international production. *Oxford Economic Papers,* 25(3): 289–336.

1981. *International production and the multinational firm.* London: Allen & Unwin.

1988. The electic paradigm of international production: A restatement and some possible extensions. *Journal of International Business Studies,* 19: 1–31.

Ghemawat, P. and Matthews, J. L. 2006. The globalization of CEMEX. Harvard Business School, Case no. 701-017.

Hymer, S. H. 1976. *The international operations of multinational firms: A study of direct foreign investment.* Cambridge, MA: The MIT Press.

Johanson, J. and Vahlne, J.-E. 1977. The internationalization process of the firm: A model of knowledge development and increasing foreign market commitments. *Journal of International Business Studies,* 8(1): 23–32.

Khanna, T. and Ishay, Y. 2007. Business groups in emerging markets: Paragons or parasites? *Journal of Economic Literature,* XLV(June): 331–372.

Khanna, T., Palepu, K. G., and Andrews, P. 2012. Haier: Taking a Chinese company global. Harvard Business School, Case no. 9-712-408.

Kogut, B. and Zander, U. 1993. Knowledge of the firm and the evolutionary theory of the multinational corporation. *Journal of International Business Studies,* 24(4): 625–645.

Lee, H. and Hoyt, D. 2005. CEMEX: Transforming a basic industry. Stanford Graduate School of Business, Case no. GS-33.

Lessard, D. 1970. *Multinational portfolio diversification for developing countries.* PhD thesis, Stanford University.

1973. International portfolio diversification: A multivariate analysis for a group of Latin American countries. *Journal of Finance,* 28: 619–633.

2003. Frameworks for global strategic analysis. *Journal of Strategic Management Education,* 1(1): 1–12.

Lessard, D. and Lucea, R. 2009. Mexican multinationals: Insights from CEMEX. In R. Ramamurti and J. V. Singh (eds.), *Emerging multinationals from emerging markets*. Cambridge University Press.

Lessard, D. and Reavis, C. 2009. Globalization "the CEMEX way." MIT Sloan School, Case no. 09-039.

Lessard, D., Lucea, R., and Vives, L. 2012. Building your company's capabilities through global expansion. *Sloan Management Review*, 54(2): 61–67.

Lundquist, E. 2007. Shih's curve can bring smiles. *eWeek*, 56.

Neto, J. S. 2008. OS18 principios de uma victoriosa cultura de Gestao do Brasil. *HSM Management*, 66 (January–February).

Pahwa, A., Haour, G., and Billington, C. 2008. Infosys: Effectively leveraging global resources. Lausanne, Switzerland: IMD. Case no. 3-1814.

Podolny, J. and Roberts, J. 1999. CEMEX, S.A. de C.V.: Global competition in a local business. Stanford University Graduate School of Business, Case no. S-IB-17.

Porter, M. C. 1990. *The competitive advantage of nations*. New York: The Free Press.

2000. Location, competition, and economic development: Local clusters in a global economy. *Economic Development Quarterly*, 14(1): 15–34.

Prahalad, C. and Hamel, G. 1990. The core competence of the corporation. *Harvard Business Review*, 68(3): 79–91.

Ramamurti, R. 2012. What really is different about emerging market multinationals? *Global Strategy Journal*, 2: 41–47.

Rugman, A. M. 1981. *Inside the multinationals: The economics of internal markets*. New York: Columbia University Press.

Rugman, A. M. and Verbeke, A. 2001. Subsidiary-specific advantages in multinational enterprises. *Strategic Management Journal*, 22(3): 237–250.

Samel, H. 2012. Upgrading under volatility in a global economy. MIT Sloan School Working Paper. Cambridge, MA: MIT Sloan School.

Santos, J. 2007. Strategy lessons from left field. *Harvard Business Review*, 85(4): 20–21.

Siegel, J. and Larson, B. Z. 2009. Labor market institutions and global strategic adaptation: Evidence from Lincoln Electric. *Management Science*, 55(9): 1527–1546.

St. George, A. and Bartlett, C. 1998. ACER, Inc.: Taiwan's rampaging dragon. Boston, MA: Harvard Business School Publishing. Case no. 3999010-PDF-ENG.

Teece, D. J. 1997. Explicating dynamic capabilities: The nature and microfoundations of (sustainable) enterprise performance. *Strategic Management Journal*, 28(13): 1319–1350.

2006. Reflections on the Hymer thesis and the multinational enterprise. *International Business Review*, 15(2): 124–139.

Teixeira, A., Hessle, C., and Oliveira, R. 2009. O legado de Lehman. Epoca Negocios. http://epocanegocios.globo.com/Revista/Epocanegocios/0,,E DR82833-8374,00.html (accessed March 14, 2013).

Vernon, R. 1966. International investment and international trade in the product cycle. *Quarterly Journal of Economics*, 80: 190–207.

1971. *Sovereignty at bay: The multinational spread of US enterprises.* New York: Basic Books.

1979. The product cycle hypothesis in a new international environment. *Oxford Journal of Economics and Statistics*, 41: 255–276.

Wells, L. T. 1983. *Third world multinationals.* Cambridge, MA: The MIT Press.

Williamson, P. and Yin, E. 2013. Innovation by Chinese EMNCs. In P. Williamson, R. Ramamurti, A. Fleury, and M. T. L. Fleury (eds.), *The competitive advantage of emerging market multinationals.* Cambridge University Press.

Zaheer, S. 1995. Overcoming the liability of foreigness. *Academy of Management Journal*, 38(2): 341–363.

7 | EMNCs and catch-up processes: the case of four Indian industries

KRISTIN BRANDL AND RAM MUDAMBI

Introduction

It has already been widely recognized, at least in the academic literature, that the set of emerging economies constitute a very diverse group, so that sweeping generalizations about the process of "emergence" almost always lead to incorrect conclusions (Ramamurti and Singh, 2009). Emerging market economies range from "middle income" countries like Brazil and Taiwan to fairly poor countries like China, India, and Indonesia. Sometimes, even wealthy economies like South Korea and Singapore are placed in this group. All these countries have different comparative advantages and specialize in different industries, so their catch-up processes are extremely country-specific. However, it is less widely acknowledged that economic activities *within* emerging market economies are also quite heterogeneous. In this chapter we focus on catch-up processes within the Indian economy and highlight three critical aspects.

Early work in development economics recognized that many developing countries were characterized by so-called "dual" economies, where backward sectors (usually subsistence agriculture) co-existed with relatively advanced export-oriented sectors (Nurkse, 1955). We expect such sectoral diversity to be even more pronounced in rapidly changing emerging market economies like India. Sectors and industries differ dramatically in terms of the extent to which they are backward relative to world standards (Lorenzen and Mudambi, 2010). Hence, in studying catch-up processes in the Indian economy, the first key aspect that we document in this chapter is the importance of industry context.

Catch-up is a process and goes through stages (Kumaraswamy, Mudambi, Saranga, and Tripathy, 2012). Hence even as the economy is liberalized, the persistence of some barriers means that it is still possible for some firms to survive by sheltering behind them. Such firms focus on the domestic market, while implementing only a limited extent of upgrading. Other firms fully grasp the opportunities presented by liberalization and aggressively implement upgrading in order to integrate into global value chains and compete on world markets. Thus, the second aspect of catch-up that we highlight is the increasing extent of intra-industry diversity in terms of firm-level capabilities.

In the popular press, the rise of emerging economies is often equated with the arrival of emerging market-based multinational companies (EMNCs) on world markets. Examples include firms like Lenovo and Huawei in China as well as Infosys and TCS in India (Ramamurti and Singh, 2009; Khanna and Palepu, 2010). These firms attract attention because they are beginning to gain market share in their competition on world markets with leading rivals from advanced markets. It is tempting to conclude that, at least in the case of these firms, the process of catch-up is complete. However, a closer examination reveals that even EMNCs that have had considerable success in terms of capturing world markets are still dependent on innovation systems in advanced market economies to maintain their competitive edge (Awate, Larsen, and Mudambi, 2012). Such dependence typically leads them to adopt what may be called "fast follower" strategies, as opposed to truly innovative strategies (Cantwell and Mudambi, 2011). Therefore, the third aspect of catch-up that we highlight is the distinction between output catch-up (the ability to produce output at current technological standards) and innovation catch-up (the ability to produce new and innovative products and services).

Taken together, these three aspects imply that emerging markets like India are fertile contexts in which to study business phenomena and the catch-up of EMNCs. First, they present a very interesting milieu for research since the extent of both inter-industry and intra-industry diversity is greater than in many advanced economies. This means that from the perspective of the practitioner, the effects of strategy are likely to be substantially greater; from the perspective of the researcher, they are easier to see and identify. Second, the strategic dichotomy between innovation and imitation is likely to arise in a much sharper form in emerging economies, since the benefits of imitation for emerging economy firms are likely to be much greater than for advanced economy firms.

Our understanding of this very basic research question of strategic management can be improved by studying the MNC versus domestic firm context in emerging markets. We will focus on four industries that differ along a number of dimensions. Some are mature, others are emerging; some are high technology driven, while others are creative. Differences along these dimensions create different catch-up dynamics.

Catch-up and internationalization after liberalization

Catch-up and internationalization

The catch-up processes of latecomer firms has been of academic interest within a general international business (IB) context (Buckley, 2002) as well as within the specific context of emerging markets (Cuervo-Cazurra, 2007). Before latecomer firms became of interest, research primarily focused on the internationalization of first mover firms and the advantages they gained by being the leaders (Lieberman and Montgomery, 1988, 1998), often to the expense of late movers. Their catch-up processes were characterized as implementing imitating strategies and struggling with a lack of resources, as well as a lack of the knowledge and capabilities to acquire or generate them. These problems were seen as accentuated in an emerging market context (Mathews, 2002). Latecomer firms are often from an underdeveloped local market with less sophisticated and poorer users (Hobday, 2010) and have less effective resources, a smaller firm size, negative country-of-origin effects, and often a lack of cutting-edge technology (Cuervo-Cazurra and Genc, 2008). However, the latecomer firms are generally determined to catch up to global standards, and also have competitive advantages such as lower labor costs due to lower living standards (Mathews, 2002).

Emerging market firms implementing catch-up processes are also able to capitalize on various late mover advantages. For instance, these firms are able to learn more rapidly from the leaders and can avoid the high cost of pathbreaking R&D, since they can profit from imitative activities (Hobday, 2010). Similarly, these firms can adapt and improve extant products for local markets and align products more closely to buyers. Other advantages apply especially to the catch-up processes of EMNCs. These firms are likely to have specific advantages when entering markets with difficult governance conditions similar to their home markets (Cuervo-Cazurra and Genc, 2008), as they have experience operating with underdeveloped market mechanisms, ineffective institutions, and heavy bureaucracy with unstable and often corrupt governments (Khanna and Palepu, 1997; Cuervo-Cazurra and Genc, 2008). Further, Abramovitz (1986) found that a greater technological gap between the first mover and the follower led to faster catch-up, at least in the early stages. This is because a large gap ensures that much of the knowledge required to begin the catch-up process has become relatively routine. However, this advantage can only be reaped if the firms acknowledge their position and capitalize on their specific latecomer advantages; in other words, they must not implement first mover strategies (Mathews, 2002).

The catch-up of these latecomer firms is argued to go through several phases. Mathews (2002) emphasizes the three stages of linkage, leverage, and learning in the catch-up process of latecomer firms. First, firms are able to acquire resources and capabilities through linkages and strategic networks (Gulati, Nohria, and Zaheer, 2001; Kumaraswamy et al., 2012). After resources are acquired it is important to leverage these resources to generate competitive advantages (Prahalad and Hamel, 1990) as well as learning capabilities that support the development of future strategies (Mathews, 2002). In line with Mathews (2002), Kumaraswamy et al. (2012) develop a three-stage process model of transition, consolidation, and global integration phases to explain EMNC catch-up processes. In the transition phase, firms acquire knowledge and capabilities from advanced economy firms through technology licensing and absorptive capacity development. The consolidation phase emphasizes developing deeper relationships with advanced economy MNCs and the integration of the firm into the industry value chain. The last phase is the global integration phase, in which firms focus on knowledge creation through R&D in order to compete globally. It is argued that EMNC catch-up strategies reflect these generic stages, which often mirror the evolution of liberalization in their home economies (Kumaraswamy et al., 2012).

Cooperation with government bodies is often perceived to be a location-bound firm-specific advantage (Rugman and Verbeke, 2001; Kumaraswamy et al., 2012), especially in emerging market economies such as India where cooperation with government agencies has been found to be one of the most important factors for firm performance (Majumdar, 1997). Government regulations and policies are a particularly important influence in the catch-up process of the EMNCs (Mathews, 2002). However, once liberalization proceeds and the regulatory bodies lose influence and importance in the catch-up process, successful firms shift away from maintaining relationships with regulators and toward efficient operations and business capabilities (Kumaraswamy et al., 2012).

Liberalization in India and catch-up processes in four industries

The Indian economy underwent rapid and discontinuous changes, starting with the first implementation of radical economic reforms in 1991. In the period since then, India has become an increasingly important part of the global economic landscape, its economy has become more open to international trade, its workforce has grown strongly, and its rate of both domestic and foreign direct investment has picked up.

The domestic economy was sheltered behind significant trade barriers through the 1980s, and both the import and export shares of GDP were below 10 percent. While these barriers protected domestic firms from foreign competition, they also limited the capacity of local firms to access current technologies and implement catch-up processes (Mudambi, 2008). Many of these barriers were lowered or removed by the reforms of the 1990s: Exchange rate controls were eased, many tariffs and duties were reduced, and most capital and intermediate goods were no longer subject to restrictive import licensing. Both the import and export shares had increased to around 15 percent of GDP by the mid-2000s. The reform process continued in the new century; between 2004 and 2008 additional reforms that included further cuts to tariffs were implemented, so that by 2009 the import and export shares of GDP had increased to levels similar to those of many advanced economies (Cagliarini and Baker, 2010).

We selected four industries within which to investigate the catch-up process of Indian firms (see Table 7.1): the auto components industry, the pharmaceutical industry, the filmed entertainment industry, and the wind turbine industry. In all four industries, established competitors

Table 7.1 *Industry matrix.*

Industry characteristic	Auto components	Pharmaceutical	Filmed entertainment	Wind turbine
Technology level	High	High	Medium	High
Technology basis	Engineering	Science	Creative	Engineering
Life cycle stage	Mature	Mature	Mature	Emerging
Clockspeed	Slow	Slow	Fast	Slow
Footprint	Global	Global	Regional	Global
Nature of competition	Dominated by majors	Dominated by majors	Mainly independents	Dominated by smaller specialists
Key success factors	Relationships with assemblers	Commercial applications of scientific knowledge	Knowledge of market tastes and trends	Grid ready solutions

from advanced economies operate on the global market and firms from emerging economies face high hurdles. These industries highlight the diversity of catch-up processes that can arise in large emerging economies like India.

Industries such as the auto components industry and the pharmaceutical industry are comparably globalized with a large amount of global competition. The wind turbine industry and the filmed entertainment industry have fewer globally operating firms and are less dispersed. The global filmed entertainment industry is strongly dominated by Hollywood productions, resulting in high market entry barriers. The wind turbine industry is a comparably young industry that has high technology dependency and is strongly dominated by European firms, also leading to high market entry barriers. Also highly dependent on technology is the auto components industry, in comparison to the relatively low dependency on technology in the filmed entertainment industry and the pharmaceutical industry. These two industries are more dependent on other elements, such as actors and marketing in the filmed entertainment industry and R&D and drug development in the pharmaceutical industry.

Catching up in the auto components industry

The auto components industry presents an ideal context to study catch-up strategies of EMNCs in a global market setting. The mature nature of the industry and its technological sophistication ensures that the competitiveness and survival of firms is often dependent on cost considerations (Mudambi and Helper, 1998). Although the dominant players of the global automobile industry are traditionally from Europe, North America, and Japan, the auto components industry has been very international almost since its inception. The industry understood the benefits of internationally dispersing a firm's value chain and sourcing components abroad early on. Instead of being domestically vertically integrated, firms internationalized and established long-term relationships abroad (Sturgeon, van Biesebroeck, and Gereffi, 2008). Many firms were therefore quick to understand the benefits of operating in emerging market economies such as India, even though market liberalization in this auto components industry has developed far more gradually in this country than in most of the other emerging economies. The Indian auto components industry is a good case to investigate how EMNCs cope with a globalized industry and how the firms catch up and get integrated into the global industry (Kumaraswamy et al., 2012).

India's liberalization and catch-up strategies in the auto components industry

In order to analyze the effects of liberalization on the Indian auto components industry, Kumaraswamy et al. (2012) divide the process into three phases, in line with the major political and economic changes in the economy as they relate to the auto industry: the economic liberalization from 1991 onwards, a clarification of an earlier automotive policy in 1997, and the implementation of a new automotive policy in 2002. Before the Indian liberalization (pre-1991), the economy consisted of a large private sector and was mainly centralized. Thus, the industry reflected several characteristics of a market economy, so that most domestic firms were already familiar with the market institutions that foreign MNCs operated under. This provided them with operational advantages when the opportunities presented by liberalization arose (Kumaraswamy et al., 2012).

During the first phase of liberalization, the Indian government adopted policies that aimed to attract MNCs through reduced regulatory constraints and modified incentives for business groups (Mahmood and Mitchell, 2004; Kumaraswamy et al., 2012). Consequently, the government allowed entering MNCs to maintain full or majority ownership in their local operations in India, which increased the level of competition in the market. In order to compete with the technologically advanced MNCs, local firms urgently needed to upgrade their technological competencies. The dominant catch-up strategy for Indian firms was the formation of technology/licensing agreements with incoming MNCs. This *transition phase* allowed local firms to gain technological knowledge as well as develop absorptive capacity (Kumaraswamy et al., 2012). Bharat Forge, a Tier-2 supplier of forged components to Indian auto engine manufacturers, established in 1961, offers a good example of this catch-up strategy. The company formed two technical knowledge and assistance agreements with MetalArt Corp. (Japan) and Lemmerze-Were (Germany) during this phase. The knowledge it gained enabled the firm to secure ISO 9002 accreditation and allowed it to implement new quality management systems in order to comply with global regulations (KalyaniGroup, 2012; Moneycontrol, 2012).

In phase two of the liberalization, from 1997 to 2002, the Indian government aimed to upgrade and grow the domestic industry through the restriction of imports of component and completely knock down (CKD) kits, with the aim of strengthening the commitment of foreign MNCs to local suppliers. The evolving institutional environment within the industry – allowing greater foreign ownership and control and increasingly fierce competition – ensured that strong customer relationships became more and more important. Consequently, the catch-up strategy of Indian firms (both automotive and component companies) was to team up with local or global suppliers or auto component firms to improve quality and productivity as well as rationalize supply chains. This *consolidation phase* resulted in the integration of many Indian firms into the industry's global value chain (Kumaraswamy et al., 2012). For example, during these years, Bharat Forge invested heavily in capacity development schemes and implemented lean manufacturing. The company further established strong relationships with various suppliers, including some in China, and became a preferred supplier to global brand name owners like Toyota, Ford, and Daimler (Moneycontrol, 2012).

In 2002, the Indian government started to further ease the pressure on domestic firms through the reduction of restrictions and custom duties, mainly to further the progress and facilitate the integration of domestic firms into the global industry (Kumaraswamy et al., 2012). As the industry became more liberalized, increasing emphasis was placed on local knowledge creation through R&D activities (Mudambi, 2008). The government tried to support the new innovation orientation of the industry with R&D-related incentives, mainly as Indian firms had not been very innovative (Kumaraswamy et al., 2012). The aim was to advance the Indian auto components industry to become a global hub for small cars and an Asian hub for auto components. Thus, in the global integration phase, the catch-up strategy of local firms focused on the creation of knowledge through R&D and the acquisition of firms and brands abroad (Kumaraswamy et al., 2012). For example, Bharat Forge acquired the innovative Carl Dan Peddinghaus GmbH & Co in Germany, Federal Forge in the USA, and Imatra Forging Group in Sweden. The firm further advanced its production operation by developing new machining capabilities (Moneycontrol, 2012).

Catching up in the pharmaceutical industry

The pharmaceutical industry is traditionally influenced by many global industry-specific factors (such as the importance of intellectual property rights – IPR) as well as local country factors (such as the nature of a country's health care system). Governments and policy makers often actively interfere in the industry to support the country's health care system, especially in emerging market economies. The catch-up strategies of EMNCs are consequently often strongly influenced by IPR factors like patent regimes and government pressures stemming from health care policies (Scherer, 1993).

In addition to these traditional issues, the industry has been challenged by low revenue growth, poor stock market performance, and a falling rate of approval of new chemical entities (NCE), particularly in recent years (Kola and Landis, 2004). Furthermore, drug discovery and development is a lengthy (up to ten years) and extremely costly process where IPR laws and patent expiration impose stringent timetables for extraction of the rents from R&D activities. However, despite these challenges, the global industry still places emphasis on R&D activities (Kola and Landis, 2004).

The Indian pharmaceutical industry and firm-level catch-up strategies

Before the 1970s, the Indian pharmaceutical industry was strongly dominated by foreign MNCs whose products were often expensive relative to the purchasing power in the Indian market. With the amendment of the Indian Patent Act in 1970, the government tried to diminish the inaccessibility or non-availability of lifesaving medicine (Kale and Little, 2007; Nair, 2008). The Indian Patent Act strengthened the domestic pharmaceutical industry and enabled Indian firms to access international intellectual property (Kale and Little, 2007). It allowed firms to patent manufacturing processes instead of complete end-products, and also allowed the development of generic equivalents to innovative products through the local development of new processes and methods (Nair, 2008). Thus, the catch-up strategy of Indian firms was to reverse-engineer and then produce products that were patented in other countries, using new and indigenously developed production processes. Consequently, the firms could produce foreign drugs at more cost effective prices and capture the domestic market from foreign MNCs by selling non-branded generics (Nair, 2008). The catch-up strategy for Indian firms was to adapt technology to firm capabilities and the local country context, and develop a basic knowledge base in the process. This adaptation was centered on process R&D, which focused on knowledge acquisition through the duplication and imitation of foreign drugs (Kale and Little, 2007). Local Indian firms such as Ranbaxy (founded in 1961) established research foundations (in 1985) in order to further develop knowledge related to drug development (Ranbaxy, 2012). Furthermore, the weak patent act and the lower drug prices forced foreign pharmaceutical MNCs to reduce operations in India, providing domestic firms with expansion opportunities in the local market. Although the Indian market became large in volume, it remained comparatively low in value (Kale and Little, 2007).

Since the liberalization of the Indian economy in the 1990s, the Indian pharmaceutical industry has undergone various institutional changes. During this phase, Indian pharmaceutical firms started to export their "imitated" generic products to emerging as well as advanced economies. Firms started to export to the US, for instance, supported by regulations such as the 1984 Waxman-Hatch Act. This Act allowed firms to sell generic drugs in the US market that are tested with less expensive and simpler "bioequivalent" and "bio-availability tests" rather than full-blown clinical trials (Kale and Little, 2007: 600).

There were two basic catch-up strategies used in generics markets by Indian firms eager to operate abroad (Kale and Little, 2007). Some firms chose the aggressive and high risk / high return route of challenging the validation of existing patents and taking on the patent holder, while others chose a more conservative approach of case filings based on expired patents or alliances and strategic ties (Kale and Little, 2007). Ranbaxy, for example, followed the more conservative approach. The company was granted its first US patent in 1990 for Doxycycline (Ranbaxy, 2012), a drug that imitated Vibramycin (doxycycline hyclate), which Pfizer introduced in 1967. This was undertaken by appealing to §2701 Patent Term, the 20-year expiration of patents paragraph at the US Patent and Trademark Office (USPTO, 2012).

A significant change in the industry was caused by India's ratification to the General Agreement on Tariffs and Trade and the TRIPs (Trade Related Aspects of Intellectual Property Rights) in 1994. India agreed to change its extant patent regime, with its loose copy and reverse-engineering regulations and a focus on processes, to a more rigorous product patent regime. As India was classified as a developing country without an existing product patent regime, it was granted a ten-year transition period, and in return the government agreed to legal protection for product patents and for trade-related intellectual property rights protection (Nair, 2008). The TRIPs regulations were applied with three amendments to the Patent Act of 1970 in 1999, 2002, and 2005 (Nair, 2008). These regulatory changes significantly affected the Indian market. Although the regulations provided more security for MNCs and thus led to more market entries, the firms also brought new and improved products and knowledge into the domestic market. Furthermore, the focus on process developments and generic drugs increased firms' awareness of the opportunities in new drug delivery systems and NCE research (Kale and Little, 2007). Additionally, Indian firms started to heavily acquire foreign firms in order to enter foreign markets. For example, in one of the first foreign acquisitions by an Indian pharmaceutical firm, Ranbaxy acquired the US firm Ohm Labs in 1995. Ranbaxy followed this with further acquisitions in Germany (Basics – Bayer's Generics business and Veratide) in 2000 and France (Aventis) in 2004 (Ranbaxy, 2012).

Catching up in the filmed entertainment industry

The filmed entertainment industry presents another ideal industry context to investigate the catch-up strategy of EMNCs. The industry is very knowledge-intensive and value is created through the capitalization and alignment of skilled labor and advanced technologies (Caves, 2000; Lorenzen, Scott, and Vang, 2008). Highly innovative products or content is at the heart of the industry, and the subjective perspective of consumers decides the real value of a film (Pratt, 2008). The industry is strongly dependent on smaller, very specialized, and high knowledge firms or individuals (freelance creative talent or technicians) that support each film, e.g., special effects specialists or small-scale editing firms (Lorenzen and Mudambi, 2013). Thus, value creation within the industry is very project based and dependent on flexible and specialized organizations as well as individuals, which are typically geographically clustered in places like Hollywood, Tokyo, London, or Mumbai/ Bollywood (Lorenzen, 2009). For many years Hollywood has been the dominant global player in the market with large worldwide revenues. This creative output typically translates into market value through film revenues and leads to further spin-off revenue from sources like DVD sales/rentals and the sales of movie-related merchandise. These marketing and distribution activities can benefit from economies of scale, and thus are often controlled by larger firms (Hoskins, McFadyen, and Finn, 1997; Lee and Waterman, 2007; Lorenzen and Mudambi, 2013).

From Bollywood to Hollywood: catch-up strategies of Indian firms

Bollywood has been a central part of India's national identity for over a century, and its origins have been traced as far back as 1912, roughly the same time as those of Hollywood. Despite its importance in India, the industry has been characterized with low growth, low exports, and a high turnover of companies. From its establishment through the 1930s, the Indian filmed entertainment industry had a comparatively good position in the global entertainment market, with many of its films displaying global appeal (Lorenzen and Mudambi, 2013). A few productive and "artistically ambitious" companies even had personal relationships with the European film scene (Lorenzen and Mudambi, 2013: 15).

This positioning changed dramatically after World War II and the emergency of the *masala* (mixed-genre), a genre that was aimed solely at the local and growing Indian audience. The films were no longer centered on scripts and technical capabilities, but rather on individual local star actors and musicians. The earlier established connection to Europe was broken off, and small-scale firms without any global linkages, which targeted only the local Indian market, took over. Thus, it became impossible to export Indian films anywhere beyond a very few close trading partners with somewhat related cultures in Asia or Africa (Lorenzen and Mudambi, 2013). The industry did profit from India's cold war political connections to the Soviet bloc, and established a niche presence in communist countries ranging from the Soviet Union to East Germany.

The immediate post-World War II period also witnessed India's independence, accompanied by restrictive economic policies that favored inward-looking strategies and led to the relative international economic isolation of the country. Further, the dispersed and highly fragmented film exhibition industry, with independent cinemas all over India, did not enable the creation of value through economies of scale in marketing and distribution. Consequently, for most of the twentieth century, Bollywood had difficulties in capturing value even from its home market, let alone globally (Lorenzen and Mudambi, 2013).

However, since 1991, the industry has awoken from its decades-long slumber. The *masala* formula has been revised and made more attractive for an international audience and for a growing Indian middle class. The change led firms to focus on shorter, script-based narratives with recognizable international locations for shootings, more state-of-the-art cinematography, and post-production comparable to Hollywood. Furthermore, the more than three million non-residential Indians (NRIs) and persons of Indian origin in North America, Saudi Arabia, the UK, Australasia, and other countries became an important market for the industry. NRIs generally strive to remain in touch with their homeland through an engagement in Indian culture, politics, and business (Taeube, 2007; Lorenzen and Mudambi, 2013). Bollywood's ties with these Diasporas were particularly strong in North America and the UK, with a rather decentralized structure "consisting of personal relations between Bollywood producers, directions, investors, and other professionals and thousands of individual consumers, investors, and skill-holders of Indian origin living abroad" (Lorenzen and Mudambi, 2013: 17). These ties became very important for the catch-up strategies of the firms in the Indian film entertainment industry, as knowledge flows about global trends and styles became possible, enabling Bollywood productions to have a more global appeal. Furthermore, creative skill-holders from the Diasporas, who had been active in their domestic entertainment industry and made Indian-flavored films popular for exports (e.g., *Bend it like Beckham* or *Monsoon Wedding*), began to target Bollywood and work for Indian companies. In addition to these talent flows, wealthy NRIs from the Diasporas also started to invest heavily in Bollywood productions, enhancing value creation and value capture in the industry (Lorenzen and Mudambi, 2013).

Change has also been evident in the Indian marketing and distribution sector, where Indian firms have understood the value of scale economies and caught up to global standards with new marketing and distribution activities that target both the local and international markets. With regards to the distribution and exhibition channels, Bollywood distributors slowly but steadily started to run multiplex cinemas in metropolitan areas and integrated vertically to generate scale economies.

Bollywood firms understood quite early on that the high geographic dispersion of the Diasporas made traditional cinema distribution unviable. This led them to recognize the importance of aggressively investing in and using innovative new distribution channels and technologies, such as pay-per-view satellite TV and online/mobile film streaming on a large scale, despite property rights disputes. A further catch-up strategy was the innovation outside of the traditional industry boundaries in complementary areas such as TV, music, computer games, and advertising (Lorenzen and Mudambi, 2013).

All these industry developments and catch-up strategies of Indian firms in the filmed entertainment industry has led to tremendous growth and the possibility for firms to use this growth for investments abroad; this is sometimes referred to as a "springboard" strategy, or the acquisition of critical assets abroad to accelerate the catch-up process (Luo and Tung, 2007). For example, Bollywood's Reliance Entertainment set out to buy a majority share of Steven Spielberg's *Dreamworks* in 2009, despite the financial crisis. Likewise, major advanced economy firms based in Hollywood and elsewhere are also setting out to invest in Bollywood, in spite of earlier unsuccessful attempts to establish themselves in the Indian market (Lorenzen and Mudambi, 2013).

Catching up in the wind turbine industry

Wind power has been growing steadily in recent years, making it the fastest-growing energy source in the world (GWEC, 2010). Influenced by the oil crises in the 1970s and periods of extremely favorable government policies around the globe, e.g., in the US in the early 1980s, the global demand for renewable energy sources such as solar and wind energy has been increasing rapidly (Garud and Karnøe, 2003; Nielsen, 2010; Awate et al., 2012).

However, in contrast to the mature industries, the wind turbine industry is still immature and rapidly growing worldwide. Thus, catch-up strategies for EMNCs go strongly in line with the global development of the industry, which is very dynamic with technologies and business models that are still evolving. Strategies need to be adapted to changing business and competitive environments (Awate et al., 2012). Consequently, the catch-up strategies of Indian firms in this industry are particularly interesting to investigate, as initially they found the domestic market to be extremely limited, forcing them to consider international activities virtually from start-up. The Indian wind energy industry, which includes the wind turbine manufacturing sector, has steadily grown and developed into an important market in terms of its share of worldwide installed wind-power capacity (Rajsekhar, Van Hulle, and Jansen, 1999).

Catch-up strategies of Indian firms in the wind turbine industry

Since the end of the twentieth century, the Indian government has supported the wind energy sector and tried to increase awareness with a nationwide program that included wind resource assessments and demonstrations to industry and state electricity boards. Additionally, in line with market liberalization in 1992, favorable policies such as five-year tax holidays, customs relief, and soft loans were implemented to encourage entry into the market (Rajsekhar et al., 1999). The dominant global players at the time were often European firms such as Vestas (Denmark) and Enercon (Germany), and these firms also became major players in the Indian wind energy market. However, Suzlon Energy Inc., a company that made its appearance in the global business environment with its inception in 1995, began by challenging foreign players in the Indian wind turbine market. At the time of Suzlon's founding, foreign firms dominated turbine production and sold final products in the Indian market. The turbines sold in India were often smaller than world standards at the time (Awate et al., 2012).

Suzlon's catch-up strategy was to manufacture turbines of comparable technological sophistication locally in India at a lower price than its competitors (Chandrasekhar and Sridharan, 2009). However, the firm did not have the necessary engineering know-how to operate in this highly knowledge intensive industry, which requires expertise in electronics, mechanics, hydraulics, advanced materials, and aerodynamics (Garud and Karnøe, 2003). In order to gain the necessary engineering know-how quickly and efficiently, Suzlon partnered with Südwind, a global player in the industry. Initially, Suzlon sold Südwind turbines in India and used this "apprenticeship" to gain further technological knowledge (Awate et al., 2012). After Südwind went bankrupt in 1997, Suzlon was able to hire the firm's engineers, finally internalizing the appropriate engineering skills to start producing turbines. The firm's catch-up strategy of partnering with an established firm to gain the necessary knowledge – also referred to as a fast-follower strategy – was very successful for Suzlon. It was able to leverage this strategy to rapidly dominate the Indian market and soon generated revenues comparable to those of the global industry leaders (Awate et al., 2012).

The next step in Suzlon's catch-up strategy was to go beyond the Indian market and start operating and selling turbines internationally, especially in northern Europe, which had developed into the most important wind power market from the late 1990s onwards. The company started alliances and licensing agreements with various MNCs from the region. The aim was to gain the newest state-of-the-art technology in the industry and be at the forefront of new developments (Kumar, Mohaparta, and Chandraskhar, 2009). Thus, Suzlon started a wave of acquisitions, such as the Dutch firm AE-Rotor Techniek BV, which provided specialized knowledge in the design and manufacture of rotor blades. Suzlon also acquired the German AX 215 Verwaltungsgesellschaft mbH in order to establish an R&D unit in Germany (close to all the important Northern European target markets). It also bought the marketing and manufacturing rights of Enron Wind, a bankrupt American turbine manufacturer. Instead of building up R&D capabilities internally, Suzlon searched and acquired these capabilities externally through a heavy acquisition strategy to catch up with the R&D capabilities of the leading European firms. In the last step of Suzlon's catch-up strategy, the company began a process of internalizing the acquired knowledge and developing its own innovation capabilities to broaden the firm's own R&D and product portfolio.

Through this development, Suzlon became the leader of the Indian wind energy sector in four years (Meyer, Mudambi, and Narula, 2011; Awate et al., 2012) and an important player in terms of productivity and kW output in the global wind energy industry. However, due to the heavy burden associated with internalizing knowledge from acquired units, the company has not yet caught up in terms of innovation capabilities (Awate et al., 2012). Its global innovation network is still a work in progress.

Conclusions

We have provided thumbnail sketches of four industries in India. It becomes evident that EMNCs in each of these industries chose different catch-up strategies and that these were strongly dependent on the industry context. The diverse catch-up stories in each of these industries illustrate the first aspect of catch-up in the Indian emerging economy context – the importance of considering industry context when discussing catch-up strategy and potential. This needs to be considered seriously when investigating how firms from emerging markets such as India cope with intra-industry factors as well as pressures from the external business and political environment.

Automobile firms started their catch-up strategies in an industry context with many foreign MNCs as potential knowledge-bearing partners within the local Indian market. Firms in the pharmaceutical industry also found many advanced economy MNCs operating in India, but the IPR regime within the industry was such that they were not able to obtain knowledge through partnering with these firms, and instead had to reverse-engineer generic versions of older drugs that had come off patent. In contrast to these two industries, wind turbine manufacturers had a very limited domestic market both in terms of foreign MNC activity and local sales. Hence, they needed to search for the necessary technology abroad.

Further, an industry's maturity does seem to play a significant role in the catch-up strategies of its EMNCs. In emerging industries such as the wind turbine sector, catch-up strategies seem less influenced by the incumbent industry leaders, so EMNCs are able to readily access knowledge and resources in advanced economy locations. In contrast, in mature industries such as pharmaceuticals, EMNCs are often constrained by substantial entry barriers created by the worldwide IPR regime, so they need to apply a more reactive than proactive approach to strategy.

As evidenced by the auto components industry, Indian firms reacted to industry changes and moved from catch-up strategies with a focus on the acquisition of basic technological know-how via licensing, to a focus on stronger ties with advanced economy MNEs via alliances, in order to gain more sophisticated and tacit knowledge as well as competencies. Indian firms needed these capabilities to compete with the MNCs that started to flood into the country as a result of liberalization in the industry and supportive government policies. After the external knowledge acquisition phase, in which the firms were successfully integrated into GVCs and increasingly operated on the global market, the focus of the firms has now shifted towards the development of R&D capabilities in order to generate knowledge internally.

Somewhat similar to the auto parts industry, global realities also influenced the catch-up strategies of Indian firms in the pharmaceutical industry. Beginning before World War II, the industry was strongly dominated by expensive foreign drug imports that were often inaccessible to the majority of the local Indian population. Consequently, the government adopted the Indian Patent Act to allow firms to focus on reverse-engineering and process patents, permitting Indian firms to produce generic non-branded drugs for the local and later also the global market. However, with the ratification of TRIPs, which drastically altered the country's existing patent regulations, the Indian pharmaceutical industry was forced to adopt global IP protection standards. Indian firms changed their strategies from reverse-engineering and began to focus on "new chemical entity" (NCE) developments in their own research centers. Moreover, Indian firms started to acquire foreign firms as a quicker route to obtaining knowledge and gaining R&D capabilities than using lengthy internal learning processes.

The auto parts and pharmaceutical industries illustrate the second aspect of catch-up strategies in the Indian context. Both of these industries are characterized by a wide variety of firms in terms of their catch-up potential and implementation capabilities. Some firms, like Bharat Forge and Ranbaxy, are becoming completely integrated into global value chains (indeed, Ranbaxy's integration is so complete that it was recently acquired by a Japanese MNE). However, many firms still struggle in the early stages of catch-up, preferring to concentrate on obtaining a larger share of the shrinking part of the market that is still protected from foreign competition.

Counter to both the auto parts and the pharmaceutical industries, the filmed entertainment industry in India was not pressured by foreign competition in the local market. Foreign firms only recently started to take interest in the Indian market and thus did not play a significant role in the catch-up strategies of Indian firms in the industry. The industry's global environment is arguably based on its special characteristics. These include its knowledge intensity, dependency on skilled, creative, and technologically sophisticated labor, subjective perspectives of consumers, and its project-based nature. Thus, Indian firms did not struggle to keep up with foreign competition on the local market; the firms needed catch-up strategies to accelerate growth and generate efficiencies on the local and global markets. Despite its success in dominating the local market, the industry's performance in terms of financial returns was not particularly impressive. Firms implemented catch-up strategies in a two-pronged manner. On the local market, they generated scale economies by consolidating operations, especially in marketing and distribution. They generated economies of scope by capitalizing on complementary areas such as TV, music, computer games, and advertisement. On the global markets, catch-up strategy focused on leveraging Indian Diasporas abroad, both in terms of importing knowledge and resources and of finding an elite group of "lead users." With a changing operational ethos and a more global focus, Indian firms became more active on the global market and also more attractive to it.

The wind turbine industry is an emerging industry that is still in the process of consolidation. From their inception, Indian firms oriented their catch-up strategies toward acquiring knowledge from firms operating in advanced market economies. In terms of marketed output range and global market share, Suzlon, the leading Indian wind turbine maker, seems to have caught up with its advanced economy competitors. However, examining the patent record indicates that while Suzlon's catch-up is complete in terms of its ability to produce the current industry output range, its knowledge base is both narrower and shallower than those of its advanced economy competitors. In other words, it is still a follower in terms of new generations of output. This illustrates the third aspect of catch-up that we mentioned at the outset. Catch-up processes are multi-dimensional and catch-up along some dimensions like output tends to occur much faster than catch-up along other dimensions like innovation.

Overall, it is evident that in all four cases the industry context plays a significant role for EMNCs' catch-up strategies. Each industry exhibits a different development profile and is influenced by different external factors, many of which are not country specific. The Indian or emerging economy context does seem to influence the strategies of firms, but only to a certain extent, and far less than one might expect. Government policies, typically unique to India, had a strong influence on firm strategies in the pre-1991 era. However, as liberalization progressed in the post-1991 period, the global industry context began to have a stronger influence on the catch-up strategies of EMNCs. This occurred both directly, as in the auto parts industry where firm success became more dependent on acquiring technological capabilities and knowledge-rich relationships with MNCs, and indirectly, as when the global IPR regime significantly impacted Indian government policies towards the pharmaceutical industry.

Future research could study how much influence the industry context and the country context have and how EMNCs cope with each of these influences on catch-up processes, recognizing the importance of institutional transition and discontinuous change. This could be done by comparing the catch-up processes of EMNCs in specific industries across country contexts, e.g., a comparison of the pharmaceutical industry of India and the pharmaceutical industry of Brazil, preferably through a longitudinal study. Such a research project could analyze if and how the country context affects the industry and enable a comparison of these impacts. It is likely that different aspects of government policy have different effects on the strategic choices of firms. Economic liberalization is likely to ensure greater commonalities in the strategies of leading EMNCs across country contexts. However, differences in macroeconomic policies may ensure that the country contexts themselves remain unique.

The comparison would provide important insights into how industry structures affect firms and their development. In particular, as we have argued above, both institutional change and the level of analysis (macro vs. micro) are important in assessing the importance of country context on firm strategy, especially in the case of leading EMNCs. Institutional change, especially at the micro-level, impacts firms directly, but it also increases the integration of the local environment into the global economy and reduces the importance of country factors. The underlying lesson is that successful policy in emerging markets needs to be formulated at the industry level. In this sense, our findings for India echo earlier studies comparing South Korea and Brazil (e.g., Moreira, 1995). These insights are of interest to the academic world but also to policy makers and managers.

Finally, research could potentially benefit from a comparison of EMNCs to firms from the so-called transition economies, mainly in Eastern Europe, such as Russia, Hungary, and Lithuania. Firms from these economies experienced a fundamental and comprehensive change in their external environment, from a centrally planned economy to free markets (Meyer and Peng, 2005). This change has affected regulations and the wider external environment, both formal and informal (Peng, 2003). If the country context becomes less important than the industry context as liberalization proceeds, as we have argued, the catch-up processes of leading MNCs from transition economies and EMNCs should converge.

References

Abramovitz, M. 1986. Catching up, forging ahead and falling behind. *The Journal of Economic History*, 46: 385–406.

Awate, S., Larsen, M. M., and Mudambi, R. 2012. EMNE catch-up strategies in the wind turbine industry: Is there a trade-off between output and innovation capabilities? *Global Strategy Journal*, 2: 205–233.

Buckley, P. 2002. Is the international business research agenda running out of steam? *Journal of International Business Studies*, 33: 365–374.

Cagliarini, A. and Baker, M. 2010. Economic change in India. *Reserve Bank of Australia Bulletin*, September: 19–24.

Cantwell, J. and Mudambi, R. 2011. Physical attraction and the geography of knowledge sourcing in multinational enterprises. *Global Strategy Journal*, 1: 206–232.

Caves, R. 2000. *Creative Industries: Contracts between Art and Commerce*. Cambridge, MA: Harvard University Press.

Chandrasekhar, R. and Sridharan, S. 2009. *Suzlon Energy Inc.* Case; 909M37. Ivey Management Services: London, Canada, pp. 1–17.

Cuervo-Cazurra, A. 2007. Sequence of value-added activities in the multinationalization of developing country firms. *Journal of International Management*, 13: 258–277.

Cuervo-Cazurra, A. and Genc, M. 2008. Transforming disadvantages into advantages: Developing-country MNEs in the least developed countries. *Journal of International Business Studies*, 39: 957–979.

Garud, R. and Karnøe, P. 2003. Bricolage versus breakthrough: Distributed and embedded agency in technology entrepreneurship. *Research Policy*, 32: 277–300.

Gulati, R., Nohria, N., and Zaheer, A. 2001. Strategic networks. *Strategic Management Journal*, 21: 203–215.

GWEC. 2010. *Global Wind Report: Annual Market Update*. Washington, DC: GWE Council.

Hobday, M. 2010. Latecomer catch-up strategies in electronics: Samsung of Korea and ACER of Taiwan. *Asia Pacific Business Review*, 4: 48–83.

Hoskins, C., McFadyen, S., and Finn, A. 1997. *Global Television and Film: An Introduction to the Economics of the Business*. Oxford: Clarendon.

Kale, D. and Little, S. 2007. From imitation to innovation: The evolution of R&D capabilities and learning processes in the Indian pharmaceutical industry. *Technology Analysis & Strategic Management*, 19: 589–609.

KalyaniGroup. 2012. Bharat Forge Limited. www.kalyanigroup.com/bharat_forge.asp. Accessed October 4, 2012.

Khanna, T. and Palepu, K. 1997. Why focused strategies may be wrong for emerging markets. *Harvard Business Review*, 75: 41–51.

2010. *Winning in Emerging Markets: A Roadmap for Strategy and Execution*. Cambridge, MA: Harvard Business Press.

Kola, I. and Landis, J. 2004. Can the pharmaceutical industry reduce the attrition rate? *Nature Reviews: Drug Discovery*, 3: 711–715.

Kumar, N., Mohaparta, P., and Chandraskhar, S. 2009. Suzlon: Conceiving the global wind energy industry. In N. Kumar (ed.), *India's Global Powerhouse: How They Are Taking on the World* (1st edn.): 145–156. Boston, MA: Harvard Business School Press.

Kumaraswamy, A., Mudambi, R., Saranga, H., and Tripathy, A. 2012. Catch-up strategies in the Indian auto components industry: Domestic firms' responses to market liberalization. *Journal of International Business Studies*, 43: 368–395.

Lee, S. W. and Waterman, D. 2007. Theatrical feature film trade in the United States, Europe and Japan since the 1950s: An empirical study of the home market effect. *Journal of Media Economics*, 20: 167–188.

Lieberman, M. B. and Montgomery, D. B. 1988. First-mover advantages. *Strategic Management Journal*, 9: 41–58.

1998. First-mover (dis)advantage: Retrospective and link with the resource-based view. *Strategic Management Journal*, 19: 1111–1126.

Lorenzen, M. 2009. Creativity in context: Content, cost, chance and collection in the organization of the film industry. In P. Jeffeut and A. Pratt (eds.), *Creativity and Innovation in the Cultural Economy*: 93–118. London: Routledge.

Lorenzen, M. and Mudambi, R. 2010. Bangalore vs. Bollywood: Connectivity and catch-up in emerging market economies. *AIB Insights*, 10: 7–11.

2013. Clusters, connectivity and catch-up: Bollywood and Bangalore in the global economy. *Journal of Economic Geography*, 13: 501–534.

Lorenzen, M., Scott, A. J., and Vang, J. 2008. Geography and the cultural economy. *Journal of Economic Geography*, 8: 389–592.

Luo, Y. and Tung, R. L. 2007. International expansion of emerging market enterprises: A springboard perspective. *Journal of International Business*, 38: 481–498.

Mahmood, I. P. and Mitchell, W. 2004. Two faces: Effects of business groups on innovation in emerging economies. *Management Science*, 50: 1348–1365.

Majumdar, S. 1997. The impact of size and age on firm-level performance. Some evidence from India. *Review of Industrial Organization*, 12: 231–247.

Mathews, J. A. 2002. Competitive advantages of the latecomer firms: A resources-based account of industrial catch-up strategies. *Asia Pacific Journal of Management*, 19: 467–488.

Meyer, K. E. and Peng, M. 2005. Probing theoretically into Central and Eastern Europe: Transactions, resources, and institutions. *Journal of International Business Studies*, 36: 600–662.

Meyer, K. E., Mudambi, R., and Narula, R. 2011. Multinational enterprises and local contexts: The opportunities and challenges of multiple embeddedness. *Journal of Management Studies*, 48: 235–252.

Moneycontrol. 2012. Bharat Forge – Company History of Bharat Forge. www.moneycontrol.com/company-facts/bharatforge/history/BF03. Accessed October 4, 2012.

Moreira, M. M. 1995. *Industrialization, Trade and Market Failures: The Role of Government Intervention in Brazil and South Korea*. New York: St. Martin's Press.

Mudambi, R. 2008. Location, control and innovation in knowledge-intensive industries. *Journal of Economic Geography*, 8: 699–725.

Mudambi, R. and Helper, S. 1998. The "closer but adversial" model of supplier relations in the US auto industry. *Strategic Management Journal*, 19: 775–792.

Nair, G. 2008. The impact of TRIPS on the Indian pharmaceutical industry. *Journal of Intellectual Property Rights*, 13: 432–441.

Nielsen, K. 2010. Technological trajectories in the making: Two cases from the contemporary history of wind power. *Centaurus*, 52: 175–205.

Nurkse, R. 1955. *Problems of Capital Formation in Underdeveloped Countries* (3rd edn.). Oxford: Basil Blackwell.

Peng, M. 2003. Institutional transitions and strategic choices. *Academy of Management Review*, 28: 275–296.

Prahalad, C. K. and Hamel, G. 1990. The core competence of the corporation. *Harvard Business Review*, May–June: 79–90.

Pratt, A. C. 2008. Cultural commodity chains, cultural industry clusters, or cultural production chains? *Growth and Change*, 39: 95–103.

Rajsekhar, B., Van Hulle, F., and Jansen, J. C. 1999. Indian wind energy programme: Performance and future directions. *Energy Policy*, 27: 669–678.

Ramamurti, R. and Singh, J. (eds.). 2009. *Emerging Multinationals from Emerging Markets*. Cambridge University Press.

Ranbaxy. 2012. About Us – History. www.ranbaxy.com/aboutus/history. aspx. Accessed October 5, 2012.

Rugman, A. M. and Verbeke, A. 1992. A note on the transnational solution and the transaction cost theory of multinational strategic management. *Journal of International Business Studies*, 23: 761–771.

2001. Subsidiary-specific advantages in multinational enterprises. *Strategic Management Journal*, 22(3): 237–250.

Scherer, F. M. 1993. Pricing, profits and technological progress in the pharmaceutical industry. *Journal of Economic Perspectives*, 7: 97–115.

Sturgeon, T., van Biesebroeck, J., and Gereffi, G. 2008. Value chains, networks and clusters: Reframing the global automotive industry. *Journal of Economic Geography*, 8: 297–321.

Taeube, F. 2007. Local clusters with non-local demand. An exploratory study of small ethnic worlds in the Indian IT industry. In S. Tallman (ed.), *A New Generation in International Strategic Management*: 263–273. Cheltenham: Edward Elgar.

USPTO. 2012. 2701 Patent Term [R-2]. www.uspto.gov/web/offices/pac/ mpep/s2701.html. Accessed October 5, 2012.

PART III

The internationalization of EMNCs: different drivers?

8 | *The global expansion of EMNCs: paradoxes and directions for future research*

PETER J. WILLIAMSON

Introduction: three fundamental paradoxes posed by EMNCs

The nature and extent of global expansion of emerging market multi-national companies (EMNCs) raises three fundamental paradoxes when viewed through the lens of extant international business (IB) theory. The first is: Why and how are they able to successfully expand globally when many commentators (Mathews, 2002a; Rugman, 2009; Madhok and Keyani, 2012) argue that they do not have the competitive advantages (i.e., the ability to operate profitably in another country in which they cannot rely on the comparative advantage of their country of origin to do so.) This question is fundamental because ownership of a rich stock of firm-specific advantages (FSAs) that can be exploited in foreign markets is postulated to be the key rationale for the very existence of a multinational enterprise by much of our existing theory (Caves, 1982).

If we were to assume the absence of these FSAs, some existing research provides an alternative explanation: that the primary rationale for EMNCs' overseas expansion is "resource seeking" (Dunning, 1980) as part of a "catch-up" strategy versus incumbent multinationals who primarily come from advanced economies (Mathews, 2002b; Bruche, 2009). In this case we would expect to see EMNCs globalizing into lower technology industries in less sophisticated markets, where the country-specific advantages (CSAs) drawn from their home markets (such as low-cost labor) would be more effective in winning market share and their paucity of sophisticated, intangible assets (such as proprietary technology and brands) relative to incumbent multinationals would pose less of a handicap. But this leads to a second key paradox: Why, if EMNCs' global expansion is based on this kind of catch-up strategy, do we find EMNCs globalizing into high technology industries as well as low technology ones, and into developed markets as well as developing ones (Williamson et al., 2013)? As will be discussed below, part of the explanation may lie in the fact that EMNCs are internationalizing in an environment that is already highly globalized (in terms of trade, investment, and knowledge flows as well as the presence of well-established global value chains). This sits uneasily, however, with the implicit assumptions of existing theories that are mostly rooted in an era where there were substantial barriers to the free flow of goods, capital, and knowledge across national borders.

The third paradox lies in the relationship between traditional entry mode theories (and the trade-offs between greenfield, joint venture, and acquisition entry modes they postulate) and the routes to international expansion that we observe EMNCs using in practice (Ramamurti, 2012: 44; Williamson et al., 2013). The dominant theories of entry mode choice focus on the relative advantages of different modes as mechanisms by which existing assets and FSAs can be exploited in new markets (Zhao et al., 2004; Canabal and White, 2008). But EMNCs often choose their entry strategies based on the mode that will best deliver other advantages such as maximized learning (that may then be deployed back in the home market) or allow them to exploit their non-traditional FSAs. As a result, EMNCs' entry mode choices are often at variance with existing theories.

In what follows, each of these ways in which the behavior of EMNCs challenges mainstream international business theory, and their implications for issues that might valuably be addressed in future research, are discussed in turn.

Recognizing non-traditional FSAs and their impacts on global competition

The FSA/CSA matrix proposed by Rugman (1981) is widely used in the international business literature to analyze what makes a firm internationally competitive. It comprises two dimensions: the first, FSAs, are the unique, proprietary capabilities of the firm built using product or process technology, marketing, or distribution skills, etc. A firm can also build advantage along a second dimension by drawing on CSAs – valuable resources that are unique to the locations in which it operates. These CSAs include natural resource endowments, the quality and quantity of the labor force, local demand conditions, and culture.

The competitive advantages of many EMNCs have their roots in the CSAs available in their home markets, such as abundant low-cost labor or favorable demand conditions that enable economies of scale to be reaped (Rugman, 2009). But it has long been recognized that CSAs act as raw material for the subsequent creation of FSAs (Porter, 1991). Historically it was contended that these CSAs were "common to all firms in a given country" (Lessard and Lucea, 2009: 282). But more recently it has been argued that firms have differential capabilities to access CSAs, with locally bred firms having an advantage in accessing CSAs in their home markets (Hennart, 2012; Wan, 2013). EMNCs also potentially have capabilities that give them advantages in accessing CSAs in other emerging markets, relative to multinationals from advanced economies.

As a result of these differential capabilities to access CSAs, EMNCs are likely to have at their disposal a different vector of CSAs which they can then convert to FSAs. This chain of causality means that the FSAs enjoyed by EMNCs are likely to be different from those normally associated with multinationals from advanced economies. Researchers looking for the FSAs that predominate in multinationals from developed countries, such as proprietary technology or brands with significant consumer equity, are therefore likely to overlook the different or "non-traditional" FSAs that are most common among EMNCs (Ramamurti, 2012). Examples of these non-traditional FSAs are increasingly being acknowledged in the literature. These include FSAs that could provide EMNCs with competitive advantage in global markets, such as: cost innovation (Zeng and Williamson, 2007; Williamson and Zeng, 2009), unlocking latent demand in low-end segments (Prahalad, 2006), optimizing products and processes for emerging markets (Ramamurti and Singh, 2009), dealing with weak institutions and infrastructure (Cuervo-Cazurra and Genc, 2008; Morck et al., 2008), or optimizing their value chains globally in ways that allow their low-cost talent and resources to be leveraged effectively in emerging markets (Williamson et al., 2013).

While these kinds of FSAs are not necessarily substitutes for those of multinationals from advanced economies, they may be particularly well attuned to the changing requirements for competitiveness in twenty-first century global markets for two reasons. First, emerging markets, especially the BRIC (Brazil, Russia, India, and China) and VISTA (Vietnam, Indonesia, South Africa, Turkey, and Argentina) countries, are becoming increasingly important as drivers of demand. As the *Economist* magazine pointed out, by 2005 the combined GDP of emerging and developing economies had risen to above half of global GDP when measured at purchasing-power parity (Economist, 2006). On average, developing country markets are also growing an order of magnitude faster than those in the developed world. The capabilities to succeed in emerging markets, therefore, will be decisive in the next round of global competition (Knight and Cavusgil, 2004).

A second important shift in the global market that might favor the FSAs of EMNCs stems from the fact that China's 1.3 billion people (including a potentially active labor force of 800 million) cannot move from economic isolation to become an integrated part of the world economy without a downward pressure on global labor rates. And that process, which began in 1978 when China started to open up to the world, still has a long way to go: there are at least 500 million Chinese still to move from low-productivity agriculture to be efficiently employed in manufacturing and services. That's before we take into account another 1 billion that might make this transition in India and other developing countries over the next decades. As long as these shifts continue, and there is little reason to suppose they will stop, downward pressure on wages will continue at the macro level. These forces have led the real income levels of a significant segment of the working population in the developed world to stall or even to decline (especially among less-skilled workers in North America and Europe). Many also feel their job security is under threat. As a result, a substantial and growing market segment of consumers in the developed world has become acutely focused on seeking out the lowest price and best "value for money." At the same time, they want to maintain interest and excitement by being able to choose products they see as keeping up with new trends, and they are loath to restrict their choice of variety. The EMNCs may be better equipped to prosper from this growing segment that demands "everyday low prices" and increased value for money for innovative products and commodities than developed country multinationals with more traditional FSAs that underpin higher-priced, differentiated offerings.

These suppositions seem to be borne out by anecdotal evidence on the success of some EMNCs in global markets characterized by booming demand in the developing world and the rise of value-for-money segments. The emergence of China's Lenovo, with the largest market share by value in personal computers and related devices, and Huawei, as number two in the global market for telecommunications equipment, are just two cases in point.

Recent developments, therefore, suggest that our theories and research agendas need to be expanded to more explicitly recognize these non-traditional FSAs and their ongoing impacts on competition within the changing global market.

Incorporating the implications of today's globalized context

The dominant theories of how companies internationalize were primarily developed in the immediate post-World War II environment when the globe was divided into national markets bounded by considerable barriers to cross-border trade and investment flows (Wilkins, 1974). Information and knowledge flows were also hampered in this environment by communication technologies that were primitive and high cost relative to those available today. Under these conditions, it is perhaps not surprising that models of the emergence and evolution of multinational firms emphasized strategies and structures designed to facilitate the transfer and exploitation of FSAs accumulated by firms in their home markets into other, discrete national markets. It was postulated that multinationals were uniquely efficient vehicles for executing the transfer of these (usually intangible) assets and advantages (Chandler, 1980). It was also accepted that the most relevant segmentation of the global market would be country-based, reflecting the (usually implicit) assumption that inter-country differences in demand patterns were more significant than intra-country differences. These constructs led to the dominance of what was later described as "global projection" strategies (Doz et al., 2001), a large literature on optimal entry modes (Canabal and White, 2008), and a concern with the trade-offs between global integration and local adaptation (Prahalad and Doz, 1987). The vast majority of entry mode studies, meanwhile, were concerned with determining the best route for a budding multinational to exploit existing FSAs developed at home by combining them with local capabilities and knowledge through green-field investment in local subsidiaries, joint ventures, or acquisitions.

The global context of the late twentieth and early twenty-first centuries in which most EMNCs have been internationalizing could not be more different from that on which these traditional theories were based. The markets in which many EMNCs are competing are already highly globalized with large flows of products and services, capital, and information knowledge across relatively porous country borders in much of the world. As a result, traditional strategies for international expansion that were successful in the different, earlier environment may well prove ineffective and unprofitable under the new conditions. For example, traditional incremental approaches as characterized by Johanson and Vahlne (1977) may not be competitive against incumbent multinationals that already enjoy the benefits of global reach. On the other hand, the globalized state of many market environments and the much freer flows of resources across national boundaries may open up opportunities for new strategies that were not available to companies globalizing in the earlier post-war era.

Moreover, existing global value chains, rather than untapped national markets, may be the dominant structures in global markets from the standpoint of global competition. Again, the existence of the global value chains may present EMNCs both with new barriers to entry (such as the need to compete with an efficient global value chain rather than constrained local competitors) as well as new gateways through which to enter and share in the value-added and profits being generated – for example, by joining an existing global value chain as a subcontractor or supplier of ancillary services (Katkalo and Medvedev, 2013).

Some of these differences in context have been highlighted by extant research, but arguably often without acknowledging their potentially profound implications. Dunning et al. (2008), for example, conclude that in the new context EMNCs have been able to globalize without substantive FSAs (or what they term "ownership advantages") by exploiting their CSAs (or "locational advantages"). But sole reliance on the kind of locational advantages to which these authors refer hardly provides a satisfactory explanation of why we observe EMNCs globalizing into high-technology industries as well as low-technology ones, into developed markets as well as developing ones, and into so-called "sunset" industries (those that are believed to have few growth prospects or expected future decline, at least in developed markets) as well as fast-growing "sunrise" ones. Such explanations leave unanswered, for example, the questions of how an EMNC can successfully win share in a high-technology industry without substantial FSAs, or how EMNCs can compete with local firms in developed countries who have access to both FSAs and many of the same CSAs exploited by EMNCs, which traditional theory argues can be freely accessed by all firms.

More recent work has begun to tease out the implications of the new global context and the resulting behavior of EMNCs for extension of existing IB theories. Cuervo-Cazurra (2012) notes, for example, that in a more globalized environment for resources and knowledge as well as competition, EMNCs may be more able and more motivated to move abroad to reduce their "ownership disadvantages" (i.e., a lack of the full complement of FSAs necessary to compete globally). He also notes that this may make EMNCs more likely to enter developed economies because these can act as a rich source of the resources they lack – such as technology or management skills – without the necessity of having to establish production subsidiaries abroad.

Despite these contributions, however, there remains considerable scope for fruitful research to better understand the implications of the more globalized environment in which EMNCs are competing compared to the conditions under which the development of multinationals from advanced economies was mostly observed. First, it may be that in a more open global market for resources and knowledge with better and cheaper communications technologies, it becomes more viable to pursue internationalization strategies based on creating new kinds of advantages by combining existing FSAs with resources and knowledge accessed from abroad. Thus the potential advantages EMNCs can gain from globalization go beyond both exploiting existing FSAs in new markets and seeking resources that fill gaps in their existing bundles to include the possibility of creating entirely new FSAs through the interaction and melding of diverse resources in ways that fuel innovation. In other words, in a more globalized environment we should explore the role of internationalization as a mechanism to stimulate innovation (Doz et al., 2001).

A second example of the kind of research that might result from more fully incorporating the implications of the more globalized environment EMNCs operate in as latecomers would be to consider the possibility that opportunities to join existing global value chains might offer a new gateway to eventually becoming a successful orchestrator of the whole chain. Zeng and Williamson (2007), for example, describe how the Chinese auto components manufacturer Wanxiang entered the global automotive value chain as a supplier of a single, humdrum component: universal joints for steering systems. Despite a very narrow range of capabilities and knowledge, by focusing all its efforts on just one activity (manufacturing) of one sub-component in the chain (universal joints) Wanxiang was able to become a globally competitive link in the chain and the largest supplier in the world with huge economies of scale. Having entered the international value chain through this gateway, it was able to use its profits to expand its knowledge and resource base. This strategy included making more than thirty acquisitions of companies in eight countries, including the United States, United Kingdom, Germany, Canada, and Australia. Leveraging this ever-expanding international resource base and combining it with its existing FSAs to innovate new products and processes, Wanxiang was able to expand along the chain to become a supplier of complete steering systems and subsequently complete braking systems and power drives for vehicles. It became a "tier one" supplier to a number of major international automakers, controlling the whole value chain for sub-assemblies from raw materials to distribution. It subsequently launched a series of complete electric vehicles under its own name, becoming an orchestrator of its own global value chain. Wanxiang continues to pursue this internationalization strategy based on incremental expansion along the value chain, most recently by acquiring lithium-ion battery developer A123 Systems, based in Massachusetts, in December 2012 against competition from America's Johnson Controls and Japan's NEC Corporation.

A third example of a potential research stream suggested by more explicitly incorporating the implications of today's more globalized context is to explore the use of global consolidation strategies as a route by which EMNCs are internationalizing in mature, sunset industries (Ramamurti, 2009). Core to this strategy is the use of acquisition by EMNCs in developed countries in order to access capabilities and knowledge that have been "orphaned" by the decline of volume production in these industries in developed markets, and to redeploy these assets (be they physical plants that are dismantled and relocated or technicians or intellectual property that can be transferred) in their vibrant home-market operations or in other emerging markets. By extending their resource bases in this way, while transferring production activities to high-volume, lower-cost sites in large, growing emerging markets, EMNCs are able to profitably globalize through cross-border industry consolidation (Williamson et al., 2013).

Given these and other options now open to EMNCs because they are internationalizing in an environment that is already relatively global, there is a real need for research that explores the implications of this new environment for alternative models of internationalization that differ significantly from those adopted by multinationals who fanned out from developed countries under the conditions and constraints associated with an earlier era.

Developing models where learning and innovation are the primary reasons for going global

In the previous section discussing the implications of the more globalized context for research on EMNC patterns of globalization, we identified a number of instances where the primary aim of global expansion was to improve and accelerate learning and innovation rather than to exploit existing FSAs or even simply to fill resource and capability gaps. Shifting our perspective to a standpoint where "learning from the world" and enhancing innovation is the primary motivation for going global also suggests a number of new and different avenues where research is required.

First, adopting learning and innovation as the primary motivators for global expansion would lead us to suspect that existing models of entry mode choice need to be fundamentally re-thought. It seems most unlikely, for example, that the relative advantages and disadvantages of greenfield investments, joint ventures, and acquisitions will remain the same when the goal is learning and innovation rather than exploitation of existing FSAs in new markets as is generally assumed. Likewise, indicators of the relative attractiveness of alternative locations would need to be re-defined.

Second, this reconceptualization indicates that in researching EMNC globalization, much more attention needs to be given to the mobility characteristics of the resources, capabilities, and knowledge being transferred. This is because, unlike the capital, products, and codified systems and processes that multinationals from developed countries typically needed to transfer in the course of exploiting new markets, the assets that EMNCs need to move are much more prone to loss or degradation during the transfer process. Moving these assets faces the well-known difficulties of transferring tacit knowledge over distance and the difficult processes of de-contextualization and re-contextualization (Kogut and Zander, 1993). A major element of any model of the globalization process where learning and innovation are primary goals, therefore, must be a characterization of the processes by which complex, messy types of knowledge can be transferred across distance. Yet while this issue has been widely researched in the context of the ongoing management of mature multinationals (e.g., Björkman et al., 2004), it has received little focus in theories seeking to explain the emergence of new multinationals. Similarly, this perspective would lead us to postulate that the absorptive capacity (Cohen and Levinthal, 1990) of the firm would be a major factor in determining the success of its globalization initiatives, despite the fact that this capacity plays little role in most theories of multinational expansion where the goal is market exploitation.

Third, if the primary goals of international expansion were to be taken as learning and innovation, then models would have to consider the interaction and melding of diverse knowledge and capabilities in ways that achieved those results, going beyond resource seeking or exploitation. Firms would no longer be conceived as assembling "bundles" of resources accessed through international expansion. The focus would need to shift from "resource assembly" to "resource interaction" and the processes of recombination and interaction in the innovation process to forge new FSAs would need to move to the forefront of internationalization models.

Finally a shift to a learning and innovation perspective would require models of multinationals' organizational structures and management processes to be re-thought. It is unlikely, for example, that a multinational whose core knowledge-generating assets and activities, such as R&D, design, and marketing, were located far from the home country, while more routine activities such as simple assembly were located in the home country (as might be the case for an EMNC expanding globally to enhance its learning and innovation), would thrive with the same organization structures and processes as a firm whose goal was the exploitation of existing FSAs in new markets. New organizational models and processes would therefore need to be explored that would be consistent with the efficient management of this new type of value chain configuration.

Conclusion: the need to re-direct future research

We began by identifying three paradoxes that the nature and extent of EMNCs' global expansion poses for existing IB theory. First, why and how have EMNCs been able to successfully expand abroad when they appear to lack the traditional sorts of competitive advantages that theory suggests are necessary for a firm to thrive when it leaves the benefits of its home market behind? Second, why do the kinds of locations and industries in which EMNCs choose to compete abroad seem to extend far beyond what is predicted by models based on the assumption that internationalization is part of a "catch-up" strategy, and how might the current highly globalized environment in which EMNCs are internationalizing help explain this behavior? Third, why do EMNCs often choose entry strategies that are different from those that would be expected based on existing theory, and that seem to be more appropriate to complex learning than market exploitation or simple resource seeking?

The analysis of these paradoxes, in turn, suggests three directions in which future research on EMNCs is likely to offer fruitful development of international business theory. The first is developing a better understanding of the nature of EMNCs' non-traditional FSAs and their implications both for likely developments in global competition and for the future behavior of EMNCs. The second fruitful direction for future research is to incorporate more explicitly the implications of "late-comer" context: the fact that EMNCs are expanding internationally in a world that has both the opportunities and challenges of markets that are often already highly globalized and where global value chains are already in place. Third is the opportunity, and most probably the necessity, to re-think the models used to describe, explain, and explore the unique issues of international expansion from the standpoint of EMNCs whose primary reasons for going global are learning, innovation, and the transfer and integration of complex knowledge back into the home country operations, rather than the exploitation of existing advantages in new markets.

References

Björkman, I., Barner-Rasmussen, W., and Li, L. 2004. Managing knowledge transfer in MNCs: The impact of headquarters control mechanisms. *Journal of International Business Studies*, 35: 443–455.

Bruche, G. 2009. The emergence of China and India as new competitors in MNCs innovation networks. *Competition and Change*, 13: 267–288.

Canabal, A. and White, G. O. 2008. Entry mode research: Past and future. *International Business Review*, 17: 267–284.

Caves, R. E. 1982. *Multinational Enterprise and Economic Analysis*. Cambridge University Press.

Chandler, A. D., Jr. 1980. *Managerial Hierarchies*. Cambridge, MA: Harvard University Press.

Cohen, W. M. and Levinthal, D. A. 1990. Absorptive capacity: A new perspective on learning and innovation. *Administrative Science Quarterly*, 35: 128–152.

Cuervo-Cazurra, A. 2012. Extending theory by analyzing developing country multinational companies: Solving the Goldilocks debate. *Global Strategy Journal*, 2: 153–167.

Cuervo-Cazurra, A. and Genc, M. 2008. Transforming disadvantages into advantages: Developing country MNEs in the least developed countries. *Journal of International Business Studies* 39: 957–979.

Cuervo-Cazurra, A. and Mehmet, G. 2008. Transforming disadvantages into advantages: Developing-country MNEs in the least developed MNEs. *Journal of International Business Studies*, 39: 957–979.

Doz, Y. L., Santos, J. and Williamson, P. 2001. *From Global to Metanational: How Companies Win in the Knowledge Economy*. Boston, MA: Harvard University Press.

Dunning, J. H. 1980. Towards an eclectic theory of international production: Some empirical tests. *Journal of International Business Studies*, 11(1): 9–31.

Dunning, J. H., Kim, C., and Park, D. 2008. Old wine in new bottles: A comparison of emerging market TNCs today and developed country TNCs thirty years ago. In K. Sauvant (ed.), *The Rise of Transnational Corporations from Emerging Markets: Threat or Opportunity?* Northampton, UK: Edward Elgar.

Economist, 2006. Emerging economies are climbing back. *The Economist*, January 21: 71–72.

Hennart, J. 2012. Emerging market multinationals and the theory of the multinational enterprise. *Global Strategy Journal*, 2: 168–187.

Johanson, J. and Vahlne, J. E. 1977. The internationalization process of the firm: A model of knowledge development and increasing foreign market commitments. *Journal of International Business Studies*, 8: 23–32.

Katkalo, V. S. and Medvedev, A. G. 2013. Value-chain configurations of Russian EMNEs. In P. J. Williamson, R. Ramamurti, A. Fleury, and M. T. L. Fleury (eds.), *The Competitive Advantage of Emerging Country Multinationals*: 116–131. Cambridge University Press.

Knight, G. A. and Cavusgil, S. T. 2004. Innovation, organizational capabilities, and the born-global firm. *Journal of International Business Studies*, 35: 124–141.

Kogut, B. and Zander, U. 1993. Knowledge of the firm and the evolutionary theory of the multinational corporation. *Journal of International Business Studies*, 24: 625–646.

Lessard, D. and Lucea, R. 2009. Mexican multinationals: Insights from CEMEX. In R. Ramamurti and J. V. Singh (eds.), *Emerging Multinationals in Emerging Markets*: 280–311. Cambridge University Press.

Madhok, A. and Keyani, M. 2012. Acquisitions as entrepreneurship: Internationalization, acquisition and multinationals from emerging economies. *Global Strategy Journal*, 2: 24–54.

Mathews, J. A. 2002a. *Dragon Multinational: A New Model for Global Growth*. Oxford University Press.

2002b. Competitive advantages of the latecomer firm: A resource-based account of industrial catch-up strategies. *Asia Pacific Journal of Management*, 19: 467–488.

Morck, R., Yeung, B., and Zhao, M. 2008. Perspectives on China's outward foreign direct investment. *Journal of International Business Studies*, 39: 337–350.

Porter, M. E. 1991. Towards a dynamic theory of strategy. *Strategic Management Journal*, 12(S2; Winter): 95–117.

Prahalad, C. K. 2006. *The Fortune at the Bottom of the Pyramid*. Philadelphia: Wharton School Publishing.

Prahalad, C. K. and Doz, Y. L. 1987. *The Multinational Mission: Balancing Local Demands and Global Vision*. New York: The Free Press.

Ramamurti, R. 2009. What have we learned about emerging market MNEs? In R. Ramamurti and J. V. Singh (eds.), *Emerging Multinationals in Emerging Markets*: 399–426. Cambridge University Press.

2012. Commentaries: What is really different about emerging market multinationals? *Global Strategy Journal*, 2: 41–47.

Ramamurti, R. and J. V. Singh (eds.). 2009. *Emerging Multinationals in Emerging Markets*. Cambridge University Press.

Rugman, A. M. 1981. *Inside the Multinationals: The Economics of Internal Markets*. New York: Columbia University Press.

2009. Theoretical aspects of MNEs from emerging markets. In R. Ramamurti and J. V. Singh (eds.), *Emerging Multinationals in Emerging Markets*: 42–63. Cambridge University Press.

Wan, F. 2013. Converting country-specific advantages into firm-specific advantages: A new perspective on developing and sustaining competitive advantage in emerging markets. Unpublished PhD Thesis. Cambridge: University of Cambridge, Judge Business School.

Wilkins, M. 1974. *The Maturing of Multinational Enterprise: American Business Abroad from 1914 to 1970*. Cambridge, MA: Harvard University Press.

Williamson, P. and Zeng, M. 2009. Chinese multinationals: Emerging through new global gateways. In R. Ramamurti and J. V. Singh (eds.), *Emerging Multinationals in Emerging Markets*: 81–109. Cambridge University Press.

Williamson, P. J., Ramamurti, R., Fleury, A., and Fleury, M. T. L. 2013. *The Competitive Advantage of Emerging Country Multinationals.* Cambridge University Press.

Zeng, M. and Williamson, P. J. 2007. *Dragons at your Door: How Chinese Cost Innovation is Disrupting Global Competition.* Boston, MA: Harvard Business School Press.

Zhao, H., Luo, Y., and Suh, T. 2004. Transaction cost determinants and ownership-based entry mode choice: A meta-analytical review. *Journal of International Business Studies*, 35: 524–544.

9 Process perspectives on the growth of emerging economy multinationals

KLAUS E. MEYER

Introduction

Recent studies of emerging market multinational companies (EMNCs) have shed new light on how origins and historical contexts shape the strategies and growth paths of MNCs (Cuervo-Cazurra, 2012; Meyer and Thaijongrak, 2013; Ramamurti, 2012; Verbeke and Kano, 2012). While we may not need new theories to explain EMNCs, they direct our attention on aspects of MNCs that may also exist elsewhere, yet were not considered typical, and thus received limited attention in the scholarly literature. Moreover, this research has highlighted the inherently static nature of mainstream theories, which thus contribute little to explaining the evolution of MNCs over time, or the difference between mature and inexperienced MNCs, such as EMNCs. Therefore, in this chapter, I review the prime dynamic model in the IB field, the internationalization process model (IPM), and discuss how it can contribute to advancing our theoretical understanding of EMNCs (and thence MNCs in general).

The IPM analyzes a firm's international business as a series of commitment decisions, driven by learning processes leading to a path of gradually changing (usually increasing) resource commitments. Specifically, the model explains the step-wise increases of commitments to foreign operations as a function of knowledge accumulated through learning processes enabled by earlier commitments (Johanson and Vahlne, 1977, 2006, 2009). It provides a powerful foundation for research explaining the growth of MNCs over time, which is highly relevant to EMNCs. Mainstream theorizing on MNCs has primarily focused on mature MNCs as they are common in Anglo-American economies, while small or early stage MNCs are relegated to specialist subfields, such as international new ventures (Chetty et al., 2006). However, smaller firms engaging in international business are commonplace in other parts of the world, e.g., in Northern Europe, where many scholars have investigated how firms start and grow their international business (Anderson, 1997; Benito et al., 2009; Forsgren, 2002; Meyer and Gelbuda, 2006).

These small and early stage MNCs have been the primary focus of process oriented international business research. However, the IPM is also highly relevant for EMNCs because although they are often quite big in terms of sales or employees due to the vast scale of their domestic operations, they are internationally still relatively inexperienced. Hence, with respect to building international business capabilities, they often are still at early stages.

The recent literature on EMNCs has developed several lines of theoretical insights that I consider quite innovative. These are respectively (a) "strategic asset seeking" as motive for EMNs (e.g., Deng, 2009; Luo and Tung, 2007; Rui and Yip, 2008), (b) the local partner perspective on the choice of organizational firms (Hennart, 2009, 2012, this book), and (c) home country institutions as a driver and constraint of EMNCs (Buckley et al., 2007; Morck et al., 2008; Wang et al., 2012). In this chapter, I will argue that these perspectives are complementary to the internationalization process perspective. Specifically, the IPM provides avenues to both add a dynamic perspective to several theories, and to explain why the above mentioned theoretical perspectives may be more relevant for EMNCs than for mature MNCs.

I start by providing some data illustrating the recent, rapid emergence of MNCs from several countries to illustrate the point that most EMNCs are still relatively immature in terms of international business experience. In section 3, I outline why I consider the IPM developed and advocated by Johanson and Vahlne (1977, 2006, 2009) to be a useful theoretical foundation for research on EMNCs. To this end I summarize my assessment of the current stage of research on the internationalization process model, drawing on Meyer and Thaijongrak (2013). In section 4, I outline how the internationalization process model can inform future research along the three lines of theorizing named above. Section 5 concludes.

Trends of FDI from emerging economies

Before engaging in the theoretical discourse, let us look at the empirical phenomenon we are trying to explain. Over the past four decades,

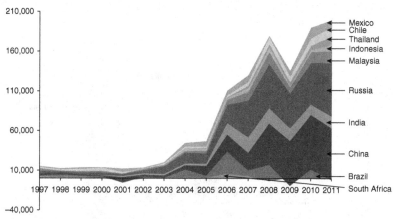

Figure 9.1 FDI flows from selected emerging markets 1997–2011 in thousands of US$.

the dominance of MNCs from a handful of industrialized economies has gradually diminished. For example, the share of the USA in global FDI outflows declined from 54% in 1970 to 23% in 2011, while the British share declined from 12% in 1970 to 3% in 2010 recovering to 6% in 2011. In their place, MNCs from a wider range of countries have become players on the global stage.

Using data from the UNCTAD database, Figure 9.1 shows FDI flows in absolute terms (not inflation adjusted) in US$ from ten selected emerging economies since 1997; while Figure 9.2 plots the percentage contributions from the same ten countries to worldwide FDI outflows from 1970 to 2011.

Two of these countries, namely South Africa and Brazil, had a small but non-negligible presence in worldwide FDI flows since the 1970s (Figure 9.2), with the largest share in global flows dating back to respectively 1980 for Brazil (1.5 percent) and 1982 for South Africa (1.4 percent). In the recent surge of FDI from emerging markets, however, both countries played only a small part; in fact both countries recorded *negative* FDI outflows in certain years. For example, South Africa had a net withdrawal of over US$3 billion in the year 2008, presumably attributable to major MNEs relocating their registration out of South Africa, for example to London (which results as them being considered as British MNCs in the balance of payments statistics that are the basis for these data).

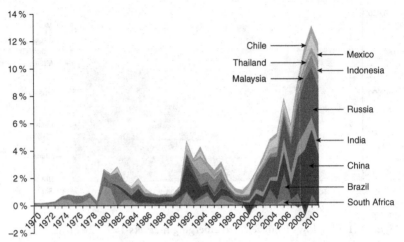

Figure 9.2 FDI flows from selected emerging markets 1970–2011 as percentage of worldwide FDI flows.

The other countries in this selection of emerging markets generated very little outward FDI until about 2005. In the middle of the decade, however, Chinese and Russian MNCs in particular emerged as substantive players as their share in global FDI flows grew to respectively 4.7 per cent and 3.6 percent in the year 2010, before falling slightly back in 2011 (Figure 9.2). In addition, several other emerging markets have increased their FDI outflows, including India, Indonesia, Thailand, and Malaysia in Asia, and Mexico and Chile in Latin America.[1] However, none of these countries exceeded 1 percent of global FDI flows in any single year.

Two empirical observations I would like to emphasize because they shape the research questions we would want to ask with respect to EMNCs. First, the recent push by MNCs onto the global stage from eight of the ten selected countries is the extension of a longer trend where MNCs from a more and more diverse range of countries of origin are investing around the world. Hence, models based solely on Anglo-American experiences lose their ability to explain the world economy. Second, with exceptions, notably in Brazil and South Africa,

---

[1] Note that the data do not include Hong Kong, which reported substantial FDI inflows and outflows over the past decade. However, as a high, yet unknown, share of the FDI is entering China indirectly, or round-tripping investment from China, Hong Kong FDI data are very difficult to interpret.

MNCs from emerging markets are still relatively recent entrants to the global economy, and they are expanding without the rich international business experience that their counterparts in industrialized economies can draw upon. This relative lack of international experience by (most) EMNCs and its theoretical implications are the main focus of this chapter.

The internationalization process model as a theoretical lens

The internationalization process model places each foreign investment decision in the context of the investing firm's own history, notably prior to a particular investment. In other words, internationalization is conceptualized as a process of learning by which firms build international business competences that enable them to profitably operate abroad (Li, 2010; Mathews, 2006). Many EMNCs are still at early stages of this process, hence the creation of competence building opportunities plays a central role in their strategy.

Johanson and Vahlne (1977, 2006, 2009) explain the dynamics of such processes as the interaction between state variables (such as capabilities of a firm at a particular point in time), and change variables (such as the learning that takes place over time, and commitment decisions taken at irregular intervals). This model is theoretically concise, but perhaps not so intuitive. In particular, the original illustration does not bring out very well the dynamic and cumulative nature of this process over time. Therefore, I prefer to depict the process in terms of the changes over time, which occurs in a discontinuous pattern (Figure 9.3). Such a representation of the model helps both to introduce the model to students (as in our textbook, Peng and Meyer, 2011) and to illustrate modifications of the model in recent research contributions (as in a special issue introduction, Meyer and Gelbuda, 2006). The inner logic of the model in Figure 9.3 is the same as in Johansen and Vahlne's model. However, I view the essence of the IPM in the dynamics of increasing resource commitments over time, and therefore prefer this timeline representation.

The critical points in the IPM are the changes in commitment at irregular intervals. Normally, these changes represent an increase of commitment, though sometimes MNCs also decrease their commitment to a particular market, though this is mostly the exception from the rule (Benito, 2005; Santangelo and Meyer, 2011). These changes in

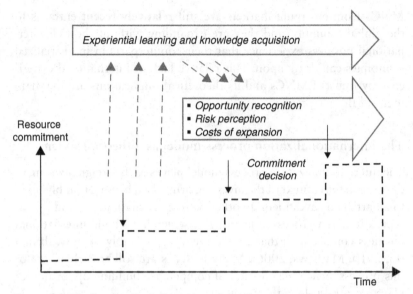

Figure 9.3 The longitudinal dimension of the internationalization process.
Source: Meyer and Thaijongrak (2013).

commitment levels go hand-in-hand with processes of learning, knowledge accumulation, and capability building. Each resource commitment enables new learning processes.

The learning enhances a firm's international business knowledge, which is the foundation for a wide range of capabilities that enable doing business outside one's own country. It includes for example knowledge of practices used in international markets, knowledge of relevant languages, and knowledge of formal and informal institutions governing the markets in which a firm is operating. Such knowledge facilitates key business challenges such as the recognition of business opportunities, and the assessment of risk, while reducing the marginal costs of further expansion moves.

Table 9.1 illustrates some types of international business knowledge that are often underestimated by inexperienced businesses. In particular, knowledge that firms fail to recognize as being important – also known as "unknown unknowns" – is often not acquired and hence leads to business failures. One way of identifying such knowledge is to consider the mistakes that Western firms made in China, and on that basis to speculate as to the problems that Chinese MNCs may run into in a Western country. For example, with respect to institutional actors, Westerners in China struggle to understand how to interact with key players such as the party or local government officials. On the other hand, Chinese companies in Europe or the US struggle to appreciate how to interact with the media and with trade unions. A dictionary will provide simple translations, and there are political parties, local governments, media, and trade unions in (most) countries. Yet, the roles that they play, the ways they influence the business environment, and how foreign investors can interact with them are fundamentally different, and require a lot of tacit knowledge that only individuals and firms experienced in international business will fully appreciate. Similarly, understanding the legal framework, consumer behavior, or employee motivations requires deep local knowledge (Table 9.1).

These examples illustrate knowledge that is specific to particular countries or societies, and is grounded in "location-bound" experience. Other international business capabilities are of a more general nature, and relevant in different geographies and hence not location bound (Clarke et al., 2013). Knowledge creation processes therefore take place both at the global level with respect to general international business competences, and at a location-specific level with respect to competences for specific locations or markets. These processes at multiple levels likely re-enforce each other.

The tacit nature of this international business knowledge implies that it is created by the key protagonists in a firm through personal experiences, and may be shared through interpersonal interactions. Johanson and Vahlne (1977) originally focused on internal experiential learning as the main process by which firms build international business competences. Other scholars have shown that the internationalization process of a firm is highly interdependent with the internationalization of its business network, especially for smaller firms (Chetty and Blankenburg-Holm, 2000; Coviello, 2006; Meyer and Skak, 2002). To some extent, such networks enable the sharing of tacit knowledge beyond organizational boundaries (Forsgren, 2002). Thus, in particular studies of smaller firms in emerging economies expanding internationally have found that home-country based networks play an important facilitating role in the process of setting up operations abroad (e.g., Prashantham and Dhanaraj, 2011; Zhou et al., 2010).

Recent studies in the tradition of the IPM have explored a broader range of processes through which firms accumulate international

Table 9.1 *Examples of tacit international business knowledge.*

Aspects of the business environment	Challenges reported by Westerns operating in China	Challenges likely to be faced by Chinese operating in Western countries
Actions of key institutional actors	Why should I spend so much time dining with officials? How to interact effectively with government officials, and the CPC (party)?	Why are the media reporting such biased stories, and why are the trade unions making so much noise? How to interact effectively with the media, and with trade unions?
Practice of the legal system	Why do Chinese competitors get away with copying our products? How to get Chinese courts to enforce our intellectual property rights?	Why are competition authorities putting their nose into our business? How can we make profits if we are not allowed to talk to our competitors?
Consumer behavior	Why are Chinese so passionate about certain brands? How to create brand loyalty among volatile consumers?	Why do Westerners not like to buy our products even if the quality seems to be just the same? How to overcome negative country-of-origin image?
Employee motivation	Why are Chinese employees so eager to switch jobs, even for small salary increases? How to cope with the unrealistic expectations of the post-1990 generation?	Why do our Western employees not follow what they are instructed to do? How to integrate highly qualified, highly autonomy-minded individuals in a hierarchical organization?

Source: Based on large numbers of mostly informal conversations with Europeans in China, and Chinese in Europe.

business knowledge. First, firms may build an entrepreneurial team that has international experience, thus acquiring knowledge through managerial recruitment. A consistent finding across the burgeoning literature on international new ventures – or born globals – is that they typically start with an entrepreneurial team with high prior international experience (e.g., Chetty et al., 2006; Meyer and Xia, 2012; Rialp et al., 2005). Extending this line of thought, several studies found that returnees play an important role in the creation of entrepreneurial businesses in emerging economies, and internationally oriented start-ups in particular (Filatotchev et al., 2009; Wang et al., 2011). More mature firms may "push" internationalization by externally recruiting key individuals, though they may face challenges integrating newly recruited senior executives with the existing team, which could be a problem if the existing team has cognitive horizon limited to the local context. However, the internationalization of the top management team is an important process that facilitates firm internationalization, and a major challenge for many EMNCs.

Second, firms can learn how to engage in international business before they formally step outside their own country by working with foreign individuals or businesses that do international business in their country. Before emerging market firms launch their international activities, they go through a process of technological catch-up with foreign investors (e.g., Kumraswamy et al., 2012). This domestic catch-up usually precedes internationalization, and may well be conceptualized as an early stage of it. In this process, the formation of joint ventures with foreign partners appears to be an important channel not only for learning about modern technologies, but about practices in international business, which in turn facilitates a firm's initial own steps abroad. This inward-outward linkage appears to have played an important role for many Chinese MNCs (Buck et al., 2009).

Third, firms like individuals can learn by imitating others (De Clercq et al., 2012). Imitation enables firms to engage in strategies the consequences of which they do not yet fully understand and a form of low risk strategy if their performance is assessed relative to these other firms. Imitating action of competitors thus not only reduces uncertainty but can accelerate learning processes about international business. However, imitation strategies also entail the risk of jumping onto a bubble that eventually will burst.

Fourth, firms may learn through collaborating with partners abroad. Such collaboration can take many forms. For example, a small firm may partner with a major multinational by joining its international supply chain; it may draw upon internationally experienced consultants or private equity investors, or it may cooperate with a local firm in the host country (Forsgren, 2002; Li and Meyer, 2009; Prashantham and Birkinshaw, 2008).

These processes of external knowledge accumulation supplement the original IPM, which was mainly focused on internal processes. The range of mechanisms by which organizations learn is very wide, and go beyond the experiential learning processes in the original model. Research on EMNCs provides new opportunities to study different means by which organizations learn, and to enhance our understanding of how firms accumulate international business knowledge.

Integrating process perspectives with other lines of theorizing

The process-oriented insights of the IPM complement other theoretical perspectives that have evolved to explain distinct features of EMNCs. These are (a) "strategic asset seeking" as motive for EMNCs, (b) the local partner perspective on the choice of organizational firms, and (c) home country institutions as a driver and constraint of EMNCs. In this section, I briefly outline how the IPM may complement the three lines of theoretical thought, and how it may inform relevant new research questions (Table 9.2). This integration highlights the critical role of the concept of experience, which may affect pivotal strategic decisions in more complex, possibly non-linear, ways than is usually hypothesized in the literature.

Strategic asset seeking FDI

Some EMNCs use foreign direct investment (FDI) to acquire strategic assets, that is target firms that have capabilities, e.g., technologies, that the acquirer intends to use not only in the host country, but in its global operations. This phenomenon challenges the view that FDI primarily aims to exploit firm-specific advantages (FSAs) as apparently in such cases the investor has no internationally exploitable FSAs (Rugman, 2009; Rugman and Nguyen, this book). This phenomenon

Table 9.2 *Innovative perspectives on EMNCs.*

	Challenges to mainstream theories	Central proposition	Research questions arising from a process perspective
Strategic asset seeking FDI perspective	Most theories explain FDI as a means to exploit firm-specific advantages overseas. Yet, for some FDI projects, exploitation of existing advantages is not the primary goal.	Some FDI projects aim to acquire assets overseas that aim not only to establish a position in a particular host country, but to enhance the global resource and capability base of the investor. These are called strategic asset seeking FDI projects. They are particularly relevant to firms that are in a (relative) catch-up situation in their respective industry.	• How can EMNCs manage strategic asset seeking FDI when they often lack internationally experienced management? • How can EMNCs use partial acquisitions to accelerate their learning processes? • How do Chinese MNCs manage the challenge of reverse transferring technology that is not only organizationally embedded, but societally embedded? • How do EMNCs learn from one acquisition to the next how to manage acquisition processes?
Host partner perspective on organizational forms	Most studies of the choice of organization form for foreign operations (such as joint venture versus wholly owned subsidiary) consider only the preferred mode from the foreign investor's perspective. Yet, it equally depends on the local partner.	The choice of organizational form is the negotiated outcome of strategies of foreign and local partners. Hence, the characteristics of the transactions between the local operations and BOTH partners, as well as BOTH partners' bargaining power shape the choice of organizational forms.	• How do the contributions sought from a local partner to an alliance change with the maturity of the investor, and how does that hence change their preferred and realized organizational form? • How does the learning taking place within an alliance shape the preferences on both sides to continue the alliance?

Table 9.2 (cont.)

	Challenges to mainstream theories	Central proposition	Research questions arising from a process perspective
Home institutional perspective	The institutional environment of host countries has been explored as a key aspect of the locational advantages that may attract or deter inward FDI. Yet, institutions in firms' home country also influence outward FDI strategies, including risk-taking propensity, location choice, and modes of entry.	Institutions in a firm's home country shape the strategies of outward FDI via, among other effects, governance structures, access to financial resources, and industrial policy. These effects may be selective for specific types of firms (e.g., state-owned firms), and may encourage or discourage FDI.	• How do home and host country institutional pressures evolve as MNCs progress along their internationalization path? • How does firms' responsiveness to specific institutional pressures evolve with shifting bargaining power between institutional and corporate actors? • How do national level and firm level processes of learning interact?

Source: Based on literature cited in the text.

has been observed before (Kogut and Chang, 1991), but only with the recent surge of EMNCs did it gain substantive attention in the scholarly literature.

The acquisition of strategic assets is a form of external knowledge accumulation outside the scope of the original IPM. It appears to be common among EMNCs that acquire target firms in Europe or North America that embody a substantially higher level of technology of brands than they themselves (Cui et al., 2014; Deng, 2009; Knoerich, 2010; Li et al., 2012; Luo and Tung, 2007). I believe we can extend the IPM to include strategic asset seeking FDI as a mechanism through which firms build their knowledge base, and thus enhance their international business capabilities.

However, this extension requires rethinking the mechanisms of knowledge accumulation and the possible sequences of different types of resource commitments. First, the implementation of an acquisition requires high level managerial resources, both in the acquisition process itself, and in the subsequent management and integration of the acquired unit (Cui et al., 2014). Even if the unit is managed "at arms' length," as appears to be common for Chinese acquisitions in Europe, the top management of the acquirer has to engage in complex intercultural leadership and negotiation challenges for which a previously mainly domestic firm is normally not well prepared. For this reason, it is somewhat surprising from the perspective of the IPM that firms with limited international business experience engage in major acquisitions. Several possible answers can be hypothesized:

- the acquiring firms may have access to relevant managerial competences from somewhere else, perhaps because they share such expertise within business groups or home country communities;
- they may have a low risk aversion and thus are consciously taking high risks in the pursuit of long term objectives, perhaps because they benefit from an implicit guarantee from a state owner;
- they may be subject to agency conflicts that allow managers to pursue their own objectives in terms of prestigious high profile deals, perhaps because systems of corporate governance offer outside shareholders only weak protection.

Either way, the IPM suggests that we are facing an empirical puzzle that merits further investigation as investment decisions are influenced by mechanisms that we do not yet understand well. Moreover, it raises interesting questions regarding the long term implications of such "big jump" commitments that occur when previously internationally inexperienced EMNCs make large scale investments abroad.

Second, talking to executives and reading case studies, I note that many corporate decision makers design their strategic asset seeking deals as partial rather than full acquisition because they expect a better learning experience (see Meyer and Thaijongrak, 2013 for an example). In other words, they acquire a controlling stake in another company but do not take full equity even though they have the necessary financial resources and the seller is willing to sell the entire firm. Such partial acquisitions create particularly complex managerial challenges because any major organizational change would have to be agreed with the co-owners (Meyer and Tran, 2006). It is, however, not clear to me theoretically why such an arrangement would enhance learning processes, and under which circumstances such learning benefits outweigh the downside of having to manage an acquired firm with limited control over that entity. There is certainly scope for further theoretical development here.

Third, I am very intrigued by the fact that large Chinese companies buy small German companies with the aim of acquiring their advanced technology, and then transfer this technology backward to improve the productivity of operations in China (for case examples see, e.g., Lynton, 2011; Schütte and Chen 2012; Sohm et al., 2009). This sought-after technology is usually only partially (or not at all) codified in patents. The knowledge of modern manufacturing and R&D processes is embedded in organizations, and thus inseparable from the organizational structure and culture. Hence, such knowledge cannot easily be disembodied and transferred, nor does it easily fit into a traditional emerging market organization (Williamson, this book). For example, flat hierarchies are often key to managing knowledge-intensive, creative organizations, yet they would be at odds with the often very hierarchical structures of many Chinese state enterprises, or Indian, Thai, and Brazilian business groups.

Hence, the transfer of organizationally embedded technology to the parent firm represents not only a challenge to knowledge transfer, but to the willingness of the acquiring organization to undergo major organizational and cultural change to be able to absorb it. Moreover, such competences may be embedded in the technology environment, for example the educational system. A major source of competitive advantage of small German manufacturing companies is, in my personal opinion, grounded in the training system that people go through, which in turn is embedded in the national economic system (Hall and Soskice, 2001). This raises the question, how to transfer an education system from Europe to an organization in China? It would require the Chinese parent company not only to change its own processes, but to implement changes in the wider community, notably the education system. It is my impression that many Chinese investors have not yet fully thought through the complexity of this challenge.

Fourth, EMNCs embarking on an acquisition spree have opportunities to learn from one acquisition to the next. Many acquisitions are not one-off deals but stepping stones within ambitious strategies of acquisition-led growth, aiming to create a major global player. This M&A knowledge is certainly part of international business knowledge accumulation. Hence, Elango and Pattnaik (2011) find that EMNCs engage in successively larger acquisition projects. However, how such knowledge is created and integrated merits further research.

Finally, when along its internationalization path is a firm most likely to benefit from strategic asset seeking FDI? Inexperienced investors can use strategic asset seeking FDI to address critical gaps that prevent them from competing effectively internationally, or in fact in their home market. At this stage, strategic asset seeking FDI is feasible *if* the firm can draw on external financial resources to pay for the acquisition, which in an emerging economy context may be obtained through past profits in a large domestic market, through financing within a business group, or (especially in China) through preferential access to bank finance from state banks. As MNCs progress along their internationalization process, such a need for strategic assets diminishes and we would expect to see a shift from strategic asset seeking to organic growth.

An experienced MNC, on the other hand, is likely to have developed managerial processes to manage international operations, including capabilities in managing acquired companies. At the same time, the MNC is likely to generate internal financial resources from its international operations that enable future growth. In other words, the mature MNC is actually much better positioned to successfully implement strategic asset seeking FDI. However, it may do so not to bridge the gap with global leaders, but to selectively acquire specific technologies, brands, or market positions that complement its asset portfolio and enable better exploitation of its resource base. The effects of needs and ability together suggest opposite hypotheses as to the stage of maturity when an MNC would be most likely to employ strategic asset seeking FDI. Moreover, the opposing effects may interact to generate a non-linear relationship, perhaps taking a u-shaped form.

Local partners and the choice of organizational form

The second line of research receiving new inspirations concerns the choice of organizational forms in international business. Traditionally, such work has taken the perspective of the foreign entrant to determine the likely costs and benefits of alternative forms, in particular the choice between a joint venture and a wholly owned subsidiary. However, as Hennart (2009, 2012, this book) eloquently explains, the organizational form by which two firms transact with each other depends on the contributions and costs faced by *both* partners. Hence, a joint venture is preferred only when both partners contribute resources that are subject to high transaction costs. This situation may apply to foreign investors seeking local knowledge in an emerging economy (the traditional focus of international business research) but also to EMNCs acquiring brands or technology overseas, which they wish to share across their global operations. The difference lies in the types of contribution made respectively by foreign and local partners. In fact, if the acquisition of tacit knowledge is a primary motive for overseas investments for EMNCs, then the perspective of the organization holding such sought-after tacit knowledge seems to be particularly relevant.

Seen through the lens of the IPM, these situations reflect a form of external learning from partners. Firms taking their first steps in international business, and having little access to international business expertise in their home environment are looking for different contributions from partners they work with abroad than do mature MNCs. In particular, they may look for partners that help them bridge the technological gap to world leaders, and know how to engage in international markets, to negotiate with various parties such as institutional investors, etc. These sorts of partner contributions are less likely to interest mature MNCs. They look more selectively for complementary resources such as specific industry expertise or specific local distribution channels. How do these differences between experienced and inexperienced MNCs affect their partnering strategies along an internationalization process?

An important difference is the likely bargaining power between the partners, and their respective exposure to information asymmetries and other sources of transaction costs. The traditional "MNC-centric theories" (Hennart, 2009) in international business implicitly assume that the local partner is in a weak bargaining position, and hence the costs and benefits that a foreign investor is facing with alternative organizational forms are determining their choice. When focusing on inexperienced investors, however, it becomes apparent that this (implicit) assumption does not hold true. Where a local partner – say a family-owned SME – is providing advanced technology, this local partner not only has considerable bargaining power (because there likely are plenty of other potential suitors for their assets; Knoerich, 2010) but its contribution is subject to high information asymmetries and hence high transaction costs. This suggests that to better understand the observed strategies of EMNCs in Europe, we need to study the objectives and motivations of European firms partnering with these inward foreign investors.

As a firm advances along its internationalization path, it not only enhances its ability to manage relationships with partners, but the types of partners and their relative bargaining power evolve. At any point in time, a firm's accumulated knowledge base provides the foundation for its next commitment decisions. However, the IPM does not provide uniform predictions as to what level and type of experience would lead to the choice of which organizational form. Some scholars working in the internationalization process tradition suggest a sequence of modes running from contractual collaboration to joint ventures and eventually to fully owned subsidiaries (e.g., Hadjikani, 1997; Millington and Bayliss, 1990). An inexperienced foreign investor would benefit most from the local knowledge and network of a local joint venture partner. However, selecting a suitable joint venture partner and managing the cross-cultural interface with a local firm is in fact very demanding in terms of managerial abilities and local knowledge, and thus greatly benefits from both local and general international business.

Hence, the ownership mode literature faces a paradox (Li and Meyer, 2009): On the one hand, the more experience a firm has, the more its internal capabilities enable it to operate in the particular host

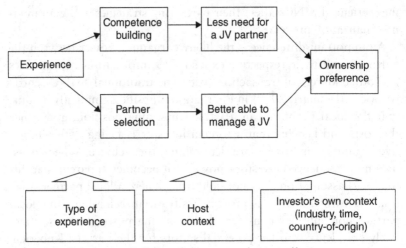

Figure 9.4 Competence building and partner selection effects.
Source: Li and Meyer (2009).

environment, and hence the less it needs access to resources from local partners. On the other hand, the more experience a firm has in a local context, the better it is able to identify suitable and trustworthy partners, and consequently to manage a relationship with such a partner (Figure 9.4). These opposing effects of strategic needs and implementation capability suggest that the relationship between a firm's international experience and the ownership modes it chooses may vary for different types of experience and in different contexts, and it may take non-linear forms. As EMNCs progress their internationalization often very rapidly, opportunities emerge to study choices of organizational form at different stages of maturity.

Institutional perspectives

The third line of research extends the institutional perspective in international business. Traditionally, institutional work on FDI has focused on the influence that the institutional setting of the host country has on the inflow of FDI (Bevan et al., 2004; Globerman and Shapiro, 2003) and on the organizational form chosen by foreign investors (Brouthers, 2002; Meyer, 2001; Meyer et al., 2009). What is new about recent work is firstly the focus on how home country institutions such as availability of bank finance and approval processes shape the flow of outward FDI from an emerging economy (Buckley et al., 2007; Luo et al., 2010; Morck et al., 2008), and how MNCs align their strategies to government policy objectives to secure such support (Cui and Jiang, 2012; Ramasamy et al., 2012; Wang et al., 2012).

How do these home and host country institutional pressures evolve while an MNC advances along its internationalization path? For businesses taking their first step abroad, support from their home environment can compensate for a lack of internal resources. Thus, both business networks and the institutions that facilitate or inhibit access to resources are likely to be critical. For example, preferential access to financial resources in the form of guarantees or loans from state banks, or to information and services from trade missions and embassies, is likely to be more critical for firms that have not yet built up such resources internally, i.e., those at an early stage of their internationalization process. However, studies of Chinese MNCs suggest that such support is often conditional on aligning outward FDI to government policy agendas (Meyer et al., 2014; Morck et al., 2008; Wang et al., 2012). For mature MNCs, these issues are less likely to be critical because they control more resources themselves, and are in stronger bargaining positions vis-à-vis external stakeholders such as governments.

Moreover, institutional environments vary in how much support they provide to internationalizing firms. Many countries have low key schemes aiming to help small and medium sized enterprises to internationalize, for example by providing export credit insurance under preferential conditions, or by providing advisory services through the country's diplomatic missions. Other countries, such as China, provide more overt support such as credit from state banks that is specifically earmarked towards international investment projects that are in line with the country's economic policy objectives (Luo et al., 2010; Sheng and Zhao, 2012). In the present context, the critical question is how does such institutional support enhance a firm's international learning processes, and hence the long term sustainability of its international operations? Financial support and match-making services identifying joint venture partners may help firms take a few big steps early in their internationalization process. But such opportunistic large steps also entail high risks as the company may lack the competences to generate learning processes that create internal competences that would support the company's economic success on the global stage in the long run.

Turning to host country institutions, research on Chinese MNCs suggests a new twist to research on host country institutions. In some cases, they appear to discriminate between different types of foreign investors both by country-of-origin and by ownership type. Low trade barriers, open and liquid financial markets, clear intellectual property rights, and low levels of corruption are usually associated with more FDI inflows. Yet, some countries that score high by these criteria, notably the USA, are said to cause most obstacles to the inflow of FDI by EMNCs (Cui and Jiang, 2012; Sauvant, 2010). Most notably, Chinese state-owned enterprises have to work extra hard to attain legitimacy in countries where they appear inconsistent with the dominant ideology (Globerman and Shapiro, 2010; Peng, 2012; Sauvant, 2010), for instance by taking lower equity stakes in subsidiaries they establish abroad (Cui and Jiang, 2012; Meyer et al., 2014). These concerns have arisen in particular in the mining industry as societies rarely appreciate if their natural resources are controlled by foreign entities, especially if entities from a particular country dominate such investment. Thus, Chinese mining firms experienced public opposition and additional regulatory barriers in resource rich countries ranging from Canada and Australia (Nyland et al., 2011; Wong, 2012) to Mongolia (Pu and Wang, 2012). This suggests that the institutions that attract US or UK investors are not the same as those that attract Chinese or Russian investors. These observations suggest revisiting institutional theory, for example to examine how and why institutions discriminate between types of investors. Moreover, we may have to revisit the way we measure institutions such as "business climate."

A critical theoretical concept in this discussion is "legitimacy." The challenges that MNCs face to being accepted by host societies as "legitimate" vary with the firm's characteristics apparently including their country or origin and their ownership type (i.e., state versus private firms). On the one hand, few host country stakeholders are concerned about the entry of small companies from a new source of origin; in fact such entrants weaken the power of big players already in the market, and possibly perceived to be a threat. Yet, large companies, especially those engaging in acquisitions and those originating from countries with different economic systems, are seen with greater suspicion, and encounter more opposition in the host country (Peng, 2012; Zhang et al., 2010). At the same time, the international growth of a firm also strengthens its ability to engage with local stakeholders and hence its ability to "earn" local legitimacy. This would suggest that as EMNCs progress along their internationalization path, threats to legitimacy may increase, while their ability to handle such threats also increases. The relationships between international experience and host country legitimacy may thus be non-linear.

Conclusion

What distinguishes the IPM from other popular theories is its focus on dynamic processes and its longitudinal angles on the phenomenon. Most contemporary strategy research is designed to study cross-sectional data sets rather than long term developments over time. This is a particular concern when it comes to EMNCs because they are not looking for advice on one-off decisions, but on how best to manage a process of internationalization that eventually leads them to a leadership role in their chosen industry. To provide managers of EMNCs with tools for strategic leadership, we as scholars ought to provide better insights into the likely long term outcomes of processes they initiate. The IPM provides a starting point for developing such insights.

Using the IPM as a theoretical perspective suggests that EMNCs command different sets of resources than mature MNCs from developed countries, in particular experiential knowledge on how to do international business. In consequence, they face different constraints and opportunities, and they rely to a larger extent on external resources such as networks and government support. However, this reliance on external resources is likely to decrease over time as they increasingly can draw upon richer internal resources. We can thus predict that the strategies of EMNCs will evolve as richer internal resources become ready to be exploited, and further needs for complementary resources focus on specific gaps.

More broadly, the IPM suggests that international experience of the firm is an important concept of international business, but not a concept that can be expected to be linearly associated with key strategic decisions over the internationalization path of a firm. Future research on EMNCs may thus explore the evolution of different strategic actions as firms mature. Such research will enhance our understanding of how and why different types of international business experience matter for different players in the global economy.

References

Andersen, O. 1997. Internationalization and market entry mode: A review of theories and conceptual frameworks. *Management International Review*, 37: 27–42.

Benito, G. R. G. 2005. Divestment and international business strategy. *Journal of Economic Geography*, 5: 235–251.

Benito, G. R. G., Petersen, B., and Welch, L. S. 2009. Towards more realistic conceptualization of foreign operation modes. *Journal of International Business Studies*, 40: 1455–1470.

Bevan, A. A., Estrin, S., and Meyer, K. E. 2004. Foreign investment location and institutional development in transition economies. *International Business Review*, 13: 43–64.

Brouthers, K. D. 2002. Institutional, cultural and transaction cost influences on entry mode choice and performance. *Journal of International Business Studies*, 33: 203–221.

Buck, T., Liu, X., Wei, Y., and Liu, X. 2009. The trade development path and export spillovers in China. *Management International Review*, 47: 683–706.

Buckley, P. J., Clegg, J., Cross, A., Liu, X., Voss, H., and Zheng, P. 2007. The determinants of Chinese outward FDI. *Journal of International Business Studies*, 38: 499–518.

Chetty, S. and Blankenburg-Holm, D. 2000. Internationalization of small to medium-sized firms: A network approach. *International Business Review*, 9: 77–93.

Chetty, S., Eriksson, K., and Lindbergh, J. 2006. The effect of specificity of experience on a firm's perceived importance of institutional knowledge in an ongoing business. *Journal of International Business Studies*, 37: 699–712.

Clarke, J. E., Tamaschke, R., and Liesch, P. 2013. International experience in international business research: A conceptualization and exploration of key themes. *International Journal of Management Reviews*, 15: 265–279.

Coviello, N. E. 2006. The network dynamics of international new ventures. *Journal of International Business Studies*, 37: 713–731.

Cuervo-Cazurra, A. 2012. Extending theory by analyzing developing country multinational companies: Solving the Goldilocks debate. *Global Strategy Journal*, 2: 153–167.

Cui, L. and Jiang, F. 2012. State ownership effect on firms' FDI ownership decisions under institutional pressure: A study of Chinese outward-investing firms. *Journal of International Business Studies*, 43: 264–284.

Cui, L., Meyer, K. E., and Hu, H. 2014. What drives firms' intent to seek strategic assets by foreign direct investment? A study of emerging economy firms. *Journal of World Business*, 49(4): advance online.

De Clercq, D., Sapienza, H. J., Yavuz, R. I., and Zhou, L. X., 2012. Learning and knowledge in early internationalization research: Past accomplishments and future directions. *Journal of Business Venturing*, 27: 143–165.

Deng, P. 2009. Why do Chinese firms tend to acquire strategic assets in international expansion? *Journal of World Business*, 44: 74–84.

Elango, B. and Pattnaik, C. 2011. Learning before making the Big Leap: Acquisition strategies of emerging economy firms. *Management International Review*, 51: 461–482.

Filatotchev, I., Liu, X., Buck, T., and Wright, M. 2009. The export orientation and export performance of high-technology SMEs in emerging markets: The effects of knowledge transfer by returnee entrepreneurs. *Journal of International Business Studies*, 40: 1005–1021.

Forsgren, M. 2002. The concept of learning in the Uppsala internationalization process model: A critical review. *International Business Review*, 11: 257–278.

Globerman, S. and Shapiro, D. 2003. Governance infrastructure and foreign direct investment. *Journal of International Business Studies*, 34: 19–39.

2010. Modes of entry by Chinese firms in the United States: Economic and political issues. In K. P. Sauvant (ed.), *Investing in the United States: Is the US Ready for FDI from China?* Cheltenham: Edward Elgar.

Hadjikani, A. 1997. A note on the criticisms against the internationalization process model. *Management International Review*, 37: 1–23.

Hall, P. A. and Soskice, D. 2001. *Varieties of Capitalism: The Institutional Foundations of Comparative Advantage*. Oxford University Press.

Hennart, J. F. 2009. Down with MNE-centric theories! Market entry and expansion as the bundling of MNE and local assets. *Journal of International Business Studies*, 40: 1432–1454.

2012. Emerging market multinationals and the theory of the multinational enterprise. *Global Strategy Journal*, 2: 168–187.

Johanson, J. and Vahlne, J.-E. 1977. The international process of the firm: A model of knowledge development and increasing foreign market commitments. *Journal of International Business Studies*, 8: 23–32.

2006. Commitment and opportunity development in the internationalization process: A note on the Uppsala internationalization process model. *Management International Review*, 46: 165–178.

2009. The Uppsala internationalization process model revisited: From liability of foreignness to liability of outsidership. *Journal of International Business Studies*, 40: 1411–1431.

Knoerich, J. 2010. Gaining from the global ambitions of emerging economy enterprises: An analysis of the decision to sell a German firm to a Chinese acquirer. *Journal of International Management*, 16: 177–191.

Kogut, B. and Chang, S. J. 1991. Technological capabilities and Japanese foreign direct investment in the United States. *Review of Economics and Statistics*, 73: 401–413.

Kumraswamy, A., Mudambi, R., Saranga, H., and Tripathy, A. 2012. Catch-up strategies in the Indian auto components industry: Domestic firms' responses to market liberalization. *Journal of International Business Studies*, 43: 368–395.

Li, J., Li, Y., and Shapiro, D. 2012. Knowledge seeking and outward FDI by emerging market firms: The moderating effect of inward FDI. *Global Strategy Journal*, 2: 277–295.

Li, P. P. 2010. Toward a learning-based view of internationalization: The accelerated trajectories of cross-border learning for latecomers. *Journal of International Management*, 16: 43–59.

Li, P. Y. and Meyer, K. E. 2009. Contextualizing experience effects in international business: A study of ownership strategies. *Journal of World Business*, 44: 370–382.

Luo, Y. D. and Tung, R. L. 2007. International expansion of emerging market enterprises: A springboard perspective. *Journal of International Business Studies*, 38: 481–498.

Luo, Y. D., Xue, Q., and Han, B. 2010. How emerging market governments promote outward FDI: Experience from China. *Journal of World Business*, 45: 68–79.

Lynton, N. 2011. *Kaper Maschinenbau*. China Europe International Business School, Case no. CC-311–014. Shanghai: China Europe International Business School.

Mathews, J. A. 2006. Dragon multinationals: New players in 21st century globalization. *Asia Pacific Journal of Management*, 23: 5–27.

Meyer, K. E. 2001. Institutions, transaction costs and entry mode choice in Eastern Europe. *Journal of International Business Studies*, 31: 357–367.

Meyer, K. E., Ding, Y., Li, J., and Zhang, H. 2013. *Home and Host Country Institutions, and the Foreign Entry of State-Owned Enterprises. Journal of International Business Studies*, 45.

Meyer, K. E., Estrin, S., Bhaumik, S. K., and Peng, M. W. 2009. Institutions, resources, and entry strategies in emerging economies. *Strategic Management Journal*, 30: 61–80.

Meyer, K. E. and Gelbuda, M. 2006. Process perspectives in international business research. *Management International Review*, 46: 142–164.

Meyer, K. E. and Skak, A. 2002. Networks, serendipity and SME entry into Eastern Europe. *European Management Journal*, 20: 179–188.

Meyer, K. E. and Thaijongrak, O. 2013. The dynamics of emerging economy MNEs: How the internationalization process model can guide future research. *Asia Pacific Journal of Management*, 30(4): 1125–1153.

Meyer, K. E. and Tran, Y. T. T. 2006. Market penetration and acquisition strategies for emerging economies. *Long Range Planning*, 39: 177–197.

Meyer, K. E. and Xia, T. 2012. British entrepreneurs: Global visions. *Business Strategy Review*, 23: 52–57.

Millington, A. I. and Bayliss, B. T. 1990. The process of internationalization: UK companies in the EC. *Management International Review*, 30: 151–161.

Morck, R., Yeung, B., and Zhao, M. 2008. Perspectives on China's outward foreign direct investment. *Journal of International Business Studies*, 39: 337–350.

Nyland, C., Forbes-Mewett, H., and Thomson, S. B. 2011. Sinophobia as corporate tactic and the response of host communities. *Journal of Contemporary Asia*, 41: 610–631.

Peng, M. W. 2012. The global strategy of emerging multinationals from China. *Global Strategy Journal*, 2: 97–107.

Peng, M. W. and Meyer, K. E. 2011. *International Business* (1st edition). London: Cengage Learning.

Prashantham, S. and Birkinshaw, J. 2008. Dancing with gorillas: How small companies can partner effectively with multinational corporations. *California Management Review*, 51: 6–23.

Prashantham, S. and Dhanaraj, C. 2011. The dynamic influence of social capital on the international growth of new ventures. *Journal of Management Studies*, 47: 967–994.

Pu, J., and Wang, D. 2012. Mining: Cold coal shower. *Caixin China Economics and Finance*, October: 38–39.

Ramamurti, R. 2012. What is really different about emerging market multinationals? *Global Strategy Journal*, 2: 41–47.

Ramasamy, B., Yeung, M., and Laforet, S. 2012. China's outward foreign direct investment: Location choice and firm ownership. *Journal of World Business*, 47: 17–25.

Rialp, A., Rialp, J., and Knight, G. A. 2005. The phenomenon of early internationalizing firms: What do we know after a decade (1994–2003) of scientific inquiry? *International Business Review*, 14: 147–166.

Rugman, A. M. 2009. Theoretical aspects of MNEs from emerging economies. In R. Ramamurti and J. V. Singh (eds.), *Emerging Multinationals in Emerging Markets*: 42–63. New York: Cambridge University Press.

Rui, H. and Yip, G. S. 2008. Foreign acquisitions by Chinese firms: A strategic intent perspective. *Journal of World Business* 43: 213–226.

Santangelo, G. and Meyer, K. E. 2011. Extending the internationalization process model: Increases and decreases of MNE commitment in emerging economies. *Journal of International Business Studies*, 42: 894–909.

Sauvant, K. P. 2010. Is the United States ready for foreign direct investment from emerging markets? The case of China. In K. P. Sauvant, W. A. Maschek, and G. McAllister (eds.), *Foreign Direct Investments From Emerging Markets*. New York: Palgrave Macmillan.

Schütte, H. and Chen, S. 2012. *Reaching High: Sany's Internationalization (A) and (B)*. China Europe International Business School, Case no. CC-312–019. Shanghai: China Europe International Business School.

Sheng, H. and Zhao, N. 2012. *China's State-Owned Enterprises: Nature, Performance and Reform*. Singapore: World Scientific.

Sohm, S., Linke, B. M., and Klossek, A. 2009. *Chinese Companies in Germany: Chances and Challenges*. Bertelsmann Foundation. www.bertelsmann-stiftung.de/sino-german-cooperation.

Verbeke, A. and Kano, L. L. 2012. *No New Theory Needed to Study MNEs from Emerging Economies*. Paper presented at the AIB Conference, Washington DC, June.

Wang, C. Q., Hong, J. J., Kafouros, M., and Wright, M. 2012. Exploring the role of government involvement in outward FDI from emerging economies. *Journal of International Business Studies*, 43: 655–676.

Wang, H., Zweig, D., and Lin, X. 2011. Returnee entrepreneurs: Impact on China's globalization process. *Journal of Contemporary China*, 20: 413–431.

Wong, L. 2012. *The Liability of Foreignness: Chinese Investment in Australia*. International conference transnational corporations and China, Wuhan, November, Proceedings pages 281–324.

Zhang, J., Zhou, C., and Ebbers, H. 2010. Completion of Chinese overseas acquisitions: Institutional perspectives and evidence. *International Business Review*, 20: 226–238.

Zhou, L. X., Barnes, B. R., and Lu, Y. 2010. Entrepreneurial proclivity, capability upgrading and performance advantage of newness among international new ventures. *Journal of International Business Studies*, 41: 882–905.

10 | Migrating EMNCs and the theory of the multinational

HELENA BARNARD

Introduction

In August 2012, a 24-year-old South African adventurer, Davey du Plessis, was almost killed in an attack in a remote Peruvian part of the Amazon. He dragged himself through the jungle until, heavily wounded and vomiting blood, he stumbled upon a village from which he was taken to Pucallpa, four hours by boat. There Du Plessis managed to call his mother in South Africa, who started lobbying for help. Soon thereafter, employees of the local subsidiary of SABMiller helped Du Plessis to get onto a chartered flight to the well-appointed Anglo-American hospital in Lima (Barbeau, 2012). The local SABMiller personnel was so supportive throughout his hospital stay that Du Plessis's mother acknowledged them in her August 28 Facebook post: "Thank you also to the constant presence of South African Breweries. SABmiller. Xxx" (see World Wonderer – The Amazon, 2013).

There is little doubt that both Anglo-American and SABMiller rushed to the aid of Du Plessis because he was South African. The two multinational corporations (MNCs) were founded in Johannesburg in 1917 and 1895 respectively, and have long been important employers in South Africa. But while Anglo-American and SABMiller may have recognized Du Plessis as a fellow South African, those MNCs are often excluded from studies of so-called "emerging multinationals" – MNCs from emerging market economies. Studies generally use the country of primary listing or the country where the headquarters are located in order to assign nationality, and because both MNCs have shifted their primary stock exchange and a substantial part (although not all) of their headquarters to London (both in 1999), they are now regarded as British. There is clearly a disconnect between how ordinary South Africans and International Business scholars assess the nationality of these firms. This study examines whether and how this disconnect matters by looking at two key roles played by MNC headquarters – control and value creation – and at how migration affects those roles.

At least since the 1990s, and with no sign that the trend is stopping, a subset of emerging market multinational companies (EMNCs), namely MNCs with origins in what are termed emerging markets, have chosen to shift their country of incorporation or primary listing to another location – almost always an advanced economy. These are not MNCs that have been acquired by advanced economy MNCs, although mergers and acquisitions are often tools to facilitate their migration. Instead, these MNCs have decided that they want a different primary location. Jones (2006: 157) uses the term "migrating multinationals" and defines them as MNCs that have "shifted their nationalities in terms of place of incorporation, seat, or nationality of shareholder."

Migrating multinationals have long been described by economic historians such as Jones (2006) and Wilkins (1988, 2004). More recently, in 2006, Birkinshaw, Braunerhjelm, Holm, and Terjesen (2006) published a paper exploring why increasing numbers of MNCs relocate their headquarters abroad. Although some of their examples involve South African MNCs, work on EMNCs has not explicitly examined whether the emergence of multinationals can be linked to their migration.

In this chapter, I analyze EMNCs that have migrated, and explain how this phenomenon provides a lens that allows us to sharpen our theory of the multinational in general. I first discuss the phenomenon of migrating MNCs, and then the roles and activities of headquarters in the MNC. I relate the migration decision to two key corporate headquarter roles: control and value creation. By examining how the migration of the head office relates to a changed nationality and affects (or not) firstly an administrative dimension, namely control, and also legitimation (a value creation dimension), I contribute to an emerging literature on what a "home" country really contributes to the MNC (see also Hirsch, 2011). I close by highlighting some of the questions that this work raises about EMNCs in particular and MNCs in general.

The phenomenon of migrating multinationals

Migrating multinationals were fairly often seen in the early part of the twentieth century. Jones (2006) highlights the case of British American

Tobacco: Although the firm was first registered in the UK in 1902, the headquarters, managers, and dominant shareholding were initially from the United States. By the 1920s the British managers and share-holders were dominant, and the company became (and remains) a British multinational with its headquarters and primary stock exchange in London. In turn, Wilkins (2004: 227) documents how the British multinational John Morrell & Co. (currently owned by the Virginia-based Smithfield foods) entered the US in 1871 as the affiliate of a UK company, and by 1928 had become American with its headquarters in the American Midwest and the bulk of its activities and managers in the US (see John Morrell Food Group, 2013). The initially Dutch, then Argentine-based and now US, agro-processing firm Bunge is another example of a migrating multinational (see Bunge, 2013).

For a long time, the discussion of migrating multinationals remained the preoccupation of economic historians. However, with the rise of MNCs from emerging markets, there has also been a surge in migrating multinationals. Not only SABMiller (the second-largest beer brewer globally) but also the world's leading brewer, Anheuser-Busch InBev, had migrated from less economically advanced coun-tries to Europe before acquiring large US breweries; Anheuser-Busch InBev chose Belgium as its place of incorporation and primary list-ing following the initial merger between the Brazilian AmBev and the Belgian Interbrew in 2004. In addition to Anglo-American, a number of migrating resource MNCs are listed on the UK's FTSE, including Vedanta Resources, which was founded in 1976 in India and oper-ates in a range of countries including India, various African countries, Ireland, and Australia, and also Fresnillo plc, which was spun off from the Mexican conglomerate Industrias Peñoles. Although Fresnillo operates exclusively in Mexico, since 2008 it has had only a secondary listing on the Mexican stock exchange, and its primary listing is in the UK. Ferrexpo, an iron producer that operates only in the Ukraine, has been UK-listed and headquartered in Switzerland since 2007.

MNCs across a range of industries migrate, not only those in low research-intensive and natural resource-based industries. The Hong Kong and Shanghai Banking Corporation became HSBC when it shifted its place of registration and head office from Hong Kong to London in 1991. Although it has a global footprint, it strategically still emphasizes the "faster-growing" emerging markets (see HSBC, 2012). In 1999, the mutual insurance company Old Mutual demutualized, listed on both the Johannesburg and London stock exchanges, and shifted its headquarters from Cape Town to London, although the bulk of its income is still derived from Africa (and indeed, South Africa). VimpelCom, a Russian telecommunications firm, was founded in Russia in 1992, listed on the New York Stock Exchange in 1996, and shifted its headquarters to the Netherlands in 2010. Its operations remain concentrated in Central and Eastern Europe, but it has started to expand to various other low-income countries such as Burundi and Bangladesh (see VimpelCom, 2013).

Because migrating multinationals operate on the fault lines of our existing theories, their increased incidence offers a useful opportunity to advance theory, especially around the purpose of the MNC headquarters. One of the fundamental points of departure in international business research is that MNCs are differentiated from other forms of cross-border economic activity by the fact that there is cross-border control (Wilkins, 1988): An MNC is not only a collection of businesses in different countries, but one in which the activities of the various businesses across the different countries are influenced, directed, and controlled from a given location. Chandler (1991) argues that MNC headquarters have two core roles/activities: One is control, i.e., the prevention of loss, but another important role is creating value through "strategies to create and then to utilize for the long-term the organization's skills, facilities and capital and to allocate resources – capital and product-specific technical and managerial skills – to pursue these strategies" (Chandler, 1991: 33).

Birkinshaw et al. (2006) suggest that the core division in terms of roles is around internally versus externally focused tasks. They agree that headquarters are intimately involved in controlling the activities of the MNC (i.e., a set of internally focused activities), but argue that another key role of the MNC headquarters is to act "as the interface between the activities of the MNC's business units and the capital markets" (Birkinshaw et al., 2006: 697), i.e., to present the MNC in the best possible light to external stakeholders.

I argue that migrating MNCs offer a useful lens to better theorize about both the loss preventing (control) and value creating dimensions of headquarter activity. Migration brings into relief some of the assumptions that are made in the literature about the link between home country and control, and the first section of this chapter is concerned with understanding how a shift in the location of the headquarters affects (or not) the nationality of and control in the MNC.

As regards the second core activity of MNC headquarters, I argue that for emerging MNCs, the Chandlerian dimension of entrepreneurial growth is very closely tied to the management of external stakeholders, as highlighted by Birkinshaw et al. (2006). Because emerging market MNCs come from regions that are not known to be economically successful, I argue that legitimation in the eyes of external stakeholders is a key driver in their creation of value. I analyze how migration enables EMNCs to address concerns about their legitimacy, and suggest that issues of legitimacy more generally need to be taken seriously in work on emerging market MNCs.

The nationality of the multinational company

Views of the nationality of multinationals

Jones (2006) argues that multinationals have operated with clearly defined national identities from about 1914 onwards. Although internationally traded brands and the emergence of global value chains are blurring the clarity of national identity (especially at the level of individual products), Jones argues that the nationality of MNCs remains both clear and relevant in the current era. However, Birkinshaw et al. (2006) argue that it is possible to conceptualize MNC headquarters along a continuum from being entirely located in the original home country to being entirely relocated, requiring a rethinking of the very concept of a "home" country.

A first step is to get a clearer understanding of where the nationality of an MNC resides, and this section analyzes five indicators of nationality: I first discuss three relatively accessible indicators, namely the country of incorporation and primary stock exchange listing of the MNC, and the location of its main market. I then discuss two less accessible but potentially more accurate indicators, the history of the MNC and the nationality of its senior management. Given the broad agreement that control is one of the key roles of the MNC headquarters, in each case I link the discussion on nationality to possible implications for where such control lies.

The country of incorporation as an indicator of nationality. Both the country where the firm is incorporated and the country of primary listing are relatively accessible indicators of control, and are therefore quite often used. But in a growing number of cases, incorporation is done in a tax haven like Bermuda or the Cayman Islands, and there is no link between the country of incorporation and any controlling function in the MNC. Indeed, Jones (2006) comments that this practice creates "havoc" with FDI numbers, especially in an emerging context like Hong Kong/China.

In addition, Jones (2006) points out that the country of incorporation is deemed the primary indicator of control only under Anglo-American law, not under Continental European law (where the administrative headquarters are more important). In other words, the very indicator of nationality is nationally defined. This situation is likely to become even more complex as legal systems from outside the Triad (Western Europe, North America, and Japan) are required to consider the matter of control.

The country of primary listing of the firm as an indicator of nationality. The country of primary listing is another accessible and often-used indicator of the nationality of an MNC. However, it offers a perhaps even less rigorous indicator of nationality than the country of incorporation. A first assumption of such a view is that shareholders exercise control over the MNC, whereas the body of research on governance (e.g., Sachs, Rühli, and Meier, 2010) suggests that a stakeholder rather than shareholder view is perhaps more appropriate when considering control.

In the case of migrating EMNCs, many come from countries that have only recently opened up to global economic activity. Assuming that shareholders do indeed exercise non-trivial control over the MNC, it can therefore be expected that a substantial proportion of the shareholders have citizenship in the country of origin rather than the adopted country. Any shift in the nationality of shareholders (and with it, any shift in possible nationality and control of the multinational) is likely to occur only over time.

However, this assumes that the majority of new shareholders will be citizens of the country of primary listing. Such an assumption must be tested in an area of globalization and relatively free participation in stock exchanges. It is possible that the post-migration broadening in the shareholding base of an EMNC results from investments from around the world, and does not result in the emergence of a clear alternative home country.

The main market as a proxy for nationality. Given the centrality of decisions made in pursuit of the market, the potential to use the main market as an indicator of the nationality of an MNC should not be dismissed. Rugman and Verbeke (2004) have already argued that sales of even the largest MNCs are regionally concentrated, and in the case of the generally smaller EMNCs, the home-region and home-country biases are likely to be even clearer. Of course, sales reflect the (successful) outcomes of managerial decisions, and are not true indicators of control. In addition, the proportion of regional sales is sensitive to market size and market conditions, and the location of sales is rarely a useful measure for the commodities generally sold by natural resource firms. Finally, given the ongoing fragmentation of the value chain (Beugelsdijk, Pedersen, and Petersen, 2008; Jones and Kierzkowski, 2005), the location of sales may be a less useful indicator for the many MNCs that supply intermediate goods. These provisos suggest that the location where the greatest proportion of sales is generated is likely to be a useful indicator of control only under certain circumstances and in certain industries. However, in terms of the type of data that large-scale databases can provide, sales may sometimes be a useful proxy indicator for the nationality of the firm.

History as indicator of nationality. Implicit in the appeal to (and response by) Anglo-American and SABMiller to help a South African in Peru is the conviction that those firms are South African by virtue of a long history in the country. It cannot be ruled out that those now-global MNCs would also have helped a citizen from elsewhere in the world, but it was because of their long history in South Africa that Du Plessis's mother had the contacts with those who could mobilize the substantial resources that those MNCs used to help an unfortunate individual. Although it is a less accessible indicator of nationality or control than some of the indicators in large-scale databases, history may be the more accurate measure. However, history reflects a past association and not necessarily a current one.

Hirsch (2011), considering the possible implications should Teva decide to relocate from Israel, points out that short-run effects of migration are likely to be minimal. However, over time there is likely to be a cumulative effect as decisions about aspects such as the transfer of product lines to new locations, the sale of existing businesses, and the engagement in mergers and acquisition are made by managers elsewhere. In other words, although some path dependency can be expected, the potential of history to be an indicator of either nationality or control is disrupted when MNCs migrate.

Nationality of senior management as an indicator of nationality of the firm. Potentially the most accurate indicator of control and nationality is the nationality of the majority of senior managers. In their historical studies on migrating multinationals, both Jones (2006) and Wilkins (1988, 2004) repeatedly highlight the role of key individuals and their nationality in determining the source of control. Hirsch (2011) argues that a home country benefits from the nationality of its MNCs through two main vehicles: the location of higher value-adding activities and the influence of senior management. But in the case of migrating MNCs from the less developed world, establishing nationality at even an individual level can be quite complex.

SABMiller is an interesting case. Since its internationalization, SABMiller has appointed almost exclusively South Africans into senior management positions. Indeed, using that indicator, the MNC should probably be considered South African. But the story is more complex than that: SABMiller had groomed a cadre of highly competent (and under the laws and logic of Apartheid, white only) managers over many years. The internationalization of SABMiller coincided with the end of apartheid in South Africa, and because the company was a large and prominent firm, it experienced substantial government pressure to appoint black managers into senior positions. Indeed, the international deployment of previously groomed white managers to create space within South Africa for black managers was recognized as a potentially positive response to the requirement for societal transformation (Selby and Sutherland, 2006).

However, the SABMiller strategy to use its existing cohort of white managers to drive internationalization was executed in the context of significant and ongoing outward middle-class and mainly white migration (Rule, 1994). South Africans concerned about the wisdom of remaining in South Africa long term often use the opportunity of a foreign posting to leave the country. They are not expatriates in the typical sense of the word, but rather they are emigrants. Consider for example Grant Harries, the president of SABMiller's subsidiary Backus in Peru. In the announcement of his appointment, he is described as a British citizen, but both his undergraduate education (at the University of Natal) and his MBA (at the University of the Free State) suggest South African roots (see SABMiller, 2012).

The role of migration as complicating factor in establishing nationality. The SABMiller example shows how specific South African socio-economic conditions affected the internationalization process of what can now be termed a global MNC. In terms of the potential generalizability of the SABMiller case, it is important to remember that emerging markets are virtually by definition characterized by substantial and rapid changes to which firms need to respond (Sun, Mellahi, and Thun, 2011; Zattoni, Pedersen, and Kumar, 2009). Given the combination of increased openness and persistent institutional weaknesses with which MNCs from emerging markets are confronted (Stal and Cuervo-Cazurra, 2011), it seems almost certain that firms will be shaped by socio-economic conditions, even though the nature of societal changes and their strategies in response will likely be unique to MNCs from different countries and regions.

In particular, middle-income countries are experiencing substantial outward (and some returning) migration, triggering a growing body of research on diasporas, "returnees," "argonauts," and "transnational communities" (Agrawal, Kapur, McHale, and Oettl, 2011; Flisi and Murat, 2011; Liu, Lu, Filatotchev, Buck, and Wright, 2010; Madhavan and Iriyama, 2009; Mullings, 2011; Oettl and Agrawal, 2008; Riddle and Brinkerhoff, 2011). The presence of entrepreneurs in both their home countries (such as India and China) and in Silicon Valley has received particular attention (Saxenian, 2006).

The extent of migration by citizens from economically less advanced economies suggests that the nationality of the employees of EMNCs themselves will often span more than one country. Given that the willingness to share knowledge with their homeland is influenced by how individual migrants feel about their home country (Barnard and Pendock, 2013), the extent and nature of the relationship between expatriates and/or emigrants in the case of migrating EMNCs is an area deserving of future research. To what extent, if at all, should a migrated South African multinational with migrated South African managers still be considered South African? There are likely to be some boundary conditions for the nature and extent of control from the original home country, but much additional research is required to establish what those are.

Implications of the ambiguous nationality of EMNCs

A discussion about the nationality of an MNC presupposes that nationality is consequential to how the MNC operates. The consequences can accrue to the MNC, or to its (original and/or adopted) home country. The consequences highlighted by both Jones (2006) and Hirsch (2011) relate to the home country: higher value-adding activities located there, a greater say in the strategic direction of the MNC and even tax revenues. Birkinshaw et al. (2006) highlight a consequence for the relocated MNC: It will need many years to develop the depth of institutional and social ties in its adopted home country that a headquarters typically has. Yet it may be that the social ties of EMNCs in their adopted countries are better developed than are generally acknowledged.

Regardless of whether the indicator is fairly accessible (such as country of legal incorporation, primary stock exchange listing, or greatest sales) or more nuanced (such as the history of the firm or nationality of the top management), there is repeated evidence that both the nationality of migrating EMNCs and the location of control are unclear. Jones uses the phrase "ambiguous nationality" to describe the extensive ethnic diversity of firms, in terms of individual key decision makers and also in the composition of management teams:

Ambiguous nationality was almost the norm rather than the exception in the extensive international business in services outside Western Europe and North America [in the nineteenth century]. In Latin America and some Asian ports much merchant and financial activity lay in the hands of what one author has termed a "cosmopolitan bourgeoisie." This was composed of highly ethnically mixed people with links back to their home countries as well as in the host country.

(Jones, 2006: 153)

In other words, the ambiguity of national identity is seen over a much longer period of time than just since the recent wave of outward FDI by middle-income countries. A number of the leading MNCs in middle-income countries have long had substantial input, in terms of both capital and managerial skills, from partners in more developed American and European countries. For example, Anglo-American was founded with help from the American bank JP Morgan and funds from US and UK investors, Old Mutual was founded by a Scottish immigrant to South Africa, and HSBC was founded by a mixture of British, American, German, and Indian shareholders.

The importance of immigrants extends to EMNCs still anchored in their home countries. For example, the Brazilian steelmaker Gerdau was founded by a German immigrant and later managed by his German son-in-law and grandchildren, and there are strong Italian ties with Bellini, the founder of the Brazilian automotive MNC Marcopolo. Jones (2006) finds historical examples dating from even longer ago: The Sassoons, a prominent Baghdad Jewish merchant family who moved to Bombay in British India in 1832 to escape persecution from the Ottoman Empire, established a mercantile business which stretched over large parts of Asia, but operated from the British-controlled parts in South and Southeast Asia.

Colonial and postcolonial changes to national boundaries clearly also shape the nationality of businesses. Jones (2006) points out that the largest EMNC according to many databases, the Hong Kong-based Hutchinson Whampoa, dates back to the nineteenth century and was in fact a British-founded firm; it was acquired by local Chinese in the 1970s. Indeed, from Jones' comments it is clear that what today are termed "emerging multinationals" have from the outset been especially strongly characterized by ambiguous nationality.

Jones' observation matters for how scholars make sense of EMNCs today. There is a general trend towards global value chains (Beugelsdijk et al., 2008; Pietrobelli and Rabellotti, 2011) and global production networks (Ernst and Kim, 2002), which affects not only EMNCs, but also MNCs in general. The globally more fragmented economic landscape has been ascribed to contemporary trends such as globalization, the accelerated development of technology, and increased economic openness (Rangan and Sengul, 2009). However, Jones' comment suggests that outside of the industrialized countries, firms have long relied on such rich cross-border networks (often of individuals rather than firms) to provide them with their needed capabilities.

One important implication of this insight relates to Hedlund's (1986) idea of a heterarchical MNC, or what Eden (2001: 597) describes as the "multi-headed ever-moving hydra" that is the modern MNC. As scholars highlight the rich cross-national network as a key differentiating feature of the modern MNC (Cantwell, 2009; Cantwell, Dunning, and Lundan, 2010; Zander, 2002), the ambiguous nationality of the networks of EMNCs may be an under-recognized source of their competitive advantage and a reason for their fairly rapid emergence in the global economy.

At the firm level, networks are not simply bi-national. For example, South Africans have migrated in large numbers to Europe (especially the UK), Australia, New Zealand, and North America (especially Canada). Each individual has links to two countries, but to the extent that a South African MNC taps into the expertise of South Africans abroad in a range of different countries, it gains access to fairly deep social ties in each emigrant's adopted country. Some work has been done on how EMNCs use networks to internationalize (Elango and Pattnaik, 2007; Ellis, 2011; McDermott and Corredoira, 2009), but the international composition of these networks, e.g., the role of returnees and diasporans, is an area deserving of additional attention.

At the same time, the presence of a complex and influential cross-national network presents a challenge to the very notion of a centralized location from which control is exercised, and therefore also to a core idea about what defines the multinational corporation. The increasing ambiguity of the nationality of MNCs is an area worthy of additional attention by scholars of not only EMNCs, but of MNCs in general. Migrating multinationals offer a useful window into where and how control shifts, as well as where and how it remains, and therefore offer scholars of MNCs greater visibility into the fault lines of established theories, as well as opportunities to create new theory for the field overall.

Legitimacy as core motive for migrating multinationals

In short, the very act of migrating complicates not only the nationality of the MNC, but also how a core function of the headquarters, namely control, is exercised. For migrating multinationals, the location from which control is exercised is ambiguous. Post migration, the EMNC is likely to have a different and institutionally more developed jurisdiction for tax and legal matters, but it is far from clear that a migrating multinational will have actually changed the location of control by shifting its headquarters or primary stock exchange listing. The EMNC will probably have succeeded in changing the perception of the nationality of its country, however. I argue that this changed perception and the legitimacy it accords is an important motive for migration. Indeed, I argue that achieving such a change in perception and the increased legitimacy it can accord is often a critical motive for not only migration, but also some other actions of EMNCs.

This motive relates to the second core function of the MNC headquarters. Chandler (1991) argues that besides control, value creation is the key activity of headquarters; Birkinshaw et al. (2006) suggest that the other key role of the headquarters is instead to present the MNC in the best possible light to external stakeholders. I argue that migrating multinationals demonstrate how closely linked those two dimensions – the Chandlerian dimension of entrepreneurial growth and the management of external stakeholders that Birkinshaw et al. (2006) highlighted – are for MNCs from the non-leading economies. Because emerging market MNCs come from regions that are not known to be economically successful, I argue that legitimation in the eyes of external stakeholders is a key driver in the creation of value for the EMNC. I analyze how migration enables EMNCs to address concerns about their legitimacy, and suggest that issues of legitimacy more generally need to be taken seriously in work on emerging market MNCs.

It is important to remember that the home locations of EMNCs are problematic along a number of dimensions, such that the India-based scholars Ramachandran and Pant coined the phrase "liability of origin" (2010) and scholars from the Baltic refer to "liability based on the context of origin" (Ivanova and Castellano, 2011). MNCs from middle-income countries are dynamic and ambitious firms, but come from regions of the world that are not known to be especially successful economically. As these firms that were "born on the wrong side of the tracks" strive to succeed economically, their heritage is a dimension of their firm identity that has to be managed and legitimated.

Suchman (1995: 574) defines legitimacy as "a generalized perception or assumption that the actions of an entity are desirable, proper, or appropriate within some socially constructed system of norms, values, beliefs, and definitions." However, Suchman does not address *whose* perception matters. In the case of EMNCs, that is a critical detail. EMNCs may be well-recognized and legitimate in their home countries, but because they generally lack "nation equity" (Maheswaran and Chen, 2009), their legitimacy at home is unlikely to be of use once they attempt to become global players. Instead, they need to establish their legitimacy in a very different context.

Zott and Huy regard the key actions needed to create legitimacy for new ventures as "symbolic management," and point out that such actions are performed "alongside their intrinsic dimensions, rather than instead of them" (2007: 101). For example, an office is intrinsically a shared place from which to work; a prestigious office simultaneously conveys the symbolic message that the firm is doing well.

Because the creation of legitimacy relies more on symbolic actions than on actual resources, it is often applied in the context of resource-scarce new ventures and entrepreneurship (Fan and Phan, 2007; Zott and Huy, 2007).

Although it is hard to systematically research and document what firms wish to remain opaque, conversations with the founders of "born global" firms from South Africa – i.e., young, small firms with a substantial export market (Knight and Cavusgil, 2004) – suggest that they use many of the strategies documented by Zott and Huy (2007): conveying the entrepreneur's personal credibility and organizational achievement, organizing professionally and signaling quality stake-holder relationships. These strategies take a particular form; namely, they are designed specifically to create the impression that the firm originates from a more rather than a less developed context. A meta-analysis of the country-of-origin literature finds that country-level dif-ferences in economic development are important especially in driving perceptions of quality (Verlegh and Steenkamp, 1999), and the actions of the founders of South African born global firms suggest that they are aware of and trying to manage such perceptions.

Thus many of the founders pursue further education in the UK or US, with additional skills development as only one of their goals. Another important motive for further education in an advanced econ-omy is to help develop their host-country network, and to help ensure that their personal capability and credibility is not defined by their initial South African education. Founders of these born global firms have explained that an office in the UK or US is essential to secure contracts in advanced economies. Professional organizing is thus signi-fied by locating sales offices in high profile areas such as Silicon Valley, Manhattan, or City of London, and by prominently displaying the details of those offices on business cards. The generally much larger operations in South Africa are often described as "back offices" in a lower cost location, if they are mentioned at all.

Insights from the South African born global firms can be useful to make sense of how EMNCs try to achieve legitimacy. The concep-tual parallels between entrepreneurial ventures and emerging mar-ket MNCs seeking to expand their global reach have been previously highlighted, and Madhok and Kheyani (2012) interpret the acquisi-tions of EMNCs as an act and form of entrepreneurship. Although both EMNCs and entrepreneurial ventures have some resources, they are relatively resource-poor relative to their longer-term ambition. The types of resources that EMNCs have or lack is an active area of research, and there are arguments that access to financial resources can sometimes compensate for weaker firm capabilities (e.g., Buckley et al., 2007). However, there is consensus that most EMNCs lack the depth of capabilities of advanced MNCs. To the extent that they lack not only firm resources but also legitimacy, migrating multinationals offer useful insight into the types of legitimization sought by EMNCs.

Legitimacy and symbolic management

Kostova and Zaheer (1999) extend the use of legitimacy to the MNC, and focus on the fact that MNCs, by virtue of their widespread presence, are exposed to a diversity of sources of and challenges to legitimacy. They make the point that larger MNCs often find it hard to maintain their legitimacy because they are so visible. Obscuring their origins is therefore not really feasible for the larger and better known MNCs from economically less advanced home countries, but their need for the legitimization of their home context is not likely to disappear. On the contrary: Once they wish or start to compete beyond their regional markets, the greatest challenge to the legitimacy of EMNCs may well be their economically less successful country of origin. Their "symbolic management" – the various actions taken to ensure legitimacy – will therefore have as an important goal that they be seen as legitimate even given their country of origin.

The SABMiller example is again useful. Shortly after SAB acquired Miller, Anheuser-Busch had a smear campaign that involved putting stickers saying "Miller is South African owned" in liquor stores. Clearly, being a South African beer did not resonate in the same way that being a Belgian beer would, but SABMiller did not highlight its ownership of leading brands in traditional beer-brewing countries, such as Pilsner Urquell and Radegast in the Czech Republic or Tyskie and Žubr from Poland. Instead, SABMiller's response suggests that it matters economically to not be from the "third world": It sued Anheuser-Busch, claiming that the firm was not South African but UK-based, and the court ruled that Anheuser-Busch had to remove the stickers from liquor stores (Eisenberg, Thigpen, and Robinson, 2004). In other words, one of the benefits of migration was that the previously "emerging" MNC could distance itself from its less developed country of origin and position itself as an MNC from an advanced economy.

The response by SABMiller seems to suggest that MNC migration serves not only an intrinsic purpose, but is also a form of "symbolic management" – a strategy that emerging MNCs can use to increase their legitimacy by linking themselves to economically more advanced contexts. Systematic research on migrating multinationals is needed to understand the motives for migration, and specifically to establish to what extent the hoped-for benefits are mainly intrinsic, such as easier access to capital and/or skilled employees, and to what extent and how multinational migration also serves a symbolic purpose.

Migrating multinationals from emerging markets are perhaps best conceptualized as MNCs that have been shaped by their home-country conditions, but that have grown large and influential enough along some dimension(s) to "outgrow" their less developed home context. To the extent that that is the case, it is likely that research into the intrinsic and symbolic purposes of migration can provide insights into the challenges facing not only migrating MNCs, but also into those experienced by the emerging market MNCs that remain at home. In other words, migrating multinationals are a special case that can highlight the legitimacy challenges facing EMNCs in an uneven global economy. But the reverse is also true; there is also value in using the lens of legitimacy to study emerging market MNCs still at home.

Using legitimacy insights about migrating EMNCs to make sense of EMNC acquisitions

One application of a legitimacy paradigm lies in explaining some of the acquisitions of EMNCs. There has been a slew of acquisitions of high profile targets, such as China's Lenovo acquiring IBM's PC business and Geely acquiring the Swedish Volvo, or India's Tata acquiring the UK-based Jaguar. At the same time, there is contradictory evidence about whether these types of acquisitions generate much economic value. Thus Aybar and Ficici (2009) find that acquisitions by EMNCs often destroy rather than create value, while Gubbi et al. (2010) and Pangarkar and Yuan (2009) find the reverse. Yet in spite of inconclusive evidence about the value of EMNC acquisitions, firms from less developed countries continue to engage in such acquisitions.

If they consistently fail to create value, such acquisitions are not sustainable. This raises the possibility that managers from EMNCs are simply not capable of assessing the costs and benefits of acquisitions, and that the phenomenon should be interpreted through a capabilities lens. There is already evidence that there is a substantial learning component to EMNCs' entry into the advanced economies (Barnard, 2010; Zahra, Abdelgawad, and Tsang, 2011; Zhu, Lynch, and Jin, 2011). But Ramachandran and Pant (2010) point out that EMNCs face the dual challenge of developing both capabilities and also legitimacy. In other words, the initial apparent failure and subsequent improvement in the performance of an EMNC in an advanced economy could be attributed to either the need to learn or the need to legitimize their presence in that economy.

Turning again to the example of SABMiller, the initial response to SAB's acquisition of Miller was somewhat negative. The share price dropped, and analysts expressed concern about the higher-than-expected purchase price, and about "the leopard changing its spots from a very capable emerging market player to a player with a big chunk of underperforming developed assets" (BBC News, 2002). In other words, there was a concern that SABMiller's extensive experience in lower-income countries was not relevant to operating successfully in advanced economies. With the benefit of hindsight, that concern can be seen as largely unfounded. However, it again underlines the working of country-of-origin perceptions, and suggests that the global (i.e., advanced economy) markets make a distinction between operating in lower- and middle-income countries, and operating in advanced economies. Experience managing operations in Australia seems to be perceived as more useful for entering the US than experience managing operations in Argentina.

Empirically, such a perception is not supported; prior internationalization experience in less developed countries is a useful predictor for successful internationalization into more developed countries (Rabbiosi, Elia, and Bertoni, 2012). In the context of legitimacy, however, the main consideration is how firms are perceived. Indeed, Kostova and Zaheer (1999) document the power of "negative legitimacy spillovers," namely the risk that MNCs may be tainted by their association with a less legitimate home context. To the extent that they are concerned about negative legitimacy spillovers and keen to address potentially limiting perceptions, EMNCs operating primarily on what has been termed the "periphery" (Benito and Narula, 2007) may perceive it as necessary to establish a presence in technologically and economically advanced countries for the sake of legitimacy rather than (or at least, in addition to) the sake of accessing new capabilities and technology. Operating on an ongoing basis in an advanced economy can legitimize EMNCs, allowing them to become "insiders" (Eden and Molot, 2002; Johanson and Vahlne, 2009) in high-income countries rather than remain "trapped" in lower- and middle-income countries.

If the purpose of a strong presence in the advanced economies were to create greater legitimacy for the EMNC, then the profitability of a given acquisition in a high-income country is less important than the overall profitability of that EMNC. To the extent that the legitimacy gained by a presence in the developed market translates into greater sales in core markets in less developed countries, the profitability of the acquired entity may be less important than the profitability of the portfolio of the EMNC. There is evidence suggesting that EMNCs are aware of the legitimating effect of high profile acquisitions in how they present themselves, especially for their customers in similarly technologically lagging countries. Take for example how Lenovo presents itself in the "About Lenovo" section on its South African, Indian, and Malaysian websites compared to how it presents itself to Australia, the UK, and the US (Table 10.1).

In the text for the economically less developed countries, Lenovo offers little information about Lenovo's own capabilities, but does point out its acquisition of IBM. In contrast, the corresponding text for the more developed countries is much longer, and goes into greater detail about Lenovo itself – when it was founded, its annual sales, relative market position, number of employees and the locations of sales offices, manufacturing plants, and R&D facilities. The text chosen by Lenovo suggests that its IBM acquisition establishes adequate legitimacy for economically less developed markets, but that customers in the advanced economies require more evidence of the capabilities of the firm itself.

To the extent that a key motive for acquisitions is legitimacy, it is perhaps not surprising that so many of the acquisitions of EMNCs are high profile luxury brands. There is debate in the IB literature on whether or not EMNCs have been able to extend their actual capabilities through these acquisitions (Kotabe, Jiang, and Murray, 2012; Ng,

Table 10.1 *Representation of Lenovo to different markets.*

Text on websites for South Africa, India, and Malaysia	Text on websites for Australia, the UK, and the US
Lenovo creates and builds exceptionally engineered personal technology, but we are much more than a tech company. We are defining a new way of doing things as a next generation global company. That means we are years ahead of the game in terms of understanding what it will take to win 5, 10 years from now. Formed by Lenovo Group's acquisition of the former IBM Personal Computing Division, Lenovo builds on its dominant position in China to grow globally. The expansion from East to West – such as by introducing our newest products in China and then spreading across the globe – is a new way of viewing the world, one we believe will be the way of the future.	While the Lenovo brand came into existence only in 2004, the company has a much longer history. In 1984, Legend Holdings was formed with 25,000 RMB in a guard house in China. The company was incorporated in Hong Kong in 1988 and would grow to be the largest PC company in China. Legend Holdings changed its name to Lenovo in 2004 and, in 2005, acquired the former Personal Computer Division of IBM, the company that invented the PC industry in 1981. Today, Lenovo is a US$21 billion personal technology company and the world's second-largest PC vendor. We have more than 26,000 employees in more than 60 countries serving customers in more than 160 countries. A global Fortune 500 company, we have headquarters in Beijing, China and Morrisville, North Carolina, US; major research centers in Yokohama, Japan; Beijing, Shanghai and Shenzhen, China; and Morrisville; and we have manufacturing around the world from Greensboro, North Carolina and Monterrey, Mexico to India, China and Brazil. We create and build exceptionally engineered personal technology, but we are much more than a tech company. We are defining a new way of doing things as a next generation global company. We have our core strength in China, rapid growth in emerging markets and a unique global footprint. Lenovo builds on its dominant position in China to grow globally. The expansion from East to West – introducing our newest products in China and then spreading across the globe – is a new way of viewing the world, one we believe will be the way of the future. That means we are years ahead of the game in terms of understanding what it will take to win 5 or even 10 years from now.

Table 10.1 (*cont.*)

Text on websites for South Africa, India, and Malaysia	Text on websites for Australia, the UK, and the US
www.lenovo.com/lenovo/za/en/our_company.html, accessed December 12, 2012. The text is the same on the websites for India and Malaysia	www.lenovo.com/lenovo/us/en/our_company.html, accessed December 12, 2012. The text is the same on the websites for Australia and the UK

Chatzkel, Lau, and Macbeth, 2012). Work using a legitimacy rather than learning perspective may help advance this debate by investigating how (if at all) these acquisitions have changed the way the EMNCs are perceived, and whether those changed perceptions have economic benefit.

Using legitimacy insights about migrating EMNCs in the "similar versus different" debate

Another application of the legitimacy paradigm relates to the debate about whether or not EMNCs are essentially the same as or fundamentally different from MNCs from advanced economies. Some scholars argue that EMNCs differ fundamentally from advanced economy MNCs, e.g., the "special theory" that Buckley et al. (2007) propose for Chinese MNCs to account for their unique institutional factors and capital market failures, and the linkage, leverage, and learning of Mathews' (2006) "dragon multinationals." Other scholars argue that existing theories of the multinational such as the eclectic paradigm are generally adequate, although those theories may not always adequately reflect the role of context (Narula, 2006; Ramamurti and Singh, 2009).

Yet the debate on similarity and difference is essentially anchored in a capabilities-based view of the firm, a theoretical framework that rarely considers that for MNCs from "the periphery" (Benito and Narula, 2007), the global economy could be a place marked with "old boys' clubs," residual (or persistent) prejudice, and possible exclusion. I argue that the actions that EMNCs take to navigate those dimensions of their global context are perhaps more usefully understood through the lens of a theoretical paradigm that explicitly considers legitimacy and legitimation.

Deephouse (1999) developed the "strategic balance" theory to reconcile the apparently contradictory requirements for competitive differentiation and legitimating similarity, and argues that firms seeking competitive advantage should be "as different as legitimately possible" (1999: 148). In other words, being too distinct does not signal a unique source of competitive advantage; instead it signals that the firm simply does not know how to do business. This has particular application in the case of emerging market MNCs, which are likely to face greater legitimacy challenges than their counterparts from the developed world. Regardless of any other benefits, migration ensures that MNCs like Anglo-American, HSBC, and Anheuser-Busch InBev find themselves categorized together with advanced MNCs, and no longer listed in the company of firms from underdeveloped contexts.

SABMiller's response to Anheuser-Busch's smear campaign suggests that EMNCs can gain real economic value if they are similar to rather than distinct from advanced economy MNCs. Similarity helps EMNCs to address legitimacy challenges, which in turn helps them achieve strategic balance. To the extent that that is the case, it can be expected that EMNCs will deliberately try to ensure that they are as similar as possible to advanced economy MNCs. This sheds a different light on the argument about whether EMNCs are "similar" or "different" to advanced economy MNCs, as their similarity to these competitors may be less the outcome of an evolutionary logic, and more the result of deliberate managerial action. Future research is likely to gain more by probing into how managers from EMNCs perceive and manage the differences and similarities between them and their counterparts in the advanced world than by simply examining whether or not such differences and similarities exist.

Conclusion

This chapter has highlighted the phenomenon of migrating EMNCs, which previous studies have simply categorized either as advanced (e.g., Cumming, Bettridge, and Toyne, 2005) or emerging MNCs (Goldstein and Prichard, 2009) based on an argument about their most likely nationality. I argue that it is a lost opportunity to regard cases in which the nationality is hard to define simply as "noisy" data, and I have provided evidence to suggest that although migrating EMCs are not especially common, they are also not anomalies. Instead, these migrating MNCs provide a potentially useful lens to sharpen our understanding of emerging market MNCs and MNC activity more generally.

Because they operate on the fault lines of existing theory, migrating MNCs present a useful challenge to the field (Table 10.2). Migrating EMNCs offer an opportunity to examine at least three main areas. The first has to do with the definition of nationality. Seen in historical perspective, migrating MNCs represent a return to the less nationally defined identities of nineteenth century MNCs, and today as then,

Table 10.2 *Some research questions raised by migrating EMNCs.*

1. What is the link between the institutional context/conditions and the decision of an MNC to migrate, both historically and in the current era?
2. What are the core purposes of the headquarters of an MNC, and to what extent can those roles be fulfilled by geographically distributed headquarters?
3. What are the assumptions researchers make about how the nationality of an MNC informs its actions, and how do those assumptions relate to the tools used to determine nationality?
4. In an era characterized by the increased global mobility of skilled people, how do the more fluid nationalities of individual decision makers shape how an MNC engages both locally and globally?
5. How important is legitimacy as a driver for the actions of EMNCs, and in whose eyes do EMNCs seek legitimation?
6. What symbolic management actions are taken by EMNCs to establish their legitimacy, and how are those actions intertwined with capability development?
7. How are key questions in work on EMNCs (such as the value of high profile acquisitions or whether EMNCs are similar or different to the advanced economy MNCs) advanced by using a legitimacy lens?

MNCs from less developed countries seem more prone to have an ambiguous nationality than MNCs from the leading economic centers. Their tendency to migrate highlights the extent to which the modern MNC is managed through a geographically dispersed and nationally ambiguous network, both of subsidiaries and of individuals. Understanding how (and from where) these networks are coordinated, and how they are used to develop a portfolio of capabilities that can be used for competitive positioning, are all areas for future research that can advance the field of international business in general.

In addition, there is evidence to suggest that migrating MNCs are driven at least in part by a need to legitimate their activities, and that the need for legitimacy also affects EMNCs more generally. Legitimacy has long been recognized as a dimension requiring managerial intervention in the MNC (Kostova and Zaheer, 1999), and the challenge of legitimacy for EMNCs in particular has recently been articulated (Ramachandran and Pant, 2010). However, as Ramachandran and Pant (2010) point out, EMNCs have to overcome both legitimacy-based and capability-based disadvantages. Some of the challenges in

studying legitimacy are that it is often deeply intertwined with learning, that learning and legitimization often have similar outcomes, and
that it is therefore hard to isolate legitimizing versus learning actions.
Indeed, in their study of "situated learning" at the individual level, Lave
and Wenger (1991) regard *legitimate* albeit peripheral participation as
fundamentally intertwined with learning. Still, the challenges in oper-
ationalizing legitimacy for research purposes should not be used to dis-
miss the relevance of a legitimacy perspective in the study of EMNCs.

The incidence of migrating MNCs not only co-occurs with the
rise of MNCs from middle-income countries, but migrating MNCs
also overwhelmingly originate in those countries. When MNCs from
middle-income countries are no longer based there, they test the limits of our theories. Migrating EMNCs are therefore of interest to the
field because understanding them requires a keen awareness of the
increased participation of firms from outside the advanced industrialized nations in the global economy and globalization in general. In
this chapter, I highlight two theoretical questions raised by migrating
MNCs, namely the challenges in conceptualizing MNC control once
the MNC is seen as a differentiated and globally dispersed network,
and the importance of legitimacy for new players in the global arena.
Migrating MNCs doubtless raise additional theoretical questions, and
therefore carry the promise of helping to advance international business theory more generally.

References

Agrawal, A., Kapur, D., McHale, J., and Oettl, A. 2011. Brain drain or brain
bank? The impact of skilled emigration on poor-country innovation.
Journal of Urban Economics, 69: 43–55.

Aybar, B. and Ficici, A. 2009. Cross-border acquisitions and firm value: An
analysis of emerging-market multinationals. *Journal of International
Business Studies,* 40: 1317–1338.

Barbeau, N. 2012. Mom tells of son's close call in Amazon. IOL, August
28. www.iol.co.za/news/crime-courts/mom-tells-of-son-s-close-call-in-
amazon-1.1371224. Accessed December 9, 2012.

Barnard, H. 2010. Overcoming the liability of foreignness without strong
firm capabilities: The value of market-based resources. *Journal of
International Management,* 16: 165–176.

Barnard, H. and Pendock, C. 2013. To share or not to share: The role of
affect in knowledge sharing by individuals in a diaspora. *Journal of
International Management,* 19: 47–65.

BBC News. 2002. African brewer seals Miller takeover. http://news.bbc.
co.uk/1/hi/business/2016061.stm. Accessed December 10, 2012.

Benito, G. and Narula, R. 2007. *Multinationals on the Periphery*. Houndmills,
UK: Palgrave MacMillan.

Beugelsdijk, S., Pedersen, T., and Petersen, B. 2008. *Is There a Trend Towards
Global Value Chain Specialization? An Examination of Cross Border
Sales of US Foreign Affiliates*. SMG Working Paper No. 24/2008. http://
dx.doi.org/10.2139/ssrn.1184902.

Birkinshaw, J., Braunerhjelm, P., Holm, U., and Terjesen, S. 2006. Why do
some multinational corporations relocate their headquarters overseas?
Strategic Management Journal, 27: 681–700.

Buckley, P. J., Clegg, L. J., Cross, A. R., Liu, X., Voss, H., and Zheng, P.
2007. The determinants of Chinese outward foreign direct investment.
Journal of International Business Studies, 38: 499–518.

Bunge. 2013. *Company: History*. www.bunge.com/company-history. Accessed
February 12, 2013.

Cantwell, J. 2009. Location and the multinational enterprise. *Journal of
International Business Studies*, 40: 35–41.

Cantwell, J., Dunning, J. H., and Lundan, S. M. 2010. An evolutionary approach to understanding international business activity: The
co-evolution of MNEs and the institutional environment. *Journal of
International Business Studies*, 41: 567–586.

Chandler, A. D. 1991. The functions of the HQ unit in the multibusiness
firm. *Strategic Management Journal*, 12(S2): 31–50.

Cumming, J. F., Bettridge, N., and Toyne, P. 2005. Responding to global
business critical issues: A source of innovation and transformation for
FTSE 350 companies? *Corporate Governance*, 5: 42–51.

Deephouse, D. L. 1999. To be different, or to be the same? It's a question
(and theory) of strategic balance. *Strategic Management Journal*, 20:
147–166.

Eden, L. 2001. Taxes, transfer pricing and the multinational enterprise. In A.
Rugman and T. L. Brewer (eds.), *The Oxford Handbook of International
Business*. Oxford University Press.

Eden, L. and Molot, M. A. 2002. Insiders, outsiders and host country bar-
gains. *Journal of International Management*, 8: 359–388.

Eisenberg, D., Thigpen, D., and Robinson, S. 2004. Big Brew-Haha! The bat-
tle of the beers. *Time Magazine*, 164 (2): 48.

Elango, B. and Pattnaik, C. 2007. Building capabilities for international
operations through networks: A study of Indian firms. *Journal of
International Business Studies*, 38: 541–555.

Ellis, P. D. 2011. Social ties and international entrepreneurship: Opportunities
and constraints affecting firm internationalization. *Journal of International Business Studies*, 42: 99–127.

Ernst, D. and Kim, L. 2002. Global production networks, knowledge diffusion, and local capability formation. *Research Policy*, 31: 1417–1429.

Fan, T. and Phan, P. 2007. International new ventures: Revisiting the influences behind the "born-global" firm. *Journal of International Business Studies*, 38: 1113–1131.

Flisi, S. and Murat, M. 2011. The hub continent? Immigrant networks, emigrant diasporas and FDI. *Journal of Socio-Economics*, 40: 796–805.

Goldstein, A. and Prichard, W. 2009. South African multinationals: Building on a unique legacy. In R. Ramamurti and J. V. Singh (eds.), *Emerging Multinationals in Emerging Markets*. Cambridge University Press.

Gubbi, S. R., Aulakh, P. S., Ray, S., Sarkar, M. B., and Chittoor, R. 2010. Do international acquisitions by emerging-economy firms create shareholder value? The case of Indian firms. *Journal of International Business Studies*, 41: 397–418.

Hedlund, G. 1986. The hypermodern MNC – a heterarchy? *Human Resource Management*, 25: 9–35.

Hirsch, S. 2011. If Teva changes its "nationality", would Israel's economy be affected? In R. Ramamurti and N. Hashai (eds.), *The Future of Foreign Direct Investment and the Multinational Enterprise*. Bingley, UK: Emerald Group Publishing.

HSBC. 2012. *Investor Day 2012*. www.hsbc.com/investor-relations/investing-in-hsbc/investor-day. Accessed February 12, 2013.

Ivanova, O. and Castellano, S. 2011. The impact of globalization on legitimacy signals. The case of organizations in transition environments. *Baltic Journal of Management*, 6: 105–123.

Johanson, J. and Vahlne, J.-E. 2009. The Uppsala internationalization process model revisited: From liability of foreignness to liability of outsidership. *Journal of International Business Studies*, 40: 1411–1131.

John Morrell Food Group. 2013. *About Us*. http://jmfg-careers.silkroad.com/jmfg/About_Us.html. Accessed February 12, 2013.

Jones, G. 2006. The end of nationality? Global firms and "borderless worlds". *Zeitschrift fur Unternehmensgeschichte / Journal of Business History*, 51: 149–165.

Jones, R. W. and Kierzkowski, H. 2005. International trade and agglomeration: An alternative framework. *Journal of Economics*, 10: 1–16.

Knight, G. A. and Cavusgil, S. T. 2004. Innovation, organizational capabilities, and the born-global firm. *Journal of International Business Studies*, 35: 124–141.

Kostova, T. and Zaheer, S. 1999. Organizational legitimacy under conditions of complexity: The case of the multinational enterprise. *Academy of Management Review*, 24: 64–81.

Kotabe, M., Jiang, C. X., and Murray, J. Y. 2012. Managerial ties, knowledge acquisition, realized absorptive capacity and new product market performance of emerging multinational companies: A case of China. *Journal of World Business*, 46: 166–176.

Lave, J. and Wenger, E. 1991. *Situated Learning: Legitimate Peripheral Participation*. Cambridge University Press.

Liu, X., Lu, J., Filatotchev, I., Buck, T., and Wright, M. 2010. Returnee entrepreneurs, knowledge spillovers and innovation in high-tech firms in emerging economies. *Journal of International Business Studies*, 41: 1183–1197.

Madhavan, R. and Iriyama, A. 2009. Understanding global flows of venture capital: Human networks as the "carrier wave" of globalization. *Journal of International Business Studies*, 40: 1241–1259.

Madhok, A. and Keyhani, M. 2012. Acquisitions as entrepreneurship: Asymmetries, opportunities, and the internationalization of multinationals from emerging economies. *Global Strategy Journal*, 2: 26–40.

Maheswaran, D. and Chen, C. Y. 2009. Nation equity: Country-of-origin effects and globalization. In M. Kotabe and K. Helsen (eds.), *The SAGE Handbook of International Marketing*. Thousand Oaks, CA: SAGE Publications.

Mathews, J. A. 2006. Dragon multinationals: New players in 21st century globalization. *Asia Pacific Journal of Management*, 23: 5–27.

McDermott, G. A. and Corredoira, R. A. 2009. Network composition, collaborative ties, and upgrading in emerging-market firms: Lessons from the Argentine autoparts sector. *Journal of International Business Studies*, 41: 308–329.

Mullings, B. 2011. Diaspora strategies, skilled migrants and human capital enhancement in Jamaica. *Global Networks*, 11: 24–42.

Narula, R. 2006. Globalization, new ecologies, new zoologies, and the purported death of the eclectic paradigm. *Asia Pacific Journal of Management*, 23: 143–151.

Ng, A. W., Chatzkel, J., Lau, K. F., and Macbeth, D. 2012. Dynamics of Chinese emerging multinationals in cross-border mergers and acquisitions. *Journal of Intellectual Capital*, 13: 416–438.

Oettl, A. and Agrawal, A. 2008. International labor mobility and knowledge flow externalities. *Journal of International Business Studies*, 39: 1242–1260.

Pangarkar, N. and Yuan, L. 2009. Location in internationalization strategy: Determinants and consequences. *Multinational Business Review*, 17: 37–68.

Pietrobelli, C. and Rabellotti, R. 2011. Global value chains meet innovation systems: Are there learning opportunities for developing countries? *World Development*, 39: 1261–1269.

Rabbiosi, L., Elia, S., and Bertoni, F. 2012. Acquisitions by EMNCs in developed markets. *Management International Review*, 52: 193–212.

Ramachandran, J. and Pant, A. 2010. The liabilities of origin: An emerging economy perspective on the costs of doing business abroad. In T. M. Devinney, T. Pedersen, and L. Tihanyi (eds.), *Advances in International Management: The Past, Present and Future of International Business and Management*. Bingley, UK: Emerald Group Publishing Limited.

Ramamurti, R. and Singh, J. 2009. *Emerging Multinationals in Emerging Markets*. Cambridge University Press.

Rangan, S. and Sengul, M. 2009. Information technology and transnational integration: Theory and evidence on the evolution of the modern multinational enterprise. *Journal of International Business Studies*, 40: 1496–1514.

Riddle, L. and Brinkerhoff, J. 2011. Diaspora entrepreneurs as institutional change agents: The case of Thamel.Com. *International Business Review*, 20(6): 670–680.

Riddle, L., Hrivnak, G. A., and Nielsen, T. M. 2010. Transnational diaspora entrepreneurship in emerging markets: Bridging institutional divides. *Journal of International Management*, 16: 383–397.

Rugman, A. M. and Verbeke, A. 2004. A perspective on regional and global strategies of multinational enterprises. *Journal of International Business Studies*, 35: 3–18.

Rule, S. P. 1994. A second-phase diaspora: South African migration to Australia. *Geoforum*, 25: 33–39.

SABMiller. 2012. *News*. www.sabmiller.com/index.asp?pageid=149& new sid=2061. Accessed December 9, 2012.

Sachs, S., Rühli, E., and Meier, C. 2010. Stakeholder governance as a response to wicked issues. *Journal of Business Ethics*, 96: 57–64.

Saxenian, A. 2006. *The New Argonauts: Regional Advantage in a Global Economy*. Cambridge MA: Harvard University Press.

Selby, K. and Sutherland, M. 2006. "Space creation": A strategy for achieving employment equity at senior management level. *South African Journal of Labour Relations*, 30: 1–30.

Stal, E. and Cuervo-Cazurra, A. 2011. The investment development path and FDI from developing countries: The role of pro-market reforms and institutional voids. *Latin American Business Review*, 12: 209–231.

Suchman, M. 1995. Managing legitimacy: Strategic and institutional approaches. *Academy of Management Review*, 20: 571–610.

Sun, P., Mellahi, K., and Thun, E. 2011. The dynamic value of MNE political embeddedness: The case of the Chinese automobile industry. *Journal of International Business Studies*, 41: 1161–1182.

Verlegh, P. W. J. and Steenkamp, J.-B. E. M. 1999. A review and meta-analysis of country-of-origin research. *Journal of Economic Psychology*, 20: 521–546.

VimpelCom. 2013. *Fact Sheets*. www.vimpelcom.com/pr/fs.wbp. Accessed February 12, 2013.

Wilkins, M. 1988. European and North American multinationals, 1870–1914: Comparisons and contrasts. *Business History*, 30: 8–45.

2004. *The History of Foreign Investment in the United States, 1914–1945*. Cambridge, MA: Harvard University Press.

World Wonderer – The Amazon. 2013. www.facebook.com/World.Wonderer.The.Amazon. Accessed February 9, 2013.

Zahra, S. A., Abdelgawad, S. G., and Tsang, E. W. K. 2011. Emerging multinationals venturing into developed economies: Implications for learning, unlearning, and entrepreneurial capability. *Journal of Management Inquiry*, 20: 323–330.

Zander, I. 2002. The formation of international innovation networks in the multinational corporation: An evolutionary perspective. *Industrial and Corporate Change*, 11: 327–353.

Zattoni, A., Pedersen, T., and Kumar, V. 2009. The performance of group-affiliated firms during institutional transition: A longitudinal study of Indian firms. *Corporate Governance: An International Review*, 17: 510–523.

Zhu, Y., Lynch, R., and Jin, Z. 2011. Playing the game of catching-up: Global strategy building in a Chinese company. *Asia Pacific Business Review*, 17: 511–533.

Zott, C. and Huy, Q. N. 2007. How entrepreneurs use symbolic management to acquire resources. *Administrative Science Quarterly*, 52: 70–105.

11 Business groups, institutional transition, and the internationalization of firms from emerging economies

TORBEN PEDERSEN AND TAMARA STUCCHI

Introduction

Studies on internationalization often claim that the patterns and drivers of the internationalization of firms from emerging markets (EMs) are qualitatively different from the corresponding patterns and drivers of the internationalization of firms from advanced economies (AEs). Such studies are based on the proposition that AE firms have more resources, and access to better technology and competences, while EM firms are latecomers with fewer resources and less knowledge. Along the same lines, these studies argue that the existing theories on internationalization are of less value in the context of EM firms, as they are based on the internationalization of AE firms (see, e.g., Luo and Tung, 2007; Mathews, 2002, 2006).

We believe that this view reflects stereotypes of EM and AE firms that are rather misleading. The term "EM firms" gives the false impression that these firms form a homogeneous group (Khanna, 2009). In reality, there is significant variation in almost any dimension among both EM and AE firms. For example, EM and AE firms can be large or small. EM firms may have access to substantial resources, while AE firms may have limited access to resources (and vice versa). Furthermore, in terms of the pattern of internationalization of AE firms, significant variation is evident, including "born-global firms," large MNCs, firms that conduct inward internationalization and others that undertake outward internationalization. In fact, AE firms do not follow "one

Our research on emerging economy firms has benefitted a lot from collaboration with Vikas Kumar, Sumit Kundu, and Alessandro Zattoni on different projects; their contributions are highly appreciated.

way of internationalizing," but rather many different paths. The same is true for EM firms, which also exhibit a myriad of patterns in their internationalization. EM firms span from conglomerates, such as the Taiwanese electronics contract manufacturer Foxconn and the Indian conglomerate Tata Group, to small family businesses in Chile and the Philippines.

One might question what EM firms really have in common, and why we should expect the process of internationalization for EM firms and AE firms to differ. EMs are typically low-income, rapid-growth economies that have experienced radical institutional changes in terms of increased openness and liberalization (Hoskisson, Eden, Lau, and Wright, 2000). These countries are typically found in Central and South America, Africa, and the ASEAN region. EM countries share several characteristics – they generally have poorly functioning institutional contexts relative to AEs, low average income and cost levels, low market efficiency, and diffused network-based behaviors (e.g., Fisman and Khanna, 2004; Hoskisson, Eden, Lau, and Wright, 2000; Xu and Meyer, 2012). In the past, several sectors were typically kept in the domain of the government in EMs and, often, the government still plays a major role. Furthermore, these countries are generally experiencing rapid population growth and urbanization (Dymsza, 1984). Business in EMs is associated with higher levels of risk due to corruption, institutional and infrastructural voids, and internal divides (Khanna and Palepu, 1997). EM firms started internationalizing relatively late (Cuervo-Cazurra, 2012; Narula, 2012; Ramamurti, 2009) and they did so in a world economy that was much more globalized than it was when many of their AE counterparts started down the internationalization path (Dymsza, 1984; Williamson and Zeng, 2009).

An extensive body of literature focuses on a variety of aspects of EM firms' internationalization, such as the drivers of foreign investments (Athreye and Kapur, 2009; Aulakh, 2007), entry modes (Duysters, Jacob, and Lemmens, 2009), growth rates (Arora, Arunachalam, Asundi, and Fernandes, 2001; Fortanier and van Tulder, 2009), host-location choices (Duysters, Jacob, and Lemmens, 2009), ownership structures (Morck, Yeung, and Zhao, 2008), relational assets (Arora, Arunachalam, Asundi, and Fernandes, 2001; Bhaumik, Driffield, and Pal, 2010; Douma, George, and Kabir, 2006; Elango and Pattnaik, 2007; Filatotchev, Liu, Buck, and Wright, 2009; Morck, Yeung, and

Zhao, 2008), and the performance effects of internationalization (Aulakh, 2007; Douma, George, and Kabir, 2006). This stream of literature has primarily been exploratory, with studies concentrating on the phenomenon of EM firms' internationalization, its characteristics, and its peculiarities (e.g., Aulakh, Kotabe, and Teegen, 2000; Buckley, Clegg, Cross, Liu, Voss, and Zheng, 2007; Gammeltoft, 2008).

Recently, the research focus has moved to improving our understanding of how doing business in EM countries might challenge existing explanations of internationalization given the characteristics of these countries (Cuervo-Cazurra, 2012). A debate has therefore emerged over potential explanations for the phenomenon, i.e., a debate over whether the internationalization activities of EM firms might be explained by traditional theoretical perspectives based on the internationalization of AE firms (Fortanier and van Tulder, 2009).

Some scholars argue that the differences between EM and AE firms' characteristics and behaviors warrant new, fresh perspectives on EM firm internationalization (see Madhok and Keyhani, 2012; Mathews, 2006) because the traditional perspectives are based on AEs and the companies that emerge out of those countries. Examples of alternative explanations for EM firm internationalization are found in Mathews' (2002, 2006) linkage, leverage, and learning (LLL) framework and in the springboard perspective presented by Luo and Tung (2007). In particular, Mathews (2002, 2006) explains the internationalization of EM firms with their linkages to external advantages, their ability to leverage these connections, and their iterative learning via repetition. Luo and Tung (2007) argue instead that EM firms internationalize in order to obtain the strategic assets they lack, compensate for their competitive disadvantages and successfully compete against AE firms. On the other hand, a more skeptical stream of studies claims that traditional theories are generally suitable for explaining the internationalization of EM firms (e.g., Narula, 2006; Rugman and Li, 2007). According to these researchers, the specific factors (e.g., the types of OLI factors – Ownership, Location, and Internalization) driving the internationalization of EM firms might vary from those of AE firms, but the basic mechanisms highlighted in the traditional theories are the same.

Although many of the challenges facing EM firms are relatively similar to those facing AE firms when going international, EMs represent an excellent context for studying many phenomena related to internationalization (e.g., Cuervo-Cazurra, 2012; Ramamurti, 2012).

According to this third, moderate perspective, the study of the behavior of EM firms can provide insights that extend current theory due to the unique conditions for data collection that characterize these countries. The multinational companies originating from AEs were once small companies. However, they have undergone a long process of internationalization, and are already large and widespread in international terms. We have the opportunity to observe this phenomenon of firms growing global on a larger scale among firms in EMs. This represents a unique opportunity to comprehensively study firms' internationalization behaviors and thereby enrich current theories. This does not imply that internationalization theories and mechanisms work qualitatively differently in EMs, but rather that EMs offer a better context for studying some phenomena than AEs simply because the visibility, scale, and magnitude of some phenomena are more significant in EMs. As such, EMs offer a suitable laboratory for the study of such phenomena as internationalization processes, institutional transitions, business groups, and disruptive innovations – just to mention a few phenomena that currently are more widespread and visible in EMs than in AEs.

In this chapter, therefore, we illustrate how EMs can serve as an exceptional context for the study of the internationalization of firms. In particular, we focus on two phenomena: business groups and institutional transitions. However, these phenomena are purely illustrative in the respect that EMs serve as an equally good context for studies of many other phenomena.

Business groups in emerging economies and internationalization

Business groups typically have the following three characteristics. First, they are composed of firms that are legally separate entities (Chang and Hong, 2002). Second, they are highly diversified (Xu and Meyer, 2012) and include affiliated firms that operate in unrelated industries (Ghemawat and Khanna, 1998). Third, they are composed of firms that are linked through overlapping ties, such as cross-ownership, interlocking directorates, market transactions, intercompany loans, and social relationships (Goto, 1982; Keister, 2001; La Porta, Lopez-de-Silanes, and Shleifer, 1999), which provide access to internal capital markets, reputation benefits, government connections, intermediation functions, labor markets, and credibility (Ghemawat and Khanna, 1998; Guillén, 1997; Leff, 1978). Furthermore, business groups differ from other organizational forms, such as strategic networks, in that the social and organizational relationships that tie members of a business group together do not exist among unaffiliated, independent firms, even if they organize in networks (Yiu, Lu, Bruton, and Hoskisson, 2007).

Business groups are relevant organizational forms in a variety of contexts and exist in many countries around the world (Fisman and Khanna, 2004). This organizational form has been documented and studied in terms of, for instance, European and Japanese trading companies (Jones and Khanna, 2006). Pedersen and Thomsen (1997) found that the norm among the one hundred largest companies in twelve European countries was not dispersed ownership, but rather a dominant form of cross-ownership that is more closely associated with business groups than with stand-alone firms. Dispersed ownership was only found among the majority of firms in the UK, while the picture was much more blurred, with evidence of substantial cross-ownership, in the eleven other European countries (Pedersen and Thomsen, 1997).

In fact, business groups are common in most continental European countries, as well as in countries like Japan, South Korea, and Taiwan. Consider, for example, the Wallenberg Group in Sweden or the Pirelli Group in Italy. However, business groups can also be studied in EMs, where they are a more widespread and dominant organizational form (Khanna and Rivkin, 2001). These countries therefore offer an appropriate context for the study of business groups.

In terms of internationalization, the literature argues that business-group affiliation offers advantages and disadvantages. The advantages follow from the view of business groups as a vehicle for overcoming "institutional voids," determined by poor infrastructures and the absence of specialized intermediaries, regulatory systems, and contract-enforcing mechanisms (Sheth, 2011), while the disadvantages emerge from the domestic imprint and embeddedness that follow from being affiliated with a business group. As such, whether business-group affiliation is a bane or boon for internationalization is an empirical question, and the answer might well vary by country, industry, or time frame.

The opposing effects of business-group affiliation on internationalization are summarized in Table 11.1. The basic reasoning is the

Table 11.1 *Advantages and disadvantages of business-group affiliation for internationalization.*

Advantages of group affiliation for internationalization
- Fills "institutional voids" (weak property-right regimes, underdeveloped financial markets, unorganized labor markets) in emerging economies
  - Potential support to internationalization in other emerging economies
- Promotes trust-based transactions
  - Experiential support, especially to some forms of internationalization such as joint ventures and international alliances
- Mitigates a lack of international experience
  - Support to internationalization for affiliated firms without experience
- Greater network connections – governments, local banks, and other institutions
  - Potential help to get information, financing and the like, which can support internationalization

Disadvantages of group affiliation for internationalization
- Institutional embeddedness in the economic, political, and social fabric of the home emerging economy (protectionist regimes, inefficient and bureaucratic systems, etc.)
  - Potential preclusion from internationalization opportunities
- Favorable domestic position
  - Potential lack of motivation to internationalize

following: business groups might effectively address "voids" or market failures in the domestic market, but this effectiveness carries the cost of domestic imprinting and embeddedness.

Advantages of business-group affiliation

EMs are characterized by significant imperfections in the markets for capital, final and intermediate products, and for managerial and entrepreneurial talent (e.g., Khanna, Palepu, and Sinha, 2005). In this context, transactions may be particularly costly because institutions for trade and contract enforcement are weak, and because trading partners are exposed to opportunistic behaviors (Khanna and Rivkin, 2001). The presence of information and contracting problems, which are associated with weak market institutions, enables the internal market and the group to create value. In fact, in the absence of specialized intermediaries providing trade, enforcement, and communication services, there is an opportunity for groups with appropriate resources and capabilities to fill the institutional voids (Khanna and Palepu, 2000). Business groups may therefore be seen as an organizational solution to problems arising from market failures and inadequate institutional environments (e.g., Khanna and Palepu, 1997).

In EMs, business groups are created to reduce the high transaction costs typical of markets for capital (Berglöf and Perotti, 1994), entrepreneurial skills (Leff, 1978), intermediate products (Kester, 1992), labor (Khanna and Palepu, 1997), and political lobbies (Khanna and Rivkin, 2001). In sum, business groups may be viewed as organizational and administrative devices aimed at reducing the transaction costs arising from market imperfections (Khanna and Palepu, 2000). For this reason, they play a prominent role in most EMs, where their existence is often related to the home institutional context (Xu and Meyer, 2012).

Disadvantages of business-group affiliation

Through their dense linkages with other businesses and institutions, business groups are highly embedded in the institutional fabric of EMs. Their high institutional embeddedness also implies that they maintain multiple connections with key institutions in their environment (DiMaggio and Powell, 1983). Although connections with key institutions confer advantages, such as resources and legitimacy (Scott and Meyer, 1983), these key institutions also likely shield local domestic firms in EMs from competition and confer monopolistic advantages on a privileged few. The deep institutional embeddedness of business groups, combined with their often dominant and secure domestic market position, actually limits the capability of business groups to strategically transform when faced with environmental changes (Hoskisson, Cannella, Tihanyi, and Faraci, 2004) and to operate in different institutional environments, such as those found in foreign markets.

In other words, firms affiliated with business groups cannot easily change the routines or processes that they have used to gain sustainable competitive advantages and dominant market positions over time, even when such changes are necessary. For instance, changing their way of conducting business, which is often based on social connections, in order to fit a new environment can be difficult (North, 1990). These firms may also find it more difficult to adapt their product and market strategies to an expansion into international markets because of their legacy of being able to operate successfully in domestic markets with their current product and market strategies. Therefore, affiliated firms can experience a type of buffering effect against changes due to their affiliation advantages (Hoskisson, Cannella, Tihanyi, and Faraci, 2004). An inability to change in times of economic deregulation and globalization should thus have a dampening effect on the international expansion of such groups.

Using the emerging economy context to develop new insights

The question of which of these effects has the most severe impact on firm internationalization is an empirical one. We have studied this issue in the Indian context, where we followed 403 Indian firms (listed in the Prowess database) over 21 years (Kumar, Pedersen, Stucchi, and Kundu, 2012). Of these firms, 318 are affiliated with a business group, while 85 are independent. We find relatively strong evidence that financial performance and local imprinting are significantly higher for group-affiliated firms than for unaffiliated firms. Furthermore, unaffiliated firms are associated with a significantly higher level of internationalization in the first part of our window (from 1989 to 2000). However, in the second part of our window (from 2000 to 2010), most of these two effects dissipate, as affiliated firms catch up in terms of internationalization and unaffiliated firms advance in terms of financial performance (Kumar, Pedersen, Stucchi, and Kundu, 2012; Zattoni, Pedersen, and Kumar, 2009). The bottom line is that affiliated and unaffiliated firms were differently equipped to cope with the external challenges in the first part of the window, but they then adapted so that their performance and behaviors were more alike.

In addition, we were able to tease out the relationship between domestic profit (Kumar, Pedersen, Stucchi, and Kundu, 2012) and internationalization and found that before 2000, domestic profit was negatively related to internationalization of Indian firms, which confirms that a favorable domestic position came at the expense of international growth in those years. Taken together, these results indicate that business group affiliated firms were able to exploit their specific advantages in the first part of the window (before 2000) as they clearly outperformed unaffiliated firms, and this largely seems to relate to the profit obtained domestically; however, the strong domestic position and domestic context embeddedness (e.g., as reflected in the negative relation between domestic profit and internationalization) is of lesser value in the second part of the window (after 2000).

The rich context of India, which has a substantial number of affiliated and unaffiliated firms that can be followed for an extended period, allows us to dig deeper into the advantages and disadvantages of business-group affiliation. We are able to investigate specific, important advantages (e.g., access to knowledge, capital, or network connections) and disadvantages (e.g., local imprinting or a favorable domestic position) as we follow these firms over time. Furthermore, we can detect their changing strategies and measure performance on a number of different dimensions. We can explore what type of firms might benefit most from business group affiliation and whether the advantages of business group affiliation is, in fact, vanishing as the institutional environment improves and becomes more transparent. In that sense, India offers a unique context for the study of business-group affiliation, which, abstracting from the Indian context to other countries where business groups are typically located, enhances our understanding of how business groups function.

Firms coping with institutional transition in emerging markets and internationalization

The ways in which firms cope with institutional transition is another area in which EMs offer an exceptional opportunity for profound studies that can generate new insights. This is not because institutions are only changing in EMs. In fact, institutions are changing in many countries all over the world, and in some cases these changes are dramatic, such as in Greece and Spain where, e.g., labor reforms and reforms of the financial sector have followed as a response to the budget crises. The consistency, magnitude, and time span of institutional changes are more severe in EMs, however, so EMs represent exceptional contexts for studies of firm internationalization and its interaction with institutions that are different not only from those in AEs, but also from their local predecessors, which were in place until very recently (Peng, 2003). This is an advantage common among many EMs, which have experienced widespread institutional transformations and economic and market liberalization since the early

1970s after decades of heavy governmental control (Cuervo-Cazurra and Dau, 2009; Hoskisson, Eden, Lau, and Wright, 2000; Peng, 2003; Wright, Filatotchev, Hoskisson, and Peng, 2005).

Institutional changes and organizational responses have also been studied in other contexts, including AEs. Several authors have studied how institutions change, and how they affect firm behavior and transformation. For instance, Cuervo-Cazurra and Dau (2009) argue that pro-market reforms can increase domestic firms' profitability in EMs. Newman (2000) focuses instead on transition economies in Central and Eastern Europe, and suggests an inverted U-shaped relationship between the institutional changes in these contexts and the subsequent organizational transformation. Peng (2003) studies instead how firms make strategic decisions during periods of institutional change, modeled as two-phase processes. Most of these authors draw on the institution-based view, which is an increasingly important theoretical lens in international business studies.

Although specific institutional changes vary widely across EMs (Peng, 2003), India can again serve as an illustration of the possibilities for conducting these kind of studies in EMs. By focusing on the Indian context, such studies can benefit from the presence of broadly, yet incrementally, changing institutions (Athreye and Godley, 2009). Moreover, few studies on this topic contain longitudinal data covering more than a decade. In this sense, India offers long data sets that allow us to follow firms' responses to institutional changes over several decades.

The Indian context of institutional changes

The period between India's independence in 1947 and the early 1980s was characterized by a tendency toward self-sufficiency; heavy public sector involvement in production; and constraints on firms' expansion (Kochhar, Kumar, Rajan, Subramanian, and Tokatlidis, 2006), foreign capital, and competition (Ray and Gubbi, 2009). By the 1980s, the country was suffering from low growth rates, closure to trade and investment, and a generally restrictive and unstable environment (Kochhar, Kumar, Rajan, Subramanian, and Tokatlidis, 2006). In 1991, India faced a severe economic crisis, which resulted in a government decision to restructure several sectors of the economy, thereby creating a more open and competitive economy. The incremental reforms stabilized India's macroeconomic situation (Ahluwalia, 1994). They included the abolition of industrial licensing, a reduction in the number of monopolized industries, and the liberalization of foreign direct investments (FDI) and trade (Kochhar, Kumar, Rajan, Subramanian, and Tokatlidis, 2006). In general, these reforms had a broad impact on every industry.

As a consequence of these changes, Indian outward FDI increased in the 1990s, mainly in the form of mergers and acquisitions, and again rose extraordinarily from 2000 onwards. Today, India is one of the main sources of aggressive outward FDI (Ray and Gubbi, 2009), which is often directed towards the US and the UK (Nayyar, 2007; Ray and Gubbi, 2009), and is typically concentrated in knowledge-intensive industries (Dahlman and Utz, 2005). We therefore suggest that the Indian reforms and subsequent incremental liberalization provided incentives for firms to internationalize. In this regard, institutional evolution can facilitate firms' internationalization processes by creating new opportunities for domestic firms, enhancing competition in the local market, and increasing exposure to international activities.

Using the emerging economy context to develop new insights

Our own studies on the impact of institutional changes on the internationalization behavior of Indian firms confirm that the liberalization and openness of the Indian economy towards the outside world have had a tremendous impact. However, there is a substantial time lag from the implementation of an institutional change until firms react by changing their behaviors (Kumar, Pedersen, Stucchi, and Kundu, 2012; Zattoni, Pedersen, and Kumar, 2009). Indian firms only respond to institutional changes when those changes have taken root, which implies that firms react to consistent institutional changes (like in the case of India with a relatively consistent pattern since 1991) but not necessarily to temporary changes or changes providing more mixed signals.

The results are also showing that firms are exposed very differently to the institutional environment and therefore also react differently to institutional changes. Business groups are argued to be a response to the lack of proper institutions ("institutional voids") that have therefore adapted their behavior to an environment with relatively weak institutions. Their mindset, imprint, attention, and resources are to a larger extent oriented towards the case of institutional voids, and therefore business-group firms are expected to be more reluctant and slower to change their strategies as a response to institutional changes. This is confirmed in our research indicating that business-group-affiliated firms were much slower in internationalizing than unaffiliated firms as a response to the institutional changes in India (Kumar, Pedersen, Stucchi, and Kundu, 2012). In fact, it was only after ten years of institutional changes (in 2000) that business-group-affiliated firms reached the same level of internationalization as the unaffiliated firms (Kumar, Pedersen, Stucchi, and Kundu, 2012).

Further research should look into whether there are other types of firms that are differently exposed to institutional changes (like the business-group-affiliated firms), and such patterns can be detected in the time series of Indian institutional changes and firm behavior. Along the same lines, it is warranted to study the co-evolution of the domestic firms and the institutions, as the firms might not just be equally reactive in responding to institutional changes. Firms are also engaging in institutional activity and entrepreneurship where they are involved in co-creation of institutions. This phenomenon can be beneficially studied in an EM context such as India as the co-creation of institutions does take place in these years.

More generally, this type of research needs to develop an understanding of institutions and how they work on a more disaggregated level. Studies in the literature usually apply rather aggregate proxies for institutions, where their importance is confirmed but the exact mechanism for how institutions work and affect firms as well as individuals are largely ignored. Institutions span over many things, from informal habits and social conventions at one end to formal regulation at the other end. One may say that institutions in its broadest sense is capturing so much that it almost becomes meaningless, and as such it is not at all obvious what are the mechanisms of institutions affecting firm behavior. A natural next step in this type of research would be to establish a stronger link between specific institutional changes (such as those related to intellectual property rights protection and exports) and firm behavior. What institutions support or hinder specific firm behaviors? In other words, what are the specific mechanisms affecting the relationship between institutions and firm behavior? Is it a particular regulation (e.g., in export promotion or intellectual property rights) that affects firm behavior directly, or are institutions having more of an indirect effect on firm behavior through the building of trust and accountability in the society as such? Few countries offer a better context and data for such studies than India.

Conclusions

In this chapter, we have pursued the argument that although the internationalization of EM firms might not be qualitatively different from that of AE firms in the sense that the same basic mechanisms drive internationalization in both cases, EMs still offer a unique laboratory for the study of many phenomena, an understanding of which can sharpen and extend our knowledge on firms' internationalization patterns. We have illustrated this point by discussing two cases – the impact of business-group affiliation on firms' internationalization processes and the impact of institutional changes on such processes – in which the Indian context is suitable for in-depth studies, as access to unique data allows for a deeper analysis than in many other contexts. In addition, we outline some avenues for future research that might be pursued in the context of the internationalization of EM firms.

Another example that illustrates how EMs are providing an excellent context for studying different phenomena is disruptive innovation. Disruptive innovations occur everywhere, in the sense that firms in both AEs and EMs develop "good enough" products/services that are sold cheaper than existing products/services. Consider, for example, Ryanair, Southwest Airlines, IKEA, and H&M with disruptive innovations coming out of AEs. Some illustrative examples of disruptive innovations from EMs include the handheld electrocardiogram (Mac 400) invented in General Electric's laboratory in Bangalore (India), which it calls a masterpiece of simplification, and a low-tech device for water purification that uses rice husks (a waste product), innovated by Tata Consulting Services (*Economist* 2010: 6). While disruptive innovation is not limited to EMs, they do serve as a particularly appropriate context for studies of disruptive innovations, as all of the necessary drivers are present in such countries (e.g., cost competition, growth in demand, and highly talented people).

Obviously, these are just a few illustrative cases. One can think of many other examples in which EMs would serve as a favorable context for studies of phenomena that are not necessarily unique to EMs, but which are more widespread, visible, or easily accessible in these countries. We hope this chapter contributes to a better understanding of how researchers can take advantage of the many opportunities available for conducting profound, insightful studies into the contexts of EM firms.

References

Ahluwalia, M. S. 1994. India's quiet economic revolution. *Columbia Journal of World Business*, 29: 6–12.

Arora, A., Arunachalam, V. S., Asundi, J., and Fernandes, R. 2001. The Indian software services industry. *Research Policy*, 30: 1267–1287.

Athreye, S. and Godley, A. 2009. Internationalization and technological leapfrogging in the pharmaceutical industry. *Industrial and Corporate Change*, 18: 295–323.

Athreye, S. and Kapur, S. 2009. Introduction: The internationalization of Chinese and Indian firms – trends, motivations and strategy. *Industrial and Corporate Change*, 18: 209–221.

Aulakh, P. S. 2007. Emerging multinationals from developing economies: Motivations, paths and performance. *Journal of International Management*, 13: 235–240.

Aulakh, P. S., Kotabe, M., and Teegen, H. 2000. Export strategies and performance of firms from emerging economies: Evidence from Brazil, Chile, and Mexico. *Academy of Management Journal*, 43: 342–361.

Berglöf, E., and Perotti, E. 1994. The governance structure of the Japanese financial keiretsu. *Journal of Financial Economics*, 36: 259–284.

Bhaumik, S. K., Driffield, N., and Pal, S. 2010. Does ownership structure of emerging-market firms affect their outward FDI? The case of the Indian automotive and pharmaceutical sectors. *Journal of International Business Studies*, 41: 437–450.

Buckley, P. J., Clegg, L. J., Cross, A. R., Liu, X., Voss, H., and Zheng, P. 2007. The determinants of Chinese outward foreign direct investment. *Journal of International Business Studies*, 38: 499–518.

Chang, S. J. and Hong, J. 2002. How much does the business group matter in Korea? *Strategic Management Journal*, 23: 265–274.

Cuervo-Cazurra, A. 2012. Extending theory by analyzing developing country multinational companies: Solving the goldilocks debate. *Global Strategy Journal*, 2: 153–167.

Cuervo-Cazurra, A. and Dau, A. 2009. Promarket reforms and firm profitability in developing countries. *Academy of Management Journal*, 52: 1348–1368.

Dahlman, C. J. and Utz, A. 2005. *India and the Knowledge Economy: Leveraging Strengths and Opportunities*. Washington, DC: World Bank Publications.

DiMaggio, P. J. and Powell, W. W. 1983. The iron cage revisited: Institutional isomorphism and collective rationality in organizational fields. *American Sociological Review*, 48: 147–160.

Douma, S., George, R., and Kabir, R. 2006. Foreign and domestic ownership, business groups and firm performance: Evidence from a large emerging market. *Strategic Management Journal*, 27: 637–657.

Duysters, G., Jacob, J., and Lemmens, C. 2009. Internationalization and technological catching up of emerging multinationals: A comparative case study of China's Haier group. *Industrial and Corporate Change*, 18: 325–349.

Dymsza, W. A. 1984. Trends in multinational business and global environments: A perspective. *Journal of International Business Studies*, 15: 25–46.

Economist. 2010. The world turned upside down: A special report on innovation in emerging markets. *The Economist*: 17 April.

Elango, B. and Pattnaik, C. 2007. Building capabilities for international operations through networks: A study of Indian firms. *Journal of International Business Studies*, 38: 541–555.

Filatotchev, I., Liu, X., Buck, T., and Wright, M. 2009. The export orientation and export performance of high-technology SMEs in emerging markets: The effects of knowledge transfer by returnee entrepreneurs. *Journal of International Business Studies*, 40: 1005–1021.

Fisman, R. and Khanna, T. 2004. Facilitating development: The role of business groups. *World Development*, 32: 609–628.

Fortanier, F. and van Tulder, R. 2009. Internationalization trajectories – a cross-country comparison: Are large Chinese and Indian companies different? *Industrial and Corporate Change*, 18: 223–247.

Gammeltoft, P. 2008. Emerging multinationals: Outward FDI from the BRICS countries. *International Journal of Technology and Globalization*, 4: 5–22.

Ghemawat, P. and Khanna, T. 1998. The nature of diversified business groups: A research design and two case studies. *Journal of Industrial Economics*, 46: 35–61.

Goto, A. 1982. Business groups in a market economy. *European Economic Review*, 19: 53–70.

Guillén, M. 1997. Business groups in economic development. *Academy of Management Best Paper Proceedings*: 170–174.

Hoskisson, R. E., Eden, L., Lau, C. M., and Wright, M. 2000. Strategy in emerging economies. *Academy of Management Journal*, 43: 249–267.

Hoskisson, R. E., Cannella, A. A., Tihanyi, L., and Faraci, R. 2004. Asset restructuring and business group affiliation in French civil law countries. *Strategic Management Journal*, 25: 525–539.

Jones, G. and Khanna, T. 2006. Bringing history (back) into international business. *Journal of International Business Studies*, 37: 453–468.

Keister, L. 2001. *Chinese Business Groups*. Oxford University Press.

Kester, W. C. 1992. Governance, contracting, and investment horizons: A look at Japan and Germany. *Journal of Applied Corporate Finance*, 5: 83–98.

Khanna, T. 2009. Learning from economic experiments in China and India. *Academy of Management Perspectives*, 23: 36–43.

Khanna, T. and Palepu, K. 1997. Why focused strategies may be wrong for emerging markets. *Harvard Business Review*, July/August: 41–51.

2000. Is group affiliation profitable in EMs? An analysis of diversified Indian business groups. *Journal of Finance*, 55: 867–891.

Khanna, T. and Rivkin, J. W. 2001. Estimating the performance effects of business groups in emerging markets. *Strategic Management Journal*, 22: 45–74.

Khanna, K., Palepu, G., and Sinha, J. 2005. Strategies that fit emerging markets. *Harvard Business Review*, 83: 63–76.

Kochhar, K., Kumar, U., Rajan, R., Subramanian, A., and Tokatlidis, I. 2006. India's patter of development: What happened, what follows? *Journal of Monetary Economics*, 53: 981–1019.

Kumar, V., Pedersen, T., Stucchi, T., Kundu, S., 2012. *Business Groups, Internationalization and Institutional Change: Evidence from India*. Paper presented at AIB-Meeting in Washington, DC.

La Porta, R., Lopez-de-Silanes, F., and Shleifer, A. 1999. Corporate ownership around the world. *Journal of Finance*, 54: 471–517.

Leff, N. H. 1978. Industrial organization and entrepreneurship in the developing countries: The economic groups. *Economic Development and Cultural Change*, 26: 661–675.

Luo, Y. and Tung, R. L. 2007. International expansion of EM enterprises: A springboard perspective. *Journal of International Business Studies*, 38: 481–498.

Madhok, A. and Keyhani, M. 2012. Acquisitions as entrepreneurship: Asymmetries, opportunities, and the internationalization of multinationals from emerging economies. *Global Strategy Journal*, 2: 26–40.

Mathews, J. A. 2002. Competitive advantages of the latecomer firm: A resource-based account of industrial catch-up strategies. *Asia Pacific Journal of Management*, 19: 467–488.

2006. Dragon multinationals: New players in 21st century globalization. *Asia Pacific Journal of Management*, 23: 5–27.

Morck, R., Yeung, B., and Zhao, M. 2008. Perspectives of China's outward foreign direct investment. *Journal of International Business Studies*, 39: 337–350.

Narula, R. 2006. Globalization, new ecologies, new zoologies, and the purported death of the eclectic paradigm. *Asia Pacific Journal of Management*, 23: 143–151.

2012. Do we need different frameworks to explain infant MNEs from developing countries? *Global Strategy Journal*, 2: 188–204.

Nayyar, D. 2007. *The Internationalization of Firms from India: Investment, Mergers and Acquisitions*. SLPTMD Working Paper Series, No. 004.

Newman, K. L. 2000. Organizational transformation during institutional upheaval. *Academy of Management Review*, 25: 602–619.

North, D. C. 1990. *Institutions, Institutional Change and Economic Performance*. Cambridge University Press.

Pedersen, T. and Thomsen, S. 1997. European patterns of corporate ownership: A twelve-country study. *Journal of International Business Studies*, 28: 759–778.

Peng, M. W. 2003. Institutional transitions and strategic choices. *Academy of Management Review*, 28: 275–296.

Ramamurti, R. 2009. What have we learned about emerging MNEs? In R. Ramamurti and J. Singh (eds.), *Emerging Multinationals from Emerging Markets*. Cambridge University Press.

2012. What is really different about emerging market multinationals? *Global Strategy Journal*, 2: 41–47.

Ray, S. and Gubbi, S. R. 2009. International acquisitions by Indian firms: Implications for research on emerging multinationals. *Indian Journal of Industrial Relations*, 45: 11–26.

Rugman, A. M. and Li, J. 2007. Will China's multinationals succeed globally or regionally? *European Management Journal*, 25: 333–343.

Scott, W. R. and Meyer, J. W. 1983. *Organizational Environments: Ritual and Rationality*. Beverly Hills, CA: SAGE Publications.

Sheth, J. N. 2011. Impact of emerging markets on marketing: Rethinking existing perspectives and practices. *Journal of Marketing*, 75: 166–182.

Williamson, P. J. and Zeng, M. 2009. Chinese multinationals: Emerging through new global gateways. In R. Ramamurti and J. V. Singh (eds.), *Emerging Multinationals from Emerging Markets*: 81–109. Cambridge University Press.

Wright, M., Filatotchev, I., Hoskisson, R. E., and Peng, M. W. 2005. Strategy research in emerging economies: Challenging the conventional wisdom. *Journal of Management Studies*, 42: 1–33.

Xu, D. and Meyer, K. E. 2012. Linking theory and context: Strategy research in emerging economies after Wright et al., 2005. *Journal of Management Studies*, 50: 1322–1346.

Yiu, D. W., Lu, Y., Bruton, G. D., and Hoskisson, R. E. 2007. Business groups: An integrated model to focus future research. *Journal of Management Studies*, 44: 1551–1579.

Zattoni, A., Pedersen, T., and Kumar, V. 2009. The performance of group-affiliated firms during institutional transition: A longitudinal study of Indian firms. *Corporate Governance: An International Review*, 17: 510–523.

12 | Country of origin effects on internationalization: insights from Brazil

AFONSO FLEURY AND MARIA TEREZA
LEME FLEURY

Introduction

The aim of this chapter is to tackle the question "How does a firm's home country affect its internationalization?" through the analysis of the Brazilian case. That question is particularly relevant at the current stage of International Business theory development, as the rise of emerging market multinationals has sparked an intense debate in regards to the likely contributions to theory stemming from studies about them. In this chapter, the actual findings about the internationalization of Brazilian enterprises are contrasted with what extant theories would predict. From this elaboration, some insights emerge in defense of the argument that extant theories must be extended by incorporating the specifics of emerging countries to enable a more accurate investigation of those new multinationals.

The first outcomes from studies about the internationalization of Brazilian firms suggest that: a) they develop distinct Firm Specific Advantages (FSAs) when compared to both developed country multinationals and multinationals from other emerging markets (Fleury and Fleury, 2011, 2013); b) they adopt particular internationalization strategies in what concerns country choice, entry mode, and commitment (Cuervo-Cazurra, 2008; Fleury, Fleury, and Reis, 2011; Dias, 2012); and c) they seem to be in the process of developing novel ways of configuring their international value chains and managing foreign subsidiaries (Borini, Fleury, and Fleury, 2009; Borini and Fleury, 2011; Fleury, Fleury, and Borini, 2013).

This chapter begins with an overview of the distinctive features of Brazilian multinationals (BrMNEs), which are contrasted with the predictions derived from extant theories. Following that, a brief summary of Brazilian social and economic development creates a backdrop for the understanding of why country of origin effects induced an internationalization process with characteristics distinct from those observed in other countries. Then, some suggestions for the extension of international business theories based on the findings about Brazil are sketched. The final remarks touch the limitations of this study and the way ahead.

Distinctive features of Brazilian firms' internationalization

Discovered by Europeans in the year 1500, Brazil was until 1822 a Portuguese colony based on the exploitation of natural resources. Whereas in North America the colonizers sought to build a new model of society, in Brazil the land was parceled up into strips called *capitanias hereditárias* (hereditary captaincies), each of which was given by the King of Portugal to a noble family for its commercial exploitation. The first type of riches exploited was Brazil wood, which lent its name to the country. Europeans valued this wood greatly for the highly appreciated red ink that it yielded. Besides the extraction of minerals – in particular gold, silver, and precious stones – agricultural commodities (first sugarcane, then coffee) also accounted for the generation of wealth. The exploitation system was based on large plantations and slave labor.

Immigration played an important role in the development of the country: large groups of German, Italian, and Japanese immigrants arrived in the country in the late nineteenth and early twentieth centuries. At that time, Brazil became an exporter of primary goods, especially coffee. Modern manufacturing was initiated with Ford and General Motors assembling plants established around 1920. Although industrialization policies were defined in the early 1930s, their implementation was done in a very peculiar way leading to a situation where the local industry is highly dependent on subsidiaries of foreign multinationals. All those features resulted in a very particular type of environment for industrial development and internationalization.

For the development of this chapter, three interdependent themes in international business were chosen to reveal the distinctiveness of the internationalization of Brazilian firms: Firm-Specific Advantage, Internationalization Strategy, and Value Chain Configuration. The reasons that justify those choices are: a) firms cannot internationalize successfully if they do not possess Firm-Specific Advantages (Dunning,

1993; Rugman, 2001); b) their internationalization strategies involve decisions related to entry mode and commitment (Johanson and Vahlne, 1977; Brouthers and Hennart, 2007); and c) their expansion in the international markets depends on the way they configure and manage their international value chains aiming to leverage their international competitiveness (Bartlett and Ghoshal, 1989; Nohria and Ghoshal, 1997; Doz, Santos, and Williamson, 2001).

BrMNEs brew distinctive sets of Firm-Specific Advantages

The internationalization of early-movers, the traditional multinationals, has been explained by both their market power (Hymer, 1976) and by their possession of proprietary competitive advantages, especially technology and brand (Vernon, 1966; Dunning, 1993). In particular, Vernon justified internationalization in terms of the product's life cycle and hypothesized that MNEs move sales and production from developed to developing countries as an innovation and production process becomes standardized. Today, developed country multinationals continue to follow that trend, relying on a breakthrough type of innovation to offer new products based on cutting-edge technology (Bartlett and Ghoshal, 1989; Mudambi, 2008), and offshoring production activities (Contractor et al., 2010).

Differently, Brazilian multinationals mainly operate in low-tech sectors, where brand and product innovation may not be so relevant, but other types of innovation are. Actually, studies on BrMNEs have identified two distinctive Firm-Specific Advantages: a) excellence in manufacturing and process engineering (Fleury and Fleury, 2011) and b) agile business models (Sull and Escobari, 2004; Sull, 2005).

Brazilian firms practice process innovation, meaning radical new ways of obtaining standard or slightly commoditized products which are not easily imitable, thus equipping them with a strong competitive advantage. BrMNEs invest heavily in process-oriented R&D, keep strong ties with local and foreign universities and research centers and own a significant number of patents. Petrobras (oil), Gerdau (steel), Votorantim (cement), and AmBev (beverages) are good examples of firms that became competitive in the commodity industries, from having learned how to efficiently exploit the local abundance of natural resources and extraordinary climatic conditions; and also in the wage consumer industries, from having learned with the large and idiosyncratic local markets.

Brazilian firms also developed distinctive agile business models which shape their internationalization strategies. Sull and Escobari (2004) coined metaphors such as Active Waiting, Fast Strategy Implementation, Golden Opportunities and Sudden Death, to describe how the leading Brazilian firms develop and implement their business models. They observed managers preparing for golden opportunities by managing smartly during the comparative calm of business as usual. During these periods of active waiting (Sull, 2005), managers probed the future and remained alert for anomalies that signaled potential threats or opportunities, exercised restraint to preserve their war chests, and maintained discipline to keep the troops battle-ready for fast and integrated action. When a golden opportunity or "sudden death" threat emerged, managers had the courage to declare the main effort and concentrate resources to seize the moment.

Those innovative business models are: a) being developed as a response to (Brazilian) environmental conditions (macro-conditions: political and economic; meso-conditions: conflicts and rivalry among local business groups) (Cyrino and Barcellos, 2013; Fleury and Fleury, 2013); b) focused in business where the concept of innovative capacity acquires a much broader meaning in that an existing product or service is produced, sold, financed, and serviced in wholly new ways, with costs, risks, and profits generated in ways that may not have been seen in developed countries.

Therefore, BrMNEs' internationalization is based on a set of FSAs (excellence in manufacturing and process engineering associated with agile business models) which is different from the FSAs identified for multinationals originating in other countries. That may represent interesting extensions for IB theory.

Internationalization strategies: idiosyncratic choices

For Bartlett, Ghoshal and Beamish (2008: 8) the internationalization process "is rarely well thought out in advance, and typically builds on a combination of rational analysis, opportunism and pure luck." The statement matches well with the Brazilian experience.

Internationalization strategies involve two types of decision: ownership mode (wholly owned subsidiary or joint-venture) and establishment mode (acquisition or greenfield) (Brouthers and Hennart, 2007). Over time, the process involves commitment (Johanson and Vahlne, 1977) and rhythm (Fortanier and van Tulder, 2007). Up to the moment, the studies about Brazilian multinationals reveal the following.

Country choice. The extant theories addressing country choice, like the Upsalla model (Johanson and Vahlne, 1977) or Incremental Internationalization theory (Cuervo-Cazurra, 2012) as well as Rugman and Brain's theory of regionalization (2003) predict that Brazilian multinationals would prefer to locate activities in the Latin American region. For the former authors, the smaller psychic distance as well as the cultural and geographic distances would reduce the liability of foreignness; for the latter the cost advantages in operations, logistics, and communication would reduce transaction costs.

To a certain extent, the data displayed in Table 12.1 confirm that trend: Latin America is the preferred choice for the great majority of BrMNEs. However, the reasons behind those choices may be somehow different from the assumptions adopted by the above mentioned theories. For example, Ronen and Shenkar (1985) locate Brazil in an independent cultural cluster (along with Japan, India, and Israel); these are countries which, given their diverse specificities, were not included in the other groups encountered. In their analysis, the Latin American cluster was composed of Argentina, Chile, Colombia, Mexico, Peru, and Venezuela. The grouping was associated with three interconnected dimensions: language, religion, and geographic region (Ronen and Shenkar, 1985). Hofstede's classic study (1980) identified greater cultural similarity between countries such as Argentina and Brazil with the Latin European countries (which included Belgium, France, Italy, Spain), than with the Latin American countries (which included Chile, Colombia, Mexico, Peru, Venezuela), and Portugal when defining specific cultural clusters (Hofstede, 1980). Therefore, it seems plausible to admit that, for Brazilian firms, reducing cultural distance is not such a strong factor in determining country choice. Contrarily, economic and institutional distance would play a greater role in that decision (Fleury, Fleury, and Borini, 2012). This suggests that the experience amassed by BrMNEs as a result of operating in a turbulent institutional environment induces them to search for countries with similar characteristics, thus ratifying studies such as Khanna and Palepu (1999, 2010) and Cuervo-Cazurra (2007).

Table 12.1 also shows that only a third of the investments head to developed countries, while two thirds are directed to other emerging or

Table 12.1 *Regional location of the activities of Brazilian multinationals.* *

	Latin Am.	North Am.	Europe	Africa	Asia	Oceania
2006	46.91	11.34	20.62	6.7	14.43	0
2007	40.38	14.72	20.00	8.3	16.60	0
2008	46.23	17.31	20.61	10.75	10.75	0.43
2009	52.95	9.18	16.89	5.43	14.66	0.89
2010	38.3	12.6	21.1	9.6	16.8	1.7

Source: Fundacao Dom Cabral's largest Brazilian multinationals report (several years).
* Fluctuation is mainly due to shifts in the sample of respondent companies from year to year.

less developed countries, Latin America included. Indeed, other studies reveal that, after their initial incursions into the international market, BrMNEs tend to look for operations in developed countries as a way to boost their productive, technological, and marketing efficiency, following an asset-seeking strategy in order to increase their competitive advantages (Mathews, 2006; Guillén and Garcia-Canal, 2009; Fleury and Fleury, forthcoming).

In summary, Latin America is the preferred location for the entry strategies not only for the arguments disclosed by the Nordic School and Rugman's Regionalization Theory, but also due to the capacity of Brazilian multinationals to deal with turbulent institutional environments.

Entry mode/ownership mode. Contrary to the findings of Mathews (2006) and Dunning, Kim, and Park (2008), BrMNEs usually demand full control as the preferential entry mode, instead of collaborative arrangements and networking practices. An analysis of the Mergers and Acquisitions (M&As) practiced by BrMNEs from 1990 to 2010 revealed only one hostile takeover, while 77 percent of them targeted total control or the majority of voting shares (Cyrino and Barcellos, 2013); this shows the difficulty that Brazilian firms have with engaging in collaborative arrangements.

Entry mode/establishment mode. The evidences are contradictory in what concerns BrMNEs' preferred establishment mode. In a recent study, Dias (2012) concluded the majority of BrMNEs' operations are greenfields (in number). However, the volume of OFDI (Outward Foreign Direct Investment) shows a superior investment in acquisitions rather than greenfields (SOBEET, 2012).

The reasons that support one course of action in relation to the other vary. BrMNEs are eager for acquisitions, especially when opportunities arise: there are several cases of BrMNEs acquiring developed country companies that were facing problematic situations. The propensity to embark in acquisitions is justified by two factors. First, BrMNEs are risk-averse and prefer to rely on their own finance (SOBEET, 2012) which reduces the range of potential acquisitions and privileges cheap deals. The second factor reinforces the first: BrMNEs display distinctive competences in manufacturing and finance, which are the key factors to effect a turnaround of firms on the brink of failure due to production inefficiency and dire finances.

Acquisitions are also preferred because managers consider that international asset prices are undervalued in relation to domestic prices. In addition, cross-border acquisitions create positive reputational effects in the home market, a point frequently neglected in the literature (Cyrino and Barcellos, 2013).

Commitment to internationalization. Authors like Mathews (2006) admit that emerging country multinationals would be characterized by fast internationalization. However, even though the number of Brazilian multinationals may be increasing, the gradient is low. Moreover, Brazilian OFDI has fluctuated strongly: after a peak in 2006, in both 2009 and 2011 a repatriation of resources was observed. In addition, the degree of internationalization of individual BrMNEs is not high, as revealed by Table 12.2 below.

Those figures are symptomatic of some intrinsic characteristics of Brazilian firms: distinctive financial competence, high organizational flexibility, and a relative commitment to internationalization. Most BrMNEs could be categorized as displaying stable-volatile internationalization trajectories, according to the Fortanier and van Tulder typology (2007). The fact that Brazilian firms internationalized autonomously, e.g., in accordance with their own drivers and decisions and without any cooperative arrangement or governmental support, may be another fact to justify that outcome.

BrMNEs configure value chains and manage subsidiaries in a different way

The very fact that BrMNEs are infant or immature multinationals (Ramamurti, 2009a; Williamson et al., 2013) creates a huge gap in

Table 12.2 *The TNI of Brazilian multinationals.*

	2011	2010	2009	2008	2007
The most internationalized	0.538	0.596	0.616	0.570	0.541
Top 23 (average)	0.291	0.282	0.260	0.254	0.219
Top 40 (average)	0.185	0.184	0.160	0.153	0.137

Source: Fundacao Dom Cabral (several years).

relation to theories derived from the behavior of mature multinationals in what concerns international management models (Bartlett and
Ghoshal, 1989; Doz, Santos, and Williamson, 2001). For these, the
transition from an era of early internationalization, characterized by
the International Division Departments, to the adoption of divisional-
ized structures (Chandler, 1962; Stopford and Wells, 1972) and then
to networked structures (Bartlett and Ghoshal, 1989; Nohria and
Ghoshal, 1997; Doz, Santos, and Williamson, 2001) constitutes a long
learning experience. That is not the case of BrMNEs. As late-movers
into international markets, the movements of BrMNEs are not only
immersed in a very turbulent environment, but also heavily influenced
by the positioning strategy of early-movers who have already established their international value chains.

International management models involve configuration and coordination. Configuration relates to the establishment of the subsidiaries'
network mission and the roles subsidiaries play, individually and collectively. Coordination refers to the dynamic interaction between headquarters and subsidiaries for the accomplishment of the enterprises' goals
(Bartlett and Ghoshal, 1989; Doz, Santos, and Williamson, 2001).

In terms of configuration, BrMNEs:

1. Acquire in developed countries, occupying positions opened when
   developed country incumbents move up their value chains towards
   knowledge-intensive industries and thus create acquisition opportunities for emerging country multinationals. That is the case
   for Braskem (chemicals) and JBR-Friboi (meat industry), among
   others. Their subsidiaries perform all organizational functions:
   production, marketing, product and service development, finance,
   and human resource management. The HQs are concerned with
   the transfer of production and finance competences to the subsidiaries, aiming to improve their operational performance.

2. Become global followers in cases where the incumbents organize global production networks. That is the case of Sabo (auto parts) and Embraco (compressors) which became global followers in the automobile and white goods industries, respectively. Internationalization strategies involve both acquisitions and greenfield investments, aiming to both supply the leading firm and upgrade within the global production network. In cases where there are acquisitions, BrMNEs tend to maintain R&D and marketing activities at the foreign subsidiary and offshore production to low-cost countries (Fleury and Fleury, forthcoming).

3. Expand to developing and less-developed countries, thus exploiting courses of action created by regionalization and globalization, like the Mercosur or Africa. In these cases, their subsidiaries perform production and logistics activities, supported by finance and human resources management; R&D and marketing are kept at home. To a certain extent, that seems to be the emulation of the internationalization strategy adopted by the developed country multinationals in their early days.

4. Conquer positions in internationally competitive markets; these include the well-known cases of Embraer, AmBev, Gerdau, and others. In those cases, BrMNEs develop innovative value chain configurations to make innovative business models operational. Among the factors that justify Embraer's success are risk-partnering and the management of a globally distributed manufacturing network; in the case of AmBev, after acquisitions (Interbrew, Anheuser-Busch, and Heinz), the global value chain configuration is restructured according to their successful business model; in the case of Gerdau, the implementation of its business model is based on an innovative manufacturing process and a particular configuration of its value chain to serve end markets in a customized way.

In summary, in subsidiaries where the production function is performed, the organizational structure is complete and encompasses all organizational functions. Subsidiaries which do not perform production activities adopt a very lean structure focused on the function that is strategic for operation in the host country. This finding suggests that BrMNEs adopt different configurations depending on the role assigned to the subsidiaries and their locations: in developing countries they adopt full function configurations to exploit their FSAs (especially manufacturing excellence), while in developed countries the configuration is optimized to explore the learning experience. That pattern is very different from the one observed for developed country multinationals, where production is offshored while R&D and marketing are kept at home.

As to value chain coordination, so far the research shows the difficulties of BrMNEs in dealing with the issue. Due to the headquarters' inability to lead, direct, and evaluate the subsidiaries' actions, these subsidiaries operate by taking initiatives based on their local business environment connections, regardless of their headquarters' consent or delegation of autonomy, which characterizes the subsidiaries as "rebellious" (Monteiro, Arvidsson, and Birkinshaw, 2008; Borini, Fleury, and Fleury, 2009). In other words, Brazilian multinationals' subsidiaries are displaying initiatives that are not actively encouraged by headquarters.

In regards to knowledge and competence transfer, Fleury, Fleury, and Borini (2013) found that the reversal flow, between subsidiaries and headquarters, is focused almost exclusively on production issues. Consequently, the learning associated with the other competences (product development, marketing, finance, and human resource management) is very limited. Therefore, Brazilian multinationals are not yet exploring their international operations as they should; the results are still limited.

In conclusion, the gradual construction of international value chains in extremely competitive and dynamic international markets associated with the transition from national to international management models is still a major challenge for BrMNEs. Notwithstanding, that becomes a particularly fertile field for studies on early-stage internationalization.

The specifics of Brazilian multinationals

The previous discussion reveals that BrMNEs display characteristics which are not foreseeable if extant theories of international business are used to predict them. These specifics of Brazilian multinationals are displayed in Table 12.3.

The above set of specifics is, to a large extent, a product of the embeddedness of firms in the Brazilian environment. In the next section, a brief overview of the most important environmental factors, the

Table 12.3 *The specifics of Brazilian multinationals.*

FSAs	Based on manufacturing excellence and innovative business models.
Internationalization strategy	Characterized by opportunistic movements associated with conservative and risk-averse decision-making processes.
Value chain configuration and subsidiary management	Diversified set of choices depending on industry and host country. BrMNEs that became global leaders implemented innovative VCCs. Coordination is still a problem and a challenge for all.

country of origin effects that induced the formation of the specifics of Brazilian multinationals, will be presented.

Country of origin effects on internationalization

In the debate about the potential contribution of research on emerging country multinationals to IB literature, Cuervo-Cazurra (2012: 154) states that "the contribution is limited to the areas in which the country of origin has a large influence on the behavior of the firm." Aiming to advance the argument, the country of origin effects over the three previously mentioned specifics will be analyzed, thus creating the basis for the identification of likely contributions to IB theory. The *pulls*, conditions related to the institutional environment which inhibit and jeopardize the internationalization of Brazilian firms, will be differentiated from the *pushes*, conditions which stimulated those processes. The Country of Origin Effects (Sethi and Elango, 1999) affecting the internationalization strategies of local firms will be portrayed at the end of this section.

The pulls: environmental factors inhibiting internationalization

The key institutional pulls affecting the internationalization of Brazilian firms are: a) industrialization policies, b) macroeconomic policies, and c) the Brazilian cultural legacies.

During most of the twentieth century, in contrast to the advanced OECD countries, Brazil was considered a Third-World Country. Industrialization began timidly in 1930, supposedly based on an

Import-Substitution Industrialization (ISI) model. Some Brazilian multinationals were born at that time, like Votorantim (cement), Gerdau (nails), and Brahma and Antarctica (beverage; merged in 1994 to become AmBev).

Brazil followed the import-substitution policy during the 1930s and 1940s, which was, to some extent, imposed by the global crisis and World War II. In that period, important state-owned enterprises like Companhia Siderurgica Nacional, Companhia Vale do Rio Doce (currently Vale), and Petrobras, as well as capital goods manufacturers like Romi (the only BrMNE in that industry), were created.

However, the actual ISI model, the one which was previously adopted by most advanced countries (Chang, 2002) was twisted twenty years after its adoption. In the 1950s, when industrialization was meant to accelerate, instead of local firms taking the leading role in the catching-up, subsidiaries of developed country multinationals were brought in to develop the high-tech industries like automobiles and durable consumer goods; these subsidiaries were seen as the locomotives of industrialization. Meanwhile, Brazilian firms stood still in the low-tech sectors. That policy had a tremendous negative impact on the development of local capabilities and, if spillover effects were expected from that policy, those were of minor relevance. From then on, the hegemony of foreign multinationals in Brazil increased continuously. Therefore, it is plausible to say that Brazil had an "Import-Substitution-Dependent Industrialization" model in which Brazilian firms, operating in traditional, low-tech economic sectors, seldom considered the perspective of internationalization. Industrial policy was essentially directed to the attraction of foreign multinationals, and there was no concern for the internationalization of Brazilian firms.

The second inhibitor was related to another dimension of policy making in Brazil. The instability and unpredictability of macroeconomic policies, especially after 1980, diverted local companies from any attention to the issue of internationalization. In that period, the Brazilian economy went through a phase of turbulence initiated by the international indebtedness incurred to finance growth in the previous period, the so-called Brazilian miracle from the 1960s to 1970s, that was intensified by the volatile conditions of the international environment due to oil shocks, world recession, etc.

The series of attempts to fix the trade balance and curb inflation then adopted – in less than a decade's time, seven macroeconomic plans were introduced and soon afterwards waned – resulted, for the firms operating in Brazil, in a roller-coaster situation where inflation rates were brought down through the freezing of prices, then rapidly increased to stratospheric levels, at which point the cycle started all over again. The key demand for firms became efficient day-to-day financial management, what was dubbed *overnight management*. Clearly, any thoughts about internationalization and its long-term prospects were out of the question.

Thirdly, the prevailing conservative and risk-averse organizational culture led to strict and rigidly controlled discipline, a lack of strategic planning, and a short-term orientation with an emphasis on crisis solutions at the firm level. That culture is considered a legacy of the Portuguese colonization, which established rigid and hierarchical organizations, depleted the colony's natural riches, and exploited the land through a slavery-based regime, among other factors. The social elements introduced back then in the formation of Brazil's rural and agricultural society subsequently influenced its urban and industrial society and the way in which Brazilian firms are managed as well (Barros and Prates, 1996; Tanure, 2005; Caldas, 2006). Clearly, such a mindset is not conducive to internationalization.

Finally, it is of paramount importance to mention the issue of natural resources and the comparative advantage of the country. Studies show that natural riches may be a handicap for development. "The natural resources curse" admits that the blessing of rich natural environments hinders diversification and innovation: "The bulk of the empirical growth literature, at the very least, does not support enthusiasm for natural-resources and the few papers that reject the natural-resource curse confirm the benefit of diversification" (Moreira, 2007: 357). Brazil is still struggling to escape that trap.

To illustrate the strength of natural resources as the key driver for Brazilian development, the case of the Brazilian Industry Competitiveness Report (Coutinho and Ferraz, 1994) is revealing. That report, and its abridged version: "Made in Brazil" (Ferraz, Kupfer, and Haguenauer, 1996), were the products of a study commissioned by the Brazilian government, following the guidelines of "Made in America" (Dertouzos, Lester, and Solow, 1989) and "Made in France" (Coriat, 1993). However, in contrast to the conceptual approach adopted by the earlier reports, the Brazilian version made the point that the economic sectors in which Brazil is internationally competitive are those related to natural resources and agribusiness (Table 12.4). Brazil also had representatives in low-tech industries considered competitive with handicaps. However, in industries considered drivers of technological progress, the subsidiaries of foreign multinationals prevailed; Brazil itself was highly underrepresented. In addition, in its recommendations, the report argued for governmental support for all categories, irrespective of leadership and technological spillovers.

At the time of its publication, the above mentioned study received severe criticisms for its conservative positioning and protectionist bias (Tavares, 1994). Notwithstanding, its assumptions and orientations still prevail; the country has yet to develop a successful alternative.

A point must be mentioned for the sake of clarity. According to Brazil's 1988 constitution, subsidiaries of foreign firms which have any share of ownership control in the hands of Brazilian citizens are considered local firms and are entitled to the same rights and obligations as native Brazilian firms. Clearly, that influences all analyses about the Brazilian industry.

In summary, industrialization policies induced Brazilian firms to look inward, attributed little importance to the external markets, and created a type of economic and cultural dependence from advanced countries and their multinationals. Macroeconomic policy making resulted in a sense of uncertainty and unpredictability that led to short term perspectives, resistance to long term investment, and management based on financial indicators. Finally, local culture stimulated conservative organization, centralization, and risk aversion. Clearly, the features of Brazilian multinationals, as analyzed in a previous section, were and are a product of that harsh environment.

The internal pushes and the external pulls driving internationalization

Together with the process of economic reforms of the 1990s (Cuervo-Cazurra, 2007), new internationalization forces came about in favor of Brazilian firms: the possibility of becoming a player in Global Production Networks (GPNs), and the creation of the Mercosur, a regional market. Therefore, the conditions for internationalization changed significantly and an increasing number of Brazilian firms internationalized.

Table 12.4 *The outcomes of the Brazilian Industry Competitiveness Study or "Made in Brazil".*

	Competitive with handicaps	
Internationally competitive	Low-tech intensity	Technology progress drivers
Agroindustry (soy, coffee, orange, ...)	Agroindustry (meat, dairy)	
Chemicals (oil, petrochemicals)	Chemicals (fertilizers)	Chemicals (pharmaceuticals,* pesticides)
Metal-mechanics (steel, aluminum, ...)	Metal-mechanics (automotive,* auto-parts)	Metal-mechanics* (machine-tools, electrical machinery)
Pulp and paper	Printing	
	Electronics (consumer electronics*)	Electronics* (computers, telecommunications, software)
		Biotechnology

Source: Coutinho and Ferraz (1994: 261).
* Dominated by subsidiaries of foreign multinationals.

Engagement in GPNs may be a powerful push for internationalization. The idea is that once a firm becomes part of a GPN, the ecosystem thus created exerts pressure for accelerated learning and upgrading, thus allowing the firm to reach the conditions necessary for international expansion. However, the experience of Brazilian firms in GPNs shows that while opportunities may appear, the challenges posed by engagement with them on a permanent basis are huge. Although a large number of firms tried, only a small group of firms were able to remain in GPNs, and those were mainly from the metal-mechanics industry: in the automobile industry, Sabo, Metagal, and Iochpe-Maxxion, among others, became global follower multinationals. In the white-goods industry Embraco became the global supplier to the Whirlpool's corporation. No firm in the shoe or apparel company succeeded in becoming an integral part of global foreign-led GPNs. That confirms Bartlett and Ghoshal's (2000) observation that the biggest challenge is not to get in, but to climb up the GPN aiming at international expansion.

Mercosur was established in 1991, when Uruguay, Paraguay, Brazil, and Argentina signed the Treaty of Asunción. In practice, Brazil and Argentina are the countries that make the most of the agreement. Uruguay and Paraguay, due to their small economies, play a less relevant role in the commercial flows. The internationalization of Brazilian enterprises in the 1990s concentrated on Argentina, which absorbed 36 percent of the country's OFDI until 2002. The tax regime added to geographic proximity and smaller cultural distance to justify the trend.

However, the positive impacts of those newly instated drivers were counterbalanced by the difficulties arising from the institutional environment. The effects of the economic reforms of the 1990s did not last for long and the Brazilian currency began to fluctuate due to the international financial crises, especially the Argentinean one, in 2001. The government then started to implement a series of policies to regulate the exchange rate, creating a battlefield with industrialists. The reason for that conflict is that the exchange rate became attached to commodities, leading to a more appreciated exchange rate than that required for the other tradable industries using state-of-the-art technology, an economic issue dubbed as "the Dutch disease" (Bresser Pereira, 2010). In other words, industry was jeopardized once more as a consequence of macroeconomic policies, and that influenced the decisions on internationalization.

As to industrial policies, after the abandonment of the import-substitution model in the 1980s and the non-policy policy of the 1990s, in compliance with the International Monetary Fund guidelines, several attempts were made since 2003 to define and implement industrial policy. The outcomes, however, are far from satisfactory due to the lack of implementation power and the reactive and short term perspective adopted in what concerns economic policy decisions.

The internationalization of Brazilian firms was never considered a strategic issue by the government until the early 2000s. At this moment in time, the significant increase in outward foreign direct investment attracted the government's attention. For fear that the internationalization of local firms would reduce investment in Brazil and send jobs abroad, the reaction of the Brazilian government was ambiguous. From then on, the issue has been brought to the fore, but "coordinated movements towards the definition of a national strategy on the theme are not yet observable, nor are the structuring of policies that could potentially support them" (Sennes and Mendes, 2009: 172). Few institutions, especially the BNDES, or National Bank for Economic and Social Development, have made a significant contribution to the fostering of Brazilian firms' internationalization.

Country of origin effects impacting the internationalization of Brazilian firms

Regardless of the role that Brazilian industrialists played, the institutional environment has been a burden for Brazilian enterprises, influencing the way in which they behave and strategize. Some firms were not able to overcome the barriers imposed by the local environment and succumbed. On the other hand, some Brazilian firms broke away from their cultural legacy and took advantage of the local resources and opportunities that created the conditions to venture in the international markets. Table 12.5 synthesizes the country of origin effects' impacts on the internationalization of Brazilian firms.

Table 12.5 portrays how the main factors related to the institutional environment influenced the conditions and strategies for internationalization in Brazil, both positively and negatively. Industrialization and macroeconomic policies, national culture, and natural resources riches generated a series of country of origin effects on firms and their internationalization processes. Fruit of a symbiotic relationship between the government and industrialists, both local and foreign, governmental policies shaped the distinct FSAs displayed by Brazilian multinationals. National culture resulted in idiosyncratic internationalization strategies while natural riches, combined with government policies, defined most of the industries in which Brazilian firms are internationally competitive.

Likely extensions of international business theory derived from BrMNEs

In the previous sections, the areas in which the country of origin (Brazil) had a large influence on the (internationalization) behavior of local firms were identified. Some likely extensions to IB theory, derived from that analysis, are suggested in Table 12.6.

The structure of Table 12.6 is based on the approach proposed by Cuervo-Cazurra (2012). From the set of international business

Table 12.5 *Country of origin effects and their impacts on internationalization.*

Macro-level		Micro-level	
Environmental factor	Country of origin effects	Negative impacts on internationalization	Positive impacts on internationalization
Industrialization policies	Inward looking; Dependence on foreign MNEs in high-tech industries	Little importance to external markets; Concentration on low-tech industries; Late-moving	FSAs based on manufacturing excellence
Macroeconomic policies	Short term perspective; Prevalence of the financial concern over any other one	Resistance to long term investment; Opportunistic movements	Agile and flexible companies; FSAs derived from innovative business models
National culture	Conservatism and risk-aversion	Conservative and risk-averse decision making; Difficulty developing international networks; Resistance to alliances	Internationalization strategies based on: Cautious decisions when entering foreign markets; Slow internationalization pace; Redundancy in value chain configuration; Global VCs operating for expansion in Brazilian market
Natural resources riches	Emphasis on nature-based industries	Handicaps for the development of technology-intensive industries	Comparative advantage in commodities and basic inputs markets

Table 12.6 *Extensions to selected IB theories raised by studies on BrMNEs.*

IB Theory: Vernon's Product Life Cycle	
Basic assumption*	MNCs move sales and production from developed to developing countries as an innovation and associated production process becomes standardized
Findings from studies of BrMNEs	BrMNEs specialize in products with long life cycles, different from assembled type of products, and invest in process innovation to remain internationally competitive
Extension suggested from studies of BrMNEs	In countries where governmental policies lead to industrialization dependent on foreign multinationals, firms will specialize in basic products with long life cycles which demand process innovation to remain competitive and will internationalize through the establishment of wholly owned subsidiaries in foreign countries
IB Theory: Incremental Internationalization	
Basic assumption*	MNCs internationalize incrementally to minimize risks and obtain experiential knowledge from abroad
Findings from studies of BrMNEs	Attitudes leading to risk minimization are intrinsic in Brazilian entrepreneurial culture; consciousness about lack of knowledge in regards to internationalization and its consequences (global mindsets and global mindedness) reinforce gradualism
Extension suggested based on studies of BrMNEs	In countries where national cultures do not stimulate the development of global mindedness and entrepreneurship, firms will internationalize slowly and opportunistically, keeping the way back home permanently opened

IB Theory: OLI	
Basic assumption*	MNCs set up production facilities abroad when they have ownership advantages, location advantages, and internalization advantages
Findings from studies of BrMNEs	**Ownership advantages:** BrMNEs have ownership advantages but their ownership advantages are not necessarily the world's best
	Location advantages: BrMNEs either move to more predictable institutional environments and find financial support in conditions similar to international competitors, or move to less predictable institutional environments and use comparative advantages
	Internalization advantages: BrMNEs internalize international operations due to the need for control and lack of experience in dealing with international affairs
Extensions suggested from studies of BrMNEs	In countries where local conditions do not stimulate and support the creation of state-of-the-art ownership advantages, firms internationalize by creating a portfolio of capabilities superior to the least competitive incumbent and the most competitive potential new entrant in the international market
	In countries where environmental conditions do not prioritize and reinforce economic reasoning, firms will approach international location decisions based on behavioral rather than economic criteria
	In countries where uncertainty and unpredictability about rules and contracts prevail, firms will choose to internationalize through wholly owned subsidiaries

Table 12.6 (*cont.*)

IB Theory: RBV and KBV	
Basic assumption*	MNCs create firm-specific assets whose services are used to create products and services, with management being the key constraint to growth at some point in time (Penrose's limits to firm growth)
Findings from studies of BrMNEs	Internationalization paths are defined according to capabilities and competences
	BrMNEs are facing the limits to growth due to the difficulties of establishing international management models
Extension suggested from studies of BrMNEs	In countries where firms internationalize as a reaction to local environmental conditions, these will tend to reinforce learning related to core competences in contrast to a broader approach that explores the learning possibilities opened by internationalization

* According to Cuervo-Cazurra (2012).

theories highlighted by the author, four will be addressed: Vernon's Product Life Cycle Theory, the Incremental Internationalization Theory, Dunning's OLI theory, and the Resources-based/Knowledge-based Theory.

For each one of those theories, its basic assumption is identified, the findings about Brazil and its multinationals are presented, and finally some likely extensions to IB theory are suggested.

Final remarks

Research on emerging country multinationals is likely to contribute to IB literature in areas in which the country of origin has a large influence on the behavior of the firm. Following that guideline, in this chapter, the Brazilian country of origin effects on the internationalization of its enterprises were analyzed and the likely contributions to IB theories were highlighted.

The analysis revealed a very strong influence of the local environment conditions on entrepreneurial behavior and actions, and vice-versa, configuring a co-evolutionary process. Under those circumstances, the rather idiosyncratic choices concerning internationalization, if measured by indicators derived from the traditional IB theories, need another explanatory framework.

However, the point stressed in this chapter is not that each country should have an internationalization theory of its own, but rather to use the specifics emerging from each country to extend existing internationalization theories. The extensions to theory suggested in the previous section may be a point of departure.

The way ahead comprises a more detailed analysis of the causal relations previously identified and the creation of more robust analytical frameworks to approach and test those relations. Only then will the contributions of studies about emerging country multinationals be effectively contributing to international business theory development.

References

Barros, B. and Prates, M. 1996. *O Estilo Brasileiro de Administrar (The Brazilian Management Style)*. São Paulo: Atlas.
Bartlett, C. A. and Ghoshal, S. 1989. *Managing across Borders: The Transnational Solution*. Boston, MA: Harvard Business School Press.

2000. Going global: Lessons from late-movers. *Harvard Business Review*, March–April: 132–142.

Bartlett, C., Ghoshal, S., and Beamish, P. 2008. *Transnational Management: Text, Cases & Readings in Cross-Border Management* (5th edition). Boston, MA: McGraw-Hill Higher Education.

Borini, F. and Fleury, M. 2011. Development of non-local competences in foreign subsidiaries of Brazilian multinationals. *European Business Review*, 23: 106–119.

Borini, F., Fleury, M., and Fleury, A. 2009. The relevance of subsidiary initiatives for Brazilian multinationals. *Revista de Administracao de Empresas*, 49: 253–265.

Bresser Pereira, L. 2010. Exchange rate war and Dutch disease. *Valor*, October 14.

Brouthers, K. and Hennart, J. 2007. Boundaries of the firm: Insights from international entry mode research. *Journal of Management*, 33: 395–425.

Caldas, M. 2006. Conceptualizing Brazilian multiple and fluid cultural profiles. *Management Research*, 4: 169–180.

Chandler, A. 1962. *Strategy and Structure: Chapters in the History of Industrial Enterprise*. Cambridge, MA: The MIT Press.

Chang, H.-J. 2002. *Kicking Away the Ladder: Development Strategy in Historical Perspective*. London: Anthem Press.

Contractor, F. J., Kumar, V., Kundu, S. K., and Pedersen, T. 2010. Reconceptualizing the firm in a world of outsourcing and offshoring: The organizational and geographical relocation of high-value company functions. *Journal of Management Studies*, 47: 1417–1433.

Coriat, B. 1993. *Made in France*. Paris: Librerie Generale Française.

Coutinho, L. and Ferraz, J. 1994. *Estudo da competitividade da indústria brasileira (Brazilian Industrial Competitiveness Study)*. Campinas: Papirus.

Cuervo-Cazurra, A. 2007. Sequence of value-added activities in the internationalization of developing country MNEs. *Journal of International Management*, 13: 258–277.

2008. The internationalization of developing country MNEs: The case of Multilatinas. *Journal of International Management*, 14: 138–154.

2012. How the analysis of developing country multinational companies helps advance theory: Solving the goldilocks debate. *Global Strategy Journal*, 2: 153–167.

Cyrino, A. and Barcellos, E. 2013. Cross-border M&A and competitive advantage of Brazilian EMNEs. In P. J. Williamson, R. Ramamurti, A. Fleury, and M. T. L. Fleury (eds.), *The Competitive Advantage of*

Emerging Market Multinationals: 191–219. Cambridge University Press.

Dertouzos, M., Lester, R., and Solow, R. 1989. *Made in America: Regaining the Productive Edge*. Cambridge: The MIT Press.

Dias, A. C. 2012. *A Escolha do Modo de Entrada no Mercado Externo e sua Relação com o Desempenho da Subsidiária: Evidências das Empresas Multinacionais Brasileiras (Entry Mode Choices in the External Market and their Relations to Subsidiary Performance: Evidence From Brazilian Multinationals)*. PhD dissertation. Rio de Janeiro: Pontifical Catholic University.

Doz, Y., Santos, J., and Williamson, P. 2001. *From Global to Metanational: How Companies Win in the Knowledge Economy*. Boston, MA: Harvard Business School Press.

Dunning, J. 1993. *Multinational Enterprises and the Global Economy*. Wokingham: Addison-Wesley.

Dunning J., Kim, C., and Park, D. 2008. Old wine in new bottles: A comparison of emerging market TNCs today and developed-country TNCs thirty years ago. In K. Sauvant (ed.), *The Rise of Transnational Corporations from Emerging Market: Threat or Opportunity?* Northampton, MA: Edward Elgar.

Ferraz, J. C., Kupfer, D., and Haguenauer, L. 1996. *Made in Brazil, Desafios Competitivos para a Indústria (Made in Brazil: Competitive Challenges for Industry)*. Rio de Janeiro: Campus.

Fleury, A. and Fleury, M. T. 2011. *Brazilian Multinationals: Competences for Internationalization*. Cambridge University Press.

2013. The Brazilian multinationals' approaches to innovation. *Journal of International Management*, 19: 260–275.

forthcoming. The importance of local enablers of business models: The experience of Brazilian multinationals acquiring in North America. *Journal of Business Research*.

Fleury, A., Fleury, M. T., and Reis, G. 2011. Europe in the internationalization strategies of the multinationals. In L. Brennan (ed.), *The Emergence of Southern Multinationals*: 59–78. Hampshire: Palgrave Macmillan.

Fleury, A., Fleury, M. T., and Borini, F. 2012. Is production the core competence for the internationalization of emerging country firms? *International Journal of Production Economics*, 140: 439–449.

2013. Value chain configurations of Brazilian EMNEs. In P. J. Williamson, R. Ramamurti, A. Fleury, and M. T. L. Fleury (eds.), *The Competitive Advantage of Emerging Market Multinationals*: 97–115. Cambridge University Press.

Fortanier, F. and van Tulder, R. 2007. Internationalization Strategies of Multinational Enterprises: 1990–2004. Paper presented at the Conference "Internationalization of Indian and Chinese Firms," Brunel Business School, April 2007.

Fundacao Dom Cabral. 2007–2011. *Ranking of Brazilian Multinationals.* Belo Horizonte.

Guillén, M. and Garcia-Canal, E. 2009. The American model of the multinational firm and the "new" multinationals from emerging economies. *Academy of Management Perspectives,* May: 23–35.

Hofstede, G. 1980. *Culture's Consequences: International Differences in Work-Related Values.* Beverly Hills, CA: Sage Publications.

Hymer, S. 1976. *International Operations of National Firms: A Study of Foreign Direct Investment.* Boston, MA: The MIT Press.

Johanson, J. and Vahlne, J. 1977. The internationalization process of the firm: A model of knowledge development and increasing foreign market commitments. *Journal of International Business Studies,* 8: 23–32.

Khanna, T. and Palepu, P. 1999. The right way to restructure conglomerates in emerging markets. *Harvard Business Review,* 125–134.

2010. *Winning in Emerging Markets: A Roadmap for Strategy and Execution.* Cambridge, MA: Harvard Business School Press.

Mathews, J. 2006. Dragon multinationals: New players in 21st century globalization. *Asia Pacific Journal of Management,* 23: 5–27.

Monteiro, F. L., Arvidsson, N., and Birkinshaw, J., 2008. Knowledge flows within multinational corporations: Explaining subsidiary isolation and its performance implications. *Organization Science,* 19: 90–107.

Moreira, M. M. 2007. Fear of China: Is there a future for manufacturing in Latin America? *World Development,* 35: 355–376.

Mudambi, R. 2008. Location, control and innovation in knowledge-intensive industries. *Journal of Economic Geography,* 8: 699–725.

Nohria, N. and Ghoshal, S. 1997. *The Differentiated Network: Organizing Multinational Corporations for Value Creation.* San Francisco: Jossey-Bass Publishers.

Ramamurti, R. 2009a. The theoretical value of studying Indian multinationals. *Indian Journal of Industrial Relations,* 45: 101–114.

2009b. What have we learned about EMNEs? In R. Ramamurti and J. Singh (eds.), *Emerging Multinationals from Emerging Markets.* Cambridge University Press.

Ronen, S. and Shenkar, O. 1985. Clustering countries on attitudinal dimensions: A review and synthesis. *Academy of Management Review,* 10: 435–454.

Rugman, A. 2001. *The End of Globalization: Why Global Strategy Is a Myth and How to Profit From the Realities of Regional Markets.* New York: AMACOM.

Rugman, A. and Brain, C. 2003. Multinationals are regional, not global. *Multinational Business Review*, 11: 3–12.

Sennes, R. and Mendes, S. 2009. Políticas Públicas e as Multinacionais Brasileiras (Public policies and the Brazilian multinationals). In J. Ramsey and A. Almeida (eds.), *A Ascenção das Multinacionais Brasileiras (The Rise of Brazilian Multinationals)*. Rio de Janeiro: Campus.

Sethi, S. and Elango, B. 1999. The influence of "country of origin" on multinational corporation global strategy: A conceptual framework. *Journal of International Management*, 5: 285–298.

SOBEET. 2012. *Multinacionais Brasileiras (Brazilian Multinationals)*. Sao Paulo: Sociedade Brasileira para o Estudo de Empresas Transnacionais.

Stopford, J. and Wells, L. 1972. *Managing the Multinational Enterprise.* New York: Basic Books.

Sull, D. 2005. Active waiting as strategy. *Harvard Business Review*, September: 120–129.

Sull, D. and Escobari, M. 2004. *Sucesso Made in Brazil: O Segredo das Empresas Brasileiras que Dão Certo (Success Made in Brazil: Secrets of Brazilian Enterprises that Have Done it Right)*. Rio de Janeiro: Elsevier.

Tanure, B. 2005. *Gestão à Brasileira: Uma Comparação entre América Latina, Estados Unidos, Europa e Ásia (Brazilian Management: A Comparison of Latin America, United States, Europe and Asia)*. São Paulo: Editora Atlas.

Tavares, J. 1994. *Livro traz Diagnostico da Ciencia Industrial Brasileira (A Diagnostic of the Industrial Science in Brazil)*. São Paulo: Folha de São Paulo, 6–11.

Vernon, R. 1966. International investment and international trade in the product cycle. *Quarterly Journal of Economics*, 80: 190–207.

Williamson, P., Ramamurti, R., Fleury, A., and Fleury, M. T. 2013. *The Competitive Advantage of Emerging Market Multinationals.* Cambridge University Press.

PART IV

A path for the future

13 | *Conclusion: an agenda for EMNC research*

ALVARO CUERVO-CAZURRA AND
RAVI RAMAMURTI

Introduction

The preceding chapters of the book provided a range of perspectives on how to understand the international behavior of EMNCs. We summarized the main ideas of each chapter in the Introduction. The goal of this concluding chapter is to pull together insights from the previous chapters and to add our own analysis of what is theoretically new or interesting about EMNCs when compared to MNCs from the advanced economies. In addition, we propose an agenda for future research on EMNCs that reflects the collective wisdom of our contributors.

One issue that ties together several of the chapters in this volume and the work of many scholars interested in EMNCs is the question of how their home country affects their competitive advantages and the dynamics of their internationalization. In other words, how does the fact that EMNCs are from emerging economies make a difference in whether and how they internationalize? In what follows, we break that discussion into two parts, consistent with how the chapters have been clustered in this volume. First, we explore how the home country influences the competitive advantage – or firm-specific advantage – of EMNCs, including what that concept means. Then we explore how the home country influences the dynamics of internationalization. The first question comes up in several of the chapters in Parts I and II of this volume, and the second question comes up in several chapters in Part III. As the reader will have gleaned by now, some of the points raised by authors are not limited to EMNCs but apply to MNCs in general. This is a valuable by-product of their work because, as we asserted in the Introduction, research on EMNCs is ultimately a way to learn more about MNCs in general.

We begin with a review of the growth of literature on EMNCs in the last few decades.

The evolving literature on EMNCs

Our understanding of EMNCs has evolved along with their evolution and transformation. Although some developing country firms had invested abroad and become multinationals as far back as the late nineteenth century,[1] scholars did not pay attention to them until much later.

As Aharoni notes in his chapter, the first attempt to systematically study EMNCs came in the 1970s, fueled by puzzlement at how such multinationals came into being at all, because extant theory argued that FDI flowed from countries with low interest rates into countries with high interest rates, i.e., from rich to poor countries (Aliber, 1970), or that only firms with a technological edge and innovative products would have the wherewithal to invest abroad (Buckley and Casson, 1976; Dunning, 1977; Vernon, 1966).

In the 1970s, many of the largest EMNCs operated in natural resources, and many were state-owned enterprises (Heenan and Keegan, 1979) that received government support for internationalization (Aggarwal and Agmon, 1990). Many other EMNCs based their exporting advantage on access to low-cost labor, and their multinationalization advantage rested on managerial practices and technologies that were well adapted to the needs of developing countries (e.g., Kumar and McLeod, 1981; Lall, 1983; Lecraw, 1977; Vernon-Wortzel and Wortzel, 1988; Wells, 1983).

In the 1980s, as Asian firms expanded abroad, the attention of scholars shifted to the question of why manufacturing EMNCs were competitive abroad. Many of these companies came from countries pursuing export-led industrialization, where government support was conditional on the firms' ability to compete internationally. These EMNCs operated in other developing countries as well as in some developed countries (Ghymn, 1980).

In the 1990s and 2000s, scholars turned their attention to how EMNCs played catch-up with advanced country firms (e.g., Aulakh, Kotabe, and Teegen, 2000; Kotabe, Jiang, and Murray, 2011; Lecraw,

---

[1] For example, the Argentinean shoe maker Alpargatas, which commenced operations in 1885 and established operations in Uruguay in 1890 and in Brazil in 1907, or the Thailand-based trading conglomerate GP (Gangjee Premjee) group, which started operations in India in the nineteenth century, established an office in Burma in 1868, and moved operations to Thailand in 1918.

1993; Ulgado, Yu, and Negandhi, 1994; Yeung, 1994, 1999; Young, Huang, and McDermott, 1996). And there was an explosion of special issues in journals devoted to EMNCs (e.g., articles reported in Aulakh, 2007; Cuervo-Cazurra, 2012; Luo and Tung, 2007) and conference volumes devoted to EMNCs, including two resulting from conferences co-organized by Northeastern University's Center for Emerging Markets (Ramamurti and Singh, 2009; Williamson et al., 2013).

Studies on the internationalization process of EMNCs revealed deviations from traditional models, as EMNCs not only invested in other developing countries with conditions similar to their home countries but also in advanced countries to gain access to markets and sophisticated resources, a possibility not considered by prevailing theoretical models (Cuervo-Cazurra, 2008). Additionally, the quest to better understand the sources of advantage to compete globally raised the possibility that these firms had different kinds of firm-specific advantage than the traditional ones of cutting-edge technology and marketing (Luo and Tung, 2007; Mathews, 2006; Ramamurti, 2009).

At present, scholars are starting to take stock of what we really know about EMNCs and what is mere speculation. Some have argued that EMNCs are just like MNCs that came before (Rugman, 2009, 2010), while others have argued that EMNCs are novel and existing theories are inadequate to explain their behavior (Guillén and Garcia-Canal, 2009; Luo and Tung, 2007; Mathews, 2006).

In an attempt to reconcile these opposing views, Ramamurti (2009) argued that contextual variables unrelated to a firm's country of origin explain some of the apparent differences between EMNCs and advanced country MNCs, but that country of origin also matters. In other words, the internationalization strategy of a firm, whether from an emerging economy or not, may be shaped by its country of origin *and* by other contextual variables, such as its industry, its stage of evolution as an MNC, and the global context in which it is internationalizing, as shown in Figure 13.1 (Ramamurti, 2012).

Cuervo-Cazurra (2012) argues that models and theories explaining the behavior of MNCs can be extended and modified to the study of EMNCs. He terms this the "Goldilocks debate" on the value of studying EMNCs, with some arguing that the study of EMNCs does not add novelty to theory, others arguing that it is completely new, and yet others arguing that some behaviors may require new theoretical understanding. To do the latter, researchers could look at the

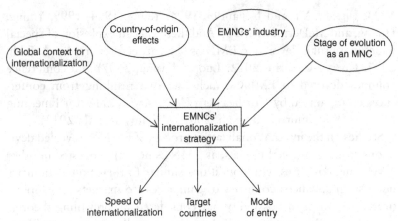

Figure 13.1 Country of origin and other determinants of EMNC internationalization.
Source: Ramamurti (2012).

underlying assumptions of existing models and theories and analyze how these may not fully hold in emerging markets and thus lead to new arguments, even if they do not lead to completely new theories, as shown in Table 13.1.

EMNCs' country of origin and firm-specific advantages

With regard to the firm-specific advantages (FSAs) of EMNCs, it is recognized that while these are often not the same as those of advanced country MNCs, they are nonetheless valuable in their own way. Williamson's chapter argues that the home-country conditions encourage EMNCs to develop FSAs that are valuable not only in other emerging economies but also in developed countries where customers seek "everyday low prices." Aharoni's chapter calls for more research into the nature of FSAs of EMNCs. Rugman (2009) argued that EMNCs lack significant FSAs and merely take advantage of their home country's location advantages or CSAs, but in his chapter with Nguyen in this volume he concedes that some EMNCs may have developed valuable FSAs at home. However, the authors go on to add that these FSAs are not as sophisticated or as valuable as those of advanced country MNCs. They distinguish between FSAs that are stand-alone, routines, and recombination capabilities, with the last being the most valuable

Table 13.1 *Key theories of the MNC and their extension from the analysis of EMNCs.*

Theory	Product life cycle	Incremental internationalization	OLI framework	Internalization theory	Integration/differentiation and legitimation models	Resource-based view and knowledge-based view
Initial argument	Vernon (1966)	Johanson and Vahlne (1977)	Dunning (1977)	Buckley and Casson (1976)	Prahalad and Doz (1987)	Penrose (1959)
Assumption on individuals' behavior	Full rationality Imperfect information Information asymmetry	Bounded rationality Imperfect information Information asymmetry	Full rationality Imperfect information Information asymmetry	Bounded rationality Imperfect information Information asymmetry Asset specificity Opportunism	Bounded rationality Imperfect information Information asymmetry Asset specificity	Bounded rationality Imperfect information Information asymmetry Asset specificity
Assumption on objective of foreign expansion	Increase sales by using innovations developed at home and benefit from lower production cost abroad	Increase sales by using knowledge developed at home	Increase sales by building on home-based ownership advantage and obtain location advantage abroad	Increase sales by using technology developed at home	Increase sales by gaining and using knowledge from multiple operations, achieving legitimation	Grow and increase sales by using already-developed firm-specific resources, especially knowledge

Table 13.1 (*cont.*)

Theory	Product life cycle	Incremental internationalization	OLI framework	Internalization theory	Integration/ differentiation and legitimation models	Resource-based view and knowledge-based view
Assumption on impact of home country conditions	Firms innovate to satisfy demanding high-income consumers	Managers develop knowledge specific to home country	Firm creates home-based ownership advantages	Firm develops technology to compete at home	Home-based headquarters pressures firm to standardize and achieve legitimacy	Home country provides inputs that determine resources and knowledge created by the firm
Assumption on impact of host country conditions	High-income consumers abroad induce export of innovation. Lowering costs induce production abroad	Differences in conditions between home and host country limit transfer of information between countries	Host country location advantages induce entry	Transaction protection in host country determines use of firm or market	Host country pressures firm to adapt to local conditions	Host country inputs and competitive conditions determine applicability of home-based resources
Key question on MNC behavior	Where does the MNC move sales and production around the world?	How does an MNC internationalize?	Why does an MNC set production facilities abroad?	How does an MNC internalize cross-border transactions?	How does an MNC solve the tension between global integration and local differentiation?	How does an MNC expand and compete across countries?

Key answer					
MNC moves sales and production from developed to developing countries as an innovation and associated production process become standardized	MNC internationalizes incrementally to minimize risks and obtain experiential knowledge from abroad MNC selects countries and entry modes that minimize risk and commitment	MNC sets up production facilities abroad when it has ownership advantages (O) at home, location advantages (L) abroad, and internalization advantages (I) of keeping the foreign operation within the firm	MNC uses a hierarchy in a cross-border transaction when the costs of using contracts exceed the costs of internalizing the transaction	MNC organizes decision making to benefit from economies of scale and from adaptation to local conditions, achieving legitimation	MNC creates firm-specific assets whose services are used to create products and services, with management being the key constraint to growth at some point in time

Table 13.1 (cont.)

Theory	Product life cycle	Incremental internationalization	OLI framework	Internalization theory	Integration/differentiation and legitimation models	Resource-based view and knowledge-based view
Differing EMNC behavior	EMNC sells innovations in advanced economies to benefit from higher income or in developing countries to benefit from similar consumer needs EMNC is already operating in low-cost countries and does not move production	EMNC chooses between a similar country but small market or dissimilar country but large market EMNC has higher tolerance for risk	EMNC is more likely to expand in search of O advantages EMNCs is more likely to expand in search of L advantages without moving production abroad	EMNC has higher tendency to internalize operations because of higher transaction costs at home	EMNC follows new strategies to take into account the pressures of the country of origin	EMNC internationalizes using resources/knowledge that cannot be protected via institutions EMNC internationalizes to access missing resources/knowledge

Potential theoretical extension from the analysis of EMNCs	Separate similarity in needs from level of income needed to pay for innovation	Separate psychic distance from market attractiveness in the selection of countries	Different types of O and L advantages depending on the country of origin determine internationalization	Managers from different countries have different attitudes toward transaction costs	Home country exerts pressures in addition to headquarters and host country pressures	Create advantages that do not rely on institutions to protect them
	Production does not move abroad to ensure proximity	Managers have levels of risk aversion influenced by home country that affect country selection and entry mode selection	Firms not only enjoy advantages but suffer from disadvantages that induce internationalization			Build advantages using acquisitions

Source: Adapted from Cuervo-Cazurra (2012). The chapters in this volume reinforce these lines of thinking, as discussed below. They help us flesh out how the country of origin of EMNCs affects their firm-specific advantages and their internationalization patterns. We review these two areas in turn.

and the kind lacking in EMNCs. They use case studies of Lenovo, Suzlon, and Tata Motors to bolster their claim that EMNCs lack recombination capabilities or the ability to create new FSAs through foreign subsidiaries based on *host* country CSAs, and show that these firms have delivered poor financial results so far. Whether or not one agrees with their conclusions, Rugman and Nguyen provoke us to think harder and deeper about the nature of FSAs of EMNCs and raise fundamental questions about our understanding of FSAs. Narula's chapter takes the analysis one step further, building on the notion that all firms in a country cannot automatically access a country's CSAs (Hennart, 2012; Ramamurti, 2009), because some CSAs have a "members only" quality that restricts their access to a select few. He argues that many CSAs are not "public goods" but "club goods," and uses this notion to explain why some FSAs are location bound. Note that Narula's point is not limited to EMNCs but a general argument about how firms can (or cannot) turn CSAs into FSAs and whether those FSAs will be internationally mobile.

A different set of interesting issues is raised with respect to the home country of EMNCs. Aharoni wonders whether American companies, if and when they are acquired by a Chinese firm, should thereafter be considered Chinese companies. He asks: "And if indeed they are now Chinese, what does that mean or imply?" Aharoni thus anticipates questions about an MNC's nationality that are explored in greater depth in Barnard's chapter on mobile MNCs. However, for many EMNCs the home country is not ambiguous, because the different criteria by which nationality might be judged are consistent, i.e., the firm's headquarters, owners, main customers, stock listings, and top management team all belong to the same country. In these cases, what can one say about the impact of the home country on a firm's ability to internationalize or the dynamics of its internationalization? Before turning to this important question in the next section, we would like to reiterate the point that "we must not assume EMNEs behave the way they do only because of their roots in emerging markets" (Ramamurti, 2012: 45).

As shown in Figure 13.1, at least two other explanatory variables besides industry are often overlooked when comparing the behavior of EMNCs and advanced country MNCs. The first is the global context in which a firm internationalizes, because the costs, risks, and challenges a firm faces in the course of internationalization are not fixed over time. Indeed, these barriers to internationalization have fallen significantly since World War II, especially in the 1990s and 2000s, making it easier for firms everywhere to internationalize more quickly and easily. Recognizing this is important when analyzing differences in the pace or mode of internationalization by EMNCs versus the way in which MNCs from Europe, the United States, or even Japan internationalized in an earlier period. In his chapter, Godley argues persuasively that historical analysis can yield valuable insights into which aspects of EMNCs' behavior are truly novel and which are not. He notes that many British firms internationalized to acquire FSAs rather than to exploit FSAs developed at home – a feature that is sometimes regarded as novel to EMNCs. Similarly, he notes that German firms went through a period of catching up with British firms in the late nineteenth century, which has parallels with contemporary examples of catch-up by emerging market firms, a topic addressed by Brandl and Mudambi in their chapter. But in making such historical comparisons researchers must take into account the greater ease with which firms can internationalize today than they could fifty or a hundred years ago. We agree with Williamson's suggestion in his chapter that "today's global context" (and its differences with prior global contexts) is an important topic for research by scholars working on EMNCs.

In the same vein, in comparing EMNCs and Western MNEs, one must keep in mind that some of the observed differences may arise from differences in their stage of evolution rather than their country of origin (Ramamurti, 2009: 419). Although some EMNCs expanded beyond their home countries several decades ago, most have done so only recently and they operate in only a few countries. In contrast, large MNCs from advanced economies operate in several countries and have years of experience with global coordination, staffing, and brand building (Chattopadhyay, Batra, and Ozsomer, 2012). One must be careful not to explain an observed behavior of EMNCs by their country of origin when in fact it is properly explained by their stage of development as a multinational firm.

Government support is a feature that the study of EMNCs highlights and that requires additional attention, as Aharoni indicates, but it is not exclusive to them. Although many of the leading EMNCs are state-owned, it is not uncommon to find state-owned multinationals in advanced economies, like in France or Italy, or to find sovereign wealth funds from advanced economies, like Norway or Singapore, investing abroad. Moreover, some large advanced economy MNCs are minority government-owned, such as Renault, which is 15 percent owned by the French state or Volkswagen, which is 20 percent owned by the German state of Lower Saxony.

Another feature incorrectly regarded as a novel feature of EMNCs is their tendency to use cross-border M&As more aggressively than did previous generations of MNCs from Europe or the US. But this again is a result of *when* EMNCs are internationalizing, i.e., in a period when global finance and capital markets were liberalized and firms everywhere found it easier to raise the capital to make bold cross-border acquisitions. In 2012, all but seven of the forty-seven cross-border deals valued at more than US$3billion were done by acquirers from advanced economies (UNCTAD, 2013).

Additionally, there seems to be a general misunderstanding of the overall importance of the rapid rise of EMNCs, which rather than being unique is part of a general trend of rising OFDI. Table 13.2 and Figure 13.2 provide a summary of the evolution of OFDI flows and stocks. Between 1970 and 2012, outward FDI flows from emerging economies did indeed grow from US$0.05bn to US$339.3bn; as a share of world flows they grew from 0.35 percent to 24.4 percent in this period. However, they still represent only a quarter of OFDI flows from advanced economies[2], which grew in these years from US$14.1bn to US$1,051.6bn. In terms of OFDI stock, between 1980 and 2012, the amounts held by emerging economies grew from US$57.6bn to US$2,928.1bn, but as a percentage of the world total it grew only slightly in this period, from 10.50 percent to 12.41 percent. Moreover, if one subtracts OFDI flows from offshore financial centers[3], which are classified as emerging economies but that are often only conduits for

----

[2] We use the list of the International Monetary Fund to classify countries as advanced economies. The IMF (2000) list includes the following: Australia, Austria, Belgium, Canada, Denmark, Finland, France, Germany, Greece, Hong Kong, Iceland, Ireland, Israel, Italy, Japan, Luxembourg, Netherlands, New Zealand, Norway, Portugal, Singapore, South Korea, Spain, Sweden, Switzerland, Taiwan, United Kingdom, and United States. Emerging economies are those that are not classified as advanced.

[3] We use the list of the International Monetary Fund to classify economies as being offshore finance centers. The IMF (2011) list includes the following: Andorra, Anguilla, Aruba, Bahamas, Belize, Bermuda, British Virgin Islands, Cayman Islands, Cook Islands, Cyprus, Gibraltar, Guernsey, Isle of Man, Jersey, Liechtenstein, Macao, Malaysia, Monaco, Montserrat, Netherlands Antilles, Palau, Panama, Samoa, Seychelles, Turks and Caicos Islands, and Vanuatu.

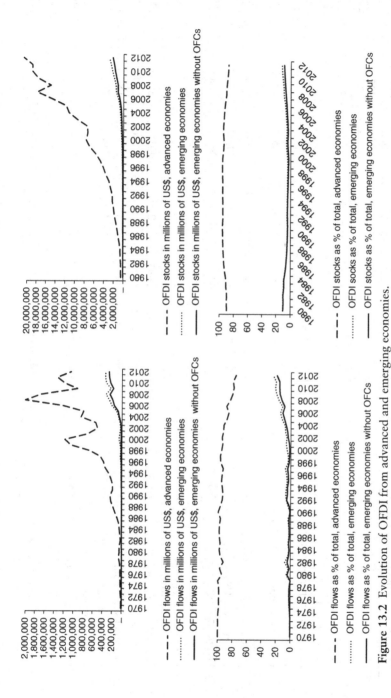

Figure 13.2 Evolution of OFDI from advanced and emerging economies.

Source: Computed using data from UNCTAD (2013) and the IMF (2000) classification of advanced economies and IMF (2011) classification of offshore finance centers (OFCs).

Table 13.2 OFDI flows and stocks from emerging and advanced economies, selected years.

Emerging economies	1970	1975	1980	1985	1990	1995	2000	2005	2010	2012
OFDI flows in US$m	50	494	2,952	2,124	1,107	7,847	62,692	109,902	322,785	339,307
OFDI stocks in US$m	n.a.	n.a.	57,672	68,306	93,291	168,727	352,351	779,372	2,280,076	2,928,130
OFDI flows as percentage of world total	0.35	1.73	5.72	3.42	0.46	4.91	5.05	12.16	21.45	24.39
OFDI stocks as percentage of world total	n.a.	n.a.	10.50	7.60	4.46	4.45	4.39	6.20	10.79	12.41
Emerging economies minus OFCs	**1970**	**1975**	**1980**	**1985**	**1990**	**1995**	**2000**	**2005**	**2010**	**2012**
OFDI flows in US$m	40	389	2,286	1,619	2,118	11,085	18,954	80,246	235,416	269,108
OFDI stocks in US$m	n.a.	n.a.	56,545	65,768	87,313	143,305	233,595	559,107	1,701,631	2,211,730
OFDI flows as percentage of world total	0.28	1.36	4.43	2.61	0.88	3.05	1.53	8.88	15.64	19.35
OFDI stocks as percentage of world total	n.a.	n.a.	10.30	7.32	4.17	3.78	2.91	4.44	8.05	9.37
Advanced economies	**1970**	**1975**	**1980**	**1985**	**1990**	**1995**	**2000**	**2005**	**2010**	**2012**
OFDI flows in US$m	14,101	28,099	48,624	59,920	240,315	345,675	1,177,624	793,862	1,182,143	1,051,649
OFDI stocks in US$m	n.a.	n.a.	491,393	830,466	1,998,205	3,623,970	7,674,210	11,799,437	18,849,974	20,664,620
OFDI flows as percentage of world total	99.65	98.27	94.28	96.58	99.54	95.09	94.95	87.84	78.55	75.61
OFDI stocks as percentage of world total	n.a.	n.a.	89.50	92.40	95.54	95.55	95.61	93.80	89.21	87.59

Source: Computed using data from UNCTAD (2013) using the IMF (2000) classification of advanced economies and IMF (2011) classification of offshore finance centers (OFCs). n.a.: not available.

investment by advanced economy firms, the share of emerging economies in global OFDI stocks drops from 10.30 percent in 1980 to 9.37 percent in 2012.

EMNCs' country of origin and internationalization dynamics

EMNCs and advanced economy MNCs share many common features as multinationals, but the country of origin of EMNCs results in some particular internationalization patterns. This is the argument made in Lessard's chapter and the RAT-CAT framework, whereby the particular resources and capabilities developed at home result in distinct internationalization needs and patterns.

We suggest two main drivers of unique EMNC internationalization. The first one is the underdeveloped economy that characterizes emerging countries, with a majority of consumers having low levels of income and an economic structure with limited providers of sophisticated technology and services. The second distinct driver is the underdeveloped institutions that bedevil many emerging countries, with unclear rules and regulations that are not predictably applied. These two drivers induce domestic firms in emerging countries to develop particular resources and capabilities that can help them internationalize; we term these positive influences. However, the underdevelopment of the country of origin on some occasions forces firms to internationalize and escape to foreign countries; we call these negative influences. Table 13.3 summarizes the resulting two-by-two classification and the ideas we discuss now. This discussion of positive and negative influences is similar to the pull and push approach adopted by Fleury and Fleury in their explanation of the particular patterns of internationalization followed by Brazilian MNCs in response to the particular conditions of the country of origin, as well as by Pedersen and Stucchi in their analysis of the dual influence of business group affiliation on the internationalization of member firms.

Undeveloped economic systems and the internationalization of EMNCs

The underdevelopment of the economy takes the form of not only a large number of relatively poor consumers, but also a lower

Table 13.3 *Impact of the economic and institutional underdevelopment of emerging countries on the EMNCs' internationalization.*

		Impact of characteristics of the home country on the firms' international competitiveness and internationalization	
		Positive: Home country characteristics induce firm to develop resources and capabilities that support its advantage and internationalization	**Negative:** Home country characteristics force firm to internationalize to solve disadvantages
Distinct characteristic of emerging countries	**Underdeveloped economy:** Prevalence of low-income consumers and underdeveloped providers of services	**Trickle-up innovation:** Managers innovate products or business models to better serve the needs of a large segment of low-income people in the emerging country and then internationalize to (1) serve low-income consumers in emerging countries, (2) serve low-income consumers in advanced countries, or (2) serve high-income consumers in advanced countries who do not want to pay a premium for products	**Technological escape:** Managers internationalize their firms to compensate for the underdeveloped infrastructure and obtain sophisticated technology from firms in advanced economies by (1) reverse engineering and copying products from advanced economy firms, (2) getting technological licenses from advanced economy firms, (3) establishing alliances with advanced economy firms, or (4) acquiring firms in advanced economies to improve home operations
		Self-reliant innovation: Managers innovate products, manufacturing process, or business models to reduce the dependence on unreliable infrastructure in the emerging country and then internationalize to (1) serve consumers with underdeveloped infrastructure in emerging economies, (2) serve consumers in advanced economies with underdeveloped infrastructure in remote areas, or (3) serve consumers in advanced economies with reliable infrastructure with a more efficient production system	**Marketing escape:** Managers internationalize their firms to compensate for the discrimination of the country of origin by customers and modify the country of origin by (1) adopting an advanced economy name, (2) claiming an advanced country of design or manufacturing, (3) obtaining an advanced economy brand that compensates for the perception of the country of origin of production

| Underdeveloped institutions: Prevalence of unclear pro-market rules and regulations and unclear application of pro-market rules and regulations | Improvisation management: Managers learn to improvise to deal with unclear rules and regulations and use this ability to internationalize the firm by (1) entering more diverse countries and (2) being more willing to take risks abroad

Self-reliance management: Managers learn to control operations to deal with the uncertainty in the application of rules and regulations and use this ability to internationalize the firm by seeking higher levels of control of foreign operations | Institutional escape: Managers internationalize their firms to compensate for the deficiencies in institutions of the country of origin and enter countries with higher corporate governance standards to signal their commitment to protecting investor rights

Discriminatory escape: Managers internationalize their firms to compensate for the discrimination of the country of origin by host country governments and move legal incorporation to an advanced economy |

sophistication of supporting infrastructure, both hard infrastructure, such as telecommunications or transportation, and soft infrastructure, such as suppliers and distributors (Khanna and Palepu, 2010). This relatively low level of economic development of emerging countries has both positive and negative influences on the firm's internationalization. Positive influences are the ones whereby companies create innovations to address the economic underdevelopment that can help them not only compete at home but also abroad. Negative influences are the ones whereby firms are forced to internationalize to address the economic underdevelopment of the home country.

Positive. A large proportion of the population with low levels of income can be seen as a competitive disadvantage, but it can also force companies to create new products that are ultra-affordable (Prahalad, 2004). Such innovation goes beyond producing a product that has a low price because the production costs in the emerging country are lower. The innovation requires the redesign of the product so that essential features are maintained and the overall price of the product is reduced (e.g., simple cell phones with multiple addresses for multiple users in developing countries), or the rethinking of the payment system so that the effective cash paid by consumers is reduced, even if the price is not (e.g., offering low-income customers the option to make biweekly payments to purchase durable goods over extended periods of time). This idea of the firm using the conditions of the location to create innovations builds on Narula's argument that the location advantages are limited to certain firms rather than being available to all firms, as many studies tend to assume. A large population with low income levels can help firms create innovations, but it is not automatic that all firms will be able to create such innovations just by being exposed to low-income customers.

These innovations not only help some firms compete and serve customers at home, but also help them become multinationals. One way is to use these innovations in other emerging economies with similar large numbers of low-income consumers. This follows a similar logic as the explanation of internationalization discussed by Vernon (1966); he argued that advanced economy firms created innovations for wealthy consumers and then sold them to wealthy consumers in other advanced economies. A more creative internationalization is via trickle-up innovation (Govindarajan and Ramamurti, 2011), when the company uses innovations generated to serve low-income consumers at home to enter advanced countries to serve wealthy customers there. Wealthy consumers purchase the innovation not because they do not have the income to buy a higher priced product, but because they prefer to pay less for a good enough product or value features such as simplicity of design and ease of use that were developed to serve low-income consumers.

In addition to innovating to serve poor consumers, a company in an emerging economy can innovate to deal with underdeveloped infrastructure. The firm may have to redesign products to be self-reliant (e.g., high alcohol content beer to ensure quality during transportation in countries with no reliable cold chains), or the firm may engage in organizational innovations in its operations and value chain, internalizing the infrastructure that in advanced countries is externalized (e.g., having back-up generators to produce electricity when the electric grid is down). These innovations addressing the constraints of the environment have been termed *jugaad* innovation (Radjou, Prabhu, and Ahuja, 2012).

Such innovations can be used to help the firm become a multinational and enter countries with similar conditions, as well as more advanced countries to serve customers that have limited access to infrastructure, for example in rural or remote areas, or to serve consumers that temporarily lack access to infrastructure, such as recreational campers or in the aftermath of natural disasters. Additionally, organizational innovations can be the basis for the advantage in other countries, not only similar developing countries with unreliable infrastructure, but also advanced countries, where local rivals may not have mastered techniques of low-cost production.

Negative. However, the economic underdevelopment of the country may alternatively detract from the firm's ability to build a competitive advantage, inducing managers to internationalize their firms and escape the underdevelopment of the home country.

The emerging market firm may engage in technological escape, entering more advanced countries to obtain technologies unavailable at home. The educational and innovation system in emerging countries is likely to not be up to par with advanced economies, limiting the ability of the firm to developed advanced technologies. Universities and technical colleges may not produce enough graduates in advanced fields; primary education may not be good, limiting the ability of employees not only to generate technology but also to use advanced imported technology; and the government may not support innovation or provide the necessary protection of intellectual property rights.

Technological escape can take several forms as the firm accesses foreign technology using alternative methods. First, it can be done by importing foreign technology, either as part of a technology transfer agreement with a provider from an advanced country or by merely reverse engineering foreign products and copying how the products are designed (Chittoor et al., 2009; Luo, Sun, and Wang, 2011). Second, the firm may establish alliances with firms from advanced economies, helping these access the local market or factors of production in exchange for learning how to produce more sophisticated products or how to organize production more efficiently (Kumaraswamy et al., 2012). Third, the firm in the developing country may choose to acquire a firm in an advanced economy to obtain sophisticated technology; by achieving control it can transfer the sophisticated technology to the home operation by training its employees in the advanced country on how to use the technology (Madhok and Keyhani, 2012).

The firm may want to engage in marketing escape to avoid the negative perception of underdevelopment of the country of origin on its products. Consumers rely on the country of origin of a product as a cue to assess its quality (Bilkey and Nes, 1982) and products from emerging markets tend to be perceived as inferior because they are associated with the lower level of development. To avoid this association, the emerging market firm may internationalize. The company can change the brandname to facilitate its association with a different country (e.g., the Chinese white goods firm Haier was originally called Qingdao Refrigerator but changed its name to the German-sounding Haier). Alternatively, the company can purchase brands in advanced countries to which consumers have a positive association to reduce the association with the emerging country. This differs from acquiring local brands to enter a country quickly, which is done not only by developing country firms but also by many advanced economy firms.

Undeveloped institutions and the internationalization of EMNCs

The underdevelopment of institutions in emerging markets has both positive and negative impacts on the internationalization of firms. Many emerging countries have underdeveloped institutions, but this does not mean that emerging countries lack institutions. Institutions are the norms and regulations that facilitate economic and social relationships, and all countries have them. However, emerging economies have less developed pro-market institutions, or norms and regulations that facilitate market transactions. In many emerging economies, rules and regulations are unclear, partly because many emerging countries have been moving from high levels of government intervention in the economy toward a more open and pro-market system, and in many cases the old rules and regulations have not been fully repealed. As a result, the application of the rules and regulations is unclear.

Positive. Underdeveloped institutions in emerging countries induce firms to improvise. To accommodate the uncertainty in rules and regulations and their application, managers develop a more flexible view of rules and regulations, being willing to bend and bypass them with some creativity. This flexibility regarding rules and regulations is captured in the Brazilian concept of *jeitinho*, with managers finding creative ways to get around rules, and asking for forgiveness later rather than for permission before.

This ability to improvise in the face of uncertain rules and regulations can then be used in the internationalization of EMNCs. Improvisation management can be used not only to enter countries in which rules are also unpredictable, like other emerging countries, which would be the natural advantage of these firms (Cuervo-Cazurra and Genc, 2008), but also to internationalize more widely and into countries that are very different from the country of origin (Luo and Tung, 2007). The manager can use this improvisation ability to deal with the differences across countries. This ability is reinforced in business groups, as the chapter by Pedersen and Stucchi highlights, because affiliated firms can draw not only on their own abilities to improvise but also those of sister firms in the group.

Alternatively, managers may develop a self-reliant management style that influences the internationalization of their firms. The application of the rules in emerging countries may not be as predictable as in advanced economies because the agencies that implement the rules and the judicial system that solves disputes are not as efficient and do not always follow the rule of law. Thus, managers in developing countries develop a self-reliant management, relying more on interpersonal relationships, the establishment of personal trust on the counterparty, and social mechanisms to enforce contracts, because they cannot rely on the legal and judicial system to enforce contracts consistently. This is reflected in developing country firms having a higher degree of vertical integration and wider diversification (Khanna and Yafeh, 2007). This experience of internalizing many of the economic relationships to reduce the potential for expropriation is carried over to foreign operations, with managers of EMNCs having a higher initial tendency to control foreign operations than managers in advanced countries.

Negative. The underdevelopment of institutions can also have a negative consequence on the firm and induce it to follow institutional escape, internationalizing into countries that have more developed institutions to deal with the limitations of the home country (Witt and Lewin, 2007). Operating in a country with underdeveloped institutions may mean that corporate governance mechanisms are not well functioning. As a result, the firm faces challenges in its ability to obtain capital because potential investors are deterred by the lack of protection for investors (Djankov et al., 2002). Managers of the best run companies in emerging markets may be forced to internationalize and seek finance in advanced economies with better corporate governance, signaling that their firms are better and willing to implement stricter corporate governance controls (Coffee, 2002).

Additionally, managers of emerging country firms may follow a discriminatory escape and invest in advanced countries to reduce the negative perception that some host governments have against investments by firms from emerging countries. This is one of the points made in Barnard's chapter about migrating MNCs and their search for legitimacy abroad. The weak institutions in the developing country may create misconceptions regarding the objective and ability of the firm in protecting rights and fulfilling contracts. Governments in advanced countries may discriminate against firms from emerging countries because they perceive that they are not able to uphold good governance standards, ensure the safety and rights of their workers, or have tight links with governments they find unsavory. To avoid the link with the home country and the discrimination by the host country the company may be forced to move headquarters to a more advanced country. This movement can also help get around politically motivated trade embargoes against particular countries, with the firm uprooting to countries not subject to the embargo.

A research agenda for the future

The preceding chapters and the ideas presented before outline several themes in which the analysis of EMNCs can help add new insights to our understanding of MNCs. Future studies can build on these ideas in several ways: uniqueness of EMNC behavior, capability development in EMNCs, internationalization of EMNCs, and the evolution of the relationship between EMNCs and their countries of origin.

First, future studies need to be more careful in making claims that EMNCs are unique. Researchers need to take a step back and reflect not only on what we already know about MNCs in general but also whether or not MNCs from advanced economies will show similar patterns of behavior. Studies of EMNCs need comparison with a control group, whether directly in the empirical analysis or indirectly in the theoretical analysis, to be able to differentiate what is truly unique about EMNCs from what advanced economy MNCs may do as well, as Aharoni and Godley caution. These comparisons have already resulted in the identification of some influences on EMNC behavior that are not the result of the country of origin but rather are driven by other influences that can affect advanced economy MNCs as well, such as industry, stage of evolution as a multinational, or the context of globalization, as Ramamurti (2012) indicates. Other influences that may be interesting to analyze and that may not be exclusive to emerging countries are the impact of belonging to a business group or being owned by the state, as Aharoni as well as Pedersen and Stucci indicate.

Second, when analyzing the development of resources and capabilities in an emerging market context, future studies can analyze the positive and negative influences of the lower level of development of the home country. On the one hand, by being in a less developed country EMNCs can benefit from the advances made by firms in developed countries and imitate what those firms have done, using them as benchmarks, as Brandl and Mudambi indicate. Additionally, operating in countries in which intellectual property rights are weakly protected can be beneficial for the firms as they can copy technology and innovations with impunity. Moreover, the company may be able to make use of large numbers of trained and relatively inexpensive engineers and scientists to reverse engineer and improve existing technologies, although the access to such location advantages may not be automatic as Narula indicates. On the other hand, the lower level of development of the country does create limitation in the firm's ability to generate sophisticated resources and capabilities and may force it to seek external support, forcing it to move abroad in search of the technology, intellectual property protection, or skilled engineers and scientists that are lacking at home, as Williamson notes. Additionally, the lack of protection of intellectual property can force firms to develop capabilities that are organizationally complex and difficult to copy by competitors because other kinds of advantage may be easily copied. These capabilities, which may be appropriate for operating at home and tied to particular conditions there, may be more difficult to move to other countries and thus limit the firm's ability to compete globally, as Rugman and Nguyen as well as Narula indicate.

Third, the internationalization process of EMNCs can shed new light on the home country's influence on the international behavior of firms, and on how the lack of development of the country has a positive and negative influence on its internationalization. The lack of development in the economy and institutions can lead EMNCs to develop product, process, organizational, and managerial innovations that support their internationalization not only in other emerging countries but also in more advanced countries, as Lessard indicates. Alternatively, this same lack of development induces firms to seek the technological, marketing, institutional, and discriminatory escape from the home country, as Williamson and Barnard note. Beyond these influences, additional topics that future research can analyze are the management of the international operations of EMNCs, and how the lower level of development of the home country affects not just the international expansion but also the management of foreign operations. Thus, in addition to limited low-cost capital that is typical of emerging countries, and that can constrain the ability of EMNCs to invest abroad, EMNCs may face limitations due to a limited supply of skilled and experienced managers in the home country who know how to manage foreign operations. This plays a large role when the firm is accessing a more advanced country for technology and needs to manage the transfer of such technology to the home country; the EMNC may lack the experience and ability to transfer much of the technology, as this is embedded within the larger innovation and educational system in the advanced country. Additionally, expatriate managers who come from emerging countries may not receive the same respect as managers who come from advanced countries, even within the foreign subsidiary of the EMNC, further complicating their international expansion. Other challenges that EMNCs are likely to experience, such as limited internationalization experience within the firm or the need to readjust the organizational structure of the company as foreign operations grow in importance, are common to advanced economy MNCs in the early stages of multinationalization, as Narula and Meyer caution in their respective chapters.

Fourth, a final area in which to analyze EMNCs is the evolution of these firms and the relationships with their countries of origin. The influence of the home country, both as the main source of resources and advantages and also a source of disadvantages, will gradually decrease over time as the EMNC operates in multiple countries and is able to draw from sources of advantages in other countries. However, it may be the case that the country of origin starts losing some of its influence on some dimensions of the firm, such as being the primary source of competitive advantage and funds, but not on others, such as having most top managers from the emerging country and influencing how the firm is run. Another interesting evolution to study is how the development of the home country alters its influence on the advantage and internationalization of the EMNC. As emerging countries achieve advanced economy status, the advantages and disadvantages of firms change and subsequently affect their internationalization process, but managers may maintain a historical memory of coming from an emerging country that results in different attitudes and decisions. The analysis of firms from, for example, Taiwan, South Korea, Hong Kong, or Singapore that have internationalized in the 2000s can offer interesting insights in this process.

Conclusion

EMNCs have received much attention in recent times but not all studies distinguish carefully between behaviors that are applicable to all MNCs and those that are truly peculiar to EMNCs. In this volume we have tried not to lose sight of that important distinction. We propose that the unique features of EMNCs result from two home country features – economic underdevelopment and institutional underdevelopment. Existing theories are appropriate for explaining much of their behavior as MNCs, but in the early stages of internationalization, when the country of origin exerts a large influence on firms, the lower level of economic and institutional development of emerging economies seems to lead to material differences between EMNCs and AMNCs.

This chapter distills many of the arguments presented in the previous chapters and tries to improve our understanding of EMNCs in particular and MNCs in general. First, it identifies distinct drivers that result in particular behaviors of EMNCs, providing not just a description of EMNC behavior but also an explanation of why these firms behave as they do. Second, it explains how the lower level of development of the home country of EMNCs results in particular sources of competitive advantage and particular patterns of evolution, as well as in positive and negative motivations for internationalization. Finally, we summarized four themes for future research to improve our theories of EMNCs and MNCs.

We hope that international business and strategy scholars will pursue these questions – and others proposed in the individual chapters of this volume – to improve our understanding of EMNCs and our theories of MNCs.

References

Aggarwal, R. and Agmon, T. 1990. The international success of developing country firms: Role of government-directed comparative advantage. *Management International Review*, 30: 163–180.

Aliber, R. Z. 1970. A theory of foreign direct investment. In C. P. Kindleberger (ed.), *The International Corporation*: 17–34. Cambridge, MA: MIT Press.

Aulakh, P. S. 2007. Emerging multinationals from developing economies: Motivations, paths and performance. *Journal of International Management*, 13: 338–355.

Aulakh, P. S., Kotabe, M., and Teegen, H. 2000. Export strategies and performance of firms from emerging economies: Evidence from Brazil, Chile, and Mexico. *Academy of Management Journal*, 43: 342–361.

Bilkey, W. J. and Nes, E. 1982. Country-of-origin effects on products evaluations. *Journal of International Business Studies*, 13: 89–99.

Buckley, P. J. and Casson, M. C. 1976. *The Future of the Multinational Enterprise*. New York: Holmes & Meier.

Chattopadhyay, A., Batra, R., and Ozsomer, A. 2012. *The New Emerging Market Multinationals: Four Strategies for Disrupting Markets and Building Brands*. New York: McGraw Hill.

Chittoor, R., Sarkar, M. B., Ray, S., and Aulakh, P. 2009. Third-World copycats to emerging multinationals: Institutional changes and organizational transformation in the Indian pharmaceutical industry. *Organization Science*, 20: 187–205.

Coffee, Jr. J. C. 2002. Racing towards the top?: The impact of cross-listings and stock market competition on international corporate governance. *Columbia Law Review*, 102: 1757–1831.

Cuervo-Cazurra, A. 2008. The multinationalization of developing country MNEs: The case of Multilatinas. *Journal of International Management*, 14: 138–154.

2012. How the analysis of developing country multinational companies helps advance theory: Solving the Goldilocks debate. *Global Strategy Journal*, 2: 153–167.

Cuervo-Cazurra, A. and Genc, M. 2008. Transforming disadvantages into advantages: Developing country MNEs in the least developed countries. *Journal of International Business Studies*, 39: 957–979.

Djankov, S., La Porta, R., Lopez-De-Silanes, F., and Shleifer, A. 2002. The regulation of entry. *Quarterly Journal of Economics*, 117: 1–37.

Dunning, J. 1977. Trade, location of economic activity and the MNE: A search for an eclectic approach. In B. Ohlin, P. O. Hesselborn, and P. M. Wijkman (eds.), *The International Allocation of Economic Activity*: 395–418. London: Macmillan.

Ghymn, K. I. 1980. Multinational enterprises from the third world. *Journal of International Business Studies*, 11: 118–122.

Govindarajan, V. and Ramamurti, R. 2011. Reverse innovation, emerging markets and global strategy. *Global Strategy Journal*, 1: 191–205.

Guillén, M. F. and Garcia-Canal, E. 2009. The American model of the multinational firm and the "new" multinationals from emerging economies. *Academy of Management Perspectives*, 23: 23–35.

Heenan, D. A. and Keegan, W. J. 1979. The rise of third world multinationals. *Harvard Business Review*, 57(1): 101–109.

Hennart, J-F. 2012. Emerging market multinationals and the theory of the multinational enterprise. *Global Strategy Journal*, 2: 168–187.

IMF. 2000. *World Economic Outlook*. Washington, DC: International Monetary Fund.

2011. Offshore Financial Centers (OFCs): IMF Staff Assessments. www.imf.org/external/NP/ofca/OFCA.aspx. Accessed September 13, 2013.

Johanson, J. and Vahlne, J. E. 1977. The internationalization process of the firm: A model of knowledge development and increasing foreign market commitments. *Journal of International Business Studies*, 8: 23–32.

Khanna, T. and Palepu, K. G. 2010. *Winning in Emerging Markets: A Road Map for Strategy and Execution*. Boston, MA: Harvard University Press.

Khanna, T. and Yafeh, Y. 2007. Business groups in emerging markets: Paragons or parasites? *Journal of Economic Literature*, 45: 331–372.

Kotabe, M., Jiang, C. X., and Murray, J. Y. 2011. Managerial ties, knowledge acquisition, realized absorptive capacity and new product market performance of emerging multinational companies: A case of China. *Journal of World Business*, 46: 166–176.

Kumar, K. R. and McLeod, M. (eds.). 1981. *Multinationals from Developing Countries*. Lexington, MA: Lexington Books.

Kumaraswamy, A., Mudambi, R., Saranga, H., and Tripathy, A. 2012. Catch-up strategies in the Indian auto components industry: Domestic firms' responses to market liberalization. *Journal of International Business Studies*, 43: 368–395.

Lall, S. 1983. *The New Multinationals: The Spread of Third World Enterprises*. New York: Wiley.

Lecraw, D. J. 1977. Direct investment by firms from less developed countries. *Oxford Economic Papers*, 29: 445–457.

1993. Outward direct investment by Indonesian firms: Motivation and effects. *Journal of International Business Studies*, 24: 589–600.

Luo, Y. and Tung, R. L. 2007. International expansion of emerging market enterprises: A springboard perspective. *Journal of International Business Studies*, 38: 481–498.

Luo, Y. D., Sun, J., and Wang, S. L. 2011. Emerging economy copycats: Capability, environment and strategy. *Academy of Management Perspective*, 25: 37–56.

Madhok, A. and Keyhani, M. 2012. Acquisitions as entrepreneurship: Asymmetries, opportunities, and the internationalization of multinationals from emerging economies. *Global Strategy Journal*, 2: 26–40.

Mathews, J. A. 2006. Dragon multinationals: New players in 21st century globalization. *Asia Pacific Journal of Management*, 23: 5–27.

Penrose, E. T. 1959. *The Theory of the Growth of the Firm*. Oxford University Press.

Prahalad, C. K. 2004. *The Fortune at the Bottom of the Pyramid: Eradicating Poverty through Profits*. Philadelphia: Wharton Business School Press.

Prahalad, C. K. and Doz, Y. L. 1987. *The Multinational Mission: Balancing Local Demands and Global Vision*. New York: The Free Press.

Radjou, N., Prabhu, J., and Ahuja, S. 2012. *Jugaad Innovation: Think Frugal, Be Flexible, Generate Breakthrough Growth*. San Francisco, CA: Jossey-Bass.

Ramamurti, R. 2009. What have we learned about emerging market multinationals? In R. Ramamurti and J. V. Singh (eds.), *Emerging Multinationals in Emerging Markets*. Cambridge University Press.

2012. What is really different about emerging market multinationals? *Global Strategy Journal*, 2: 41–47.

Ramamurti, R. and Singh, J. V. (eds.). 2009. *Emerging Multinationals in Emerging Markets*. Cambridge University Press.

Rugman, A. M. 2009. Theoretical aspects of MNEs from emerging economies. In R. Ramamurti and J. V. Singh (eds.), *Emerging Multinationals from Emerging Markets*. Cambridge University Press.

2010. Do we need a new theory to explain emerging market MNEs? In K. P. Sauvant, W. A. Maschek, and G. A. McAllister (eds.), *Foreign Direct Investments from Emerging Markets: The Challenges Ahead*. New York: Palgrave McMillan.

Ulgado, F. M., Yu, C. M. J., and Negandhi, A. R. 1994. Multinational enterprises from Asian developing countries: Management and organizational characteristics. *International Business Review*, 3: 123–133.

UNCTAD. 2013. UNCTADStat. http://unctadstat.unctad.org/Report Folders/reportFolders.aspx?sRF_ActivePath=p,5&sRF_Expanded=,p,5. Accessed September 13, 2013.

Vernon, R. 1966. International investment and international trade in the product cycle. *Quarterly Journal of Economics*, 80: 190–207.

Vernon-Wortzel, H. and Wortzel, L. H. 1988. Globalizing strategies for multinationals from developing countries. *Columbia Journal of World Business*, 23: 27–35.

Wells, L. T. 1983. *Third World Multinationals*. Cambridge, MA: MIT Press.

Williamson, P., Ramamurti, R., Fleury, A., and Fleury, M. T. (eds.). 2013. *Competitive Advantages of Emerging Country Multinationals*. Cambridge University Press.

Witt, M. A. and Lewin, A. Y. 2007. Outward foreign direct investment as escape response to home country institutional constraints. *Journal of International Business Studies*, 38: 579–594.

Yeung, H. W. C. 1994. Third World multinationals revisited: A research critique and future agenda. *Third World Quarterly*, 15: 297–317.

1999. Competing in the global economy: The globalization of business firms from emerging economies. In H. W. C. Yeung (ed.), *The Globalization of Business Firms from Emerging Economies*. Cheltenham: Edward Elgar.

Young, S., Huang, C. H., and McDermott, M. 1996. Internationalization and competitive catch-up processes: Case study evidence on Chinese multinational enterprises. *Management International Review*, 36: 295–314.

Further reading

This is an incomplete but useful guide to the literature created using recommendations from the conference speakers, especially Klaus Meyer.

Aggarwal, R. and Agmon, T. 1990. The international success of developing country firms: Role of government-directed comparative advantage. *Management International Review*, 30: 163–180.

Aharoni, Y. 1966. *The Foreign Investment Decision Process*. Harvard University, Graduate School of Business Administration, Division of Research.

2009. Israeli multinationals: Competing from a small open economy. In R. Ramamurti and J. V. Singh (eds.), *Emerging Multinationals in Emerging Markets*: 352–396. Cambridge University Press.

2010. Behavioral elements in foreign direct investment. In T. M. DeVinney, T. Pedersen, and L. Tihanyi (eds.), *The Past, Present and Future of International Business and Management*: 73–111. Bingley, UK: Emerald.

Aharoni, Y. and Ramamurti, R. 2011. Evolution of multinationals. In R. Ramamurti and N. Hashai (eds.), *The Future of Foreign Direct Investment and the Multinational Enterprise*: 113–136. Bingley, UK: Emerald.

Alon, M. T. 2010. Institutional analysis and the determinants of Chinese FDI, *Multinational Business Review*, 18: 1–24.

Ang, S. and Michailova, S. 2008. Institutional explanations of cross-border alliance modes: The case of emerging economies firms. *Management International Review*, 48: 551–576.

Athreye, S. and Cantwell, J. 2007. Creating competition? Globalisation and the emergence of new technology producers. *Research Policy*, 36: 209–226.

Athreye, S. and Kapur, S. 2009. Introduction: The internationalization of Chinese and Indian firms – trends, motivations and strategy. *Industrial and Corporate Change*, 18: 209–221.

Aulakh, P. S. 2007. Emerging multinationals from developing economies: Motivations, paths and performance. *Journal of International Management*, 13: 338–355.

Awate, S., Larsen, M., and Mudambi, R. 2012. EMNE catch-up strategies in the wind turbine industry: Is there a trade-off between output and innovation capabilities? *Global Strategy Journal*, 2: 205–223.

Aybar, B. and Ficici, A. 2009. Cross-border acquisitions and firm value: An analysis of emerging market multinationals. *Journal of International Business Studies*, 40: 1317–1338.

Banalieva, E. R. and Sarathy, R. 2011. A contingency theory of internationalization-performance for emerging market multinational enterprises. *Management International Review*, 51: 593–634.

Bangara, A., Freeman, S., and Schroder, W. 2012. Legitimacy and accelerated internationalization: An Indian perspective. *Journal of World Business*, 47(4): 623–634.

Barnard, H. 2008. Capability development and the geographic destination of outbound FDI by developing country firms. *International Journal of Technology and Globalisation*, 4: 39–55.

2010. Overcoming the liability of foreignness without strong firm capabilities – the value of market-based resources. *Journal of International Management*, 16: 165–176.

Bartlett, C. A. and Ghoshal, S. 2000. Going global: Lessons from late movers. *Harvard Business Review*, 78: 132–142.

Becker-Ritterspach, F. and Bruche, G. 2012. Capability creation and internationalization with business group embeddedness – the case of Tata Motors in passenger cars. *European Management Journal*, 30: 232–247.

Bhaumik, S. K. and Driffield, N., 2011. Direction of outward FDI of EMNEs: Evidence from the Indian pharmaceutical sector. *Thunderbird International Business Review*, 53(5): 615–628.

Bhaumik, S. K., Driffield, N., and Pal, S. 2010. Does ownership structure of emerging market firms affect their outward FDI? The case of the Indian automotive and pharmaceutical sectors. *Journal of International Business Studies*, 41: 437–450.

Boisot, M. and Meyer, W. 2008. Which way through the open door? Reflections on the internationalization of Chinese firms. *Management Organization Review*, 4: 349–366.

Bonaglia, F., Goldstein, A., and Mathews, J. A. 2007. Accelerated internationalization by emerging markets' multinationals: The case of the white goods sector. *Journal of World Business*, 42: 369–383.

BCG. 2006. *The New Global Challengers: How 100 Top Companies from Rapidly Developing Economies Are Changing the World*. Boston, MA: Boston Consulting Group.

2008. *The 2008 BCG 100 New Global Challengers: How Top Companies from Rapidly Developing Economies Are Changing the World*. Boston, MA: Boston Consulting Group.

2009. *The 2009 BCG 100 New Global Challengers: How Companies from Rapidly Developing Economies Are Contending for Global Leadership*. Boston, MA: Boston Consulting Group.

2011. *BCG Global Challengers. Companies on the Move: Rising Stars from Rapidly Developing Economies Are Reshaping Global Industries.* Boston, MA: Boston Consulting Group.

2013. *Allies and Adversaries: 2013 BCG Global Challengers*. Boston, MA: Boston Consulting Group.

Bromfield, T. and Barnard, H. 2010. The evolution of the intellectual property management strategy of an emerging multinational: Learning the purpose of patenting and scientific publications. *IEEE Transactions on Engineering Management*, 57: 118–131.

Bruche, G. 2012. Emerging Indian pharma multinationals: Latecomer catch-up strategies in a globalised high-tech industry. *European Journal of International Management*, 6: 300–322.

Buck, T., Liu, X., Wei, Y., and Liu, X. 2009. The trade development path and export spillovers in China. *Management International Review*, 47: 683–706.

Buckley, P. J., Clegg J., Cross A., Liu, X., Voss H., and Zheng, P. 2007. The determinants of Chinese outward FDI. *Journal of International Business Studies*, 38: 499–518.

Buckley, P. J., Clegg, J., Cross, A., Rhodes, H., Voss, H., and Zheng, P. 2008. Explaining China's outward FDI: An institutional perspective. In K. Sauvant (ed.), *The Rise of Transnational Corporations from Emerging Markets*. Cheltenham: Elgar.

Buckley, P. J., Cross, A. R., Tan, H., Xin, L., and Voss, H. 2008. Historic and emergent trends in Chinese outward direct investment. *Management International Review*, 48: 715–747.

Cai, K. G. 1999. Outward foreign direct investment: A novel dimension of China's integration into the regional and global economy. *China Quarterly*, 160: 856–880.

Cardoza, G. and Fornes, G. 2011. The internationalisation of SMEs from China: The case of Ningxia Hui Autonomous Region. *Asia Pacific Journal of Management*, 28: 737–759.

Chang, S. J. and Rhee, J. H. 2011. Rapid FDI expansion and firm performance. *Journal of International Business Studies*, 42: 979–994.

Chen, H., Hu, M. Y., and Hu, P. S. 2002. Ownership strategy of multinationals from ASEAN: The case of their investment in Sino-foreign joint ventures. *Management International Review*, 42: 309–326.

Chen, S. and Tan, H. 2012. Region effects in the internationalization–performance relationship in Chinese firms. *Journal of World Business*, 17: 73–80.

Chen, S. H. 2004. Taiwanese IT firms' offshore R&D in China and the connection with the global innovation network. *Research Policy*, 33: 337–349.

Chen, V. Z., Li, J., and Shapiro, D. 2012. International reverse spill-over effects on parent firms: Evidences from emerging-market MNEs in developed markets. *European Management Journal*, 30: 204–218.

Chen, W. 2011. The effect of investor origin on firm performance: Domestic and foreign investment in the United States. *Journal of International Economics*, 83: 218–228.

Chen, Y. Y. and Young, M. N. 2010. Cross-border mergers and acquisitions by Chinese listed companies: A principal–principal perspective. *Asia Pacific Journal of Management*, 27: 523–539.

Child, J. and Rodrigues, S. B. 2005. The internationalization of Chinese firms: A case for theoretical extension? *Management and Organization Review*, 1: 381–410.

Chittoor, R. and Ray, S. 2007. Internationalization paths of Indian pharmaceutical firms: A strategic group analysis. *Journal of International Management*, 13, 338–355.

Chittoor, R., Ray, S., Aulakh, P. S., and Sarkar, M. B. 2008. Strategic responses to institutional changes: "Indigenous growth" model of the Indian pharmaceutical industry. *Journal of International Marketing*, 14: 252–269.

Chittoor, R, Sarkar, M. B., Ray, S., and Aulakh, P. S. 2009. Third-world copycats to emerging multinationals: Institutional changes and organizational transformation in the Indian pharmaceutical industry. *Organization Science*, 20: 187–205.

Collinson, S. and Rugman, A. M. 2007. The regional character of Asian multinational enterprises. *Asia Pacific Journal of Management*, 24: 429–446.

Contractor, F. J., Kumar, V., and Kundu, S. K. 2007. Nature of the relationship between international expansion and performance: The case of emerging market firms. *Journal of World Business*, 42: 401–417.

Cuervo-Cazurra, A. 2006. Who cares about corruption? *Journal of International Business Studies*, 37: 803–822.

2006. Business groups and their types. *Asia Pacific Journal of Management*, 23: 419–437.

2007. Sequence of value-added activities in the internationalization of developing country MNEs. *Journal of International Management*, 13: 258–277.

2008. The multinationalization of developing country MNEs: The case of multilatinas. *Journal of International Management*, 14: 138–154.

2011. Selecting the country in which to start internationalization: The non-sequential internationalization argument. *Journal of World Business*, 46: 426–437.

2012. Extending theory by analyzing developing country multinational companies: Solving the Goldilocks debate. *Global Strategy Journal*, 2: 153–167.

Cuervo-Cazurra, A. and Dau, L. A. 2009. Pro-market reforms and firm profitability in developing countries. *Academy of Management Journal*, 52: 1348–1368.

2009. Structural reform and firm exports. *Management International Review*, 49: 479–507.

Cuervo-Cazurra, A. and Genc, M. 2008. Transforming disadvantages into advantages: Developing country MNEs in the least developed countries. *Journal of International Business Studies*, 39: 957–979.

2011. How context matters: Non-market advantages of developing-country MNEs. *Journal of Management Studies*, 48: 441–445.

Cui, L. and Jiang, F. 2009. FDI entry mode choice of Chinese firms: A strategic behavior perspective. *Journal of World Business*, 44: 434–444.

2012. State ownership effect on firms' FDI ownership decisions under institutional pressure: A study of Chinese outward-investing firms. *Journal of International Business Studies*, 43(3): 264–284.

Da Silva, J. F., Da Rocha, A., and Carneiro, J. 2009. The international expansion of firms from emerging markets: Toward a typology of Brazilian MNEs. *Latin American Business Review*, 10: 95–115.

Dau, L. A. 2012. Pro-market reforms and developing country multinational corporations. *Global Strategy Journal*, 2: 262–276.

Dawar, N. and Frost, T. 1999. Competing with Giants. *Harvard Business Review*, 77: 119–129.

De Beule, F. and Duanmu, J. L. 2012. Locational determinants of internationalization: A firm-level analysis of Chinese and Indian acquisitions. *European Management Journal*, 30: 264–277.

del Sol, P. and Kogan, J. 2007. Regional competitive advantage based on pioneering economic reforms: The case of Chilean FDI. *Journal of International Business Studies*, 38: 901–927.

Demirbag, M. and Glaister, K. W. 2010. Factors determining offshore location choice for R&D projects: A comparative study of developed and emerging regions. *Journal of Management Studies*, 47: 1534–1560.

Demirbag, M., Tatoglu, E., and Glaister, K. W. 2009. Equity-based entry modes of emerging country multinationals: Lessons from Turkey. *Journal of World Business*, 44: 445–462.

Deng, P. 2004. Outward investment by Chinese MNCs: Motivations and implications. *Business Horizons*, 47: 8–16.

2007. Investing for strategic resources and its rationale: The case of outward FDI from Chinese companies. *Business Horizons*, 50: 71–81.

2009. Why do Chinese firms tend to acquire strategic assets in international expansion? *Journal of World Business*, 44: 74–84.

2012. The internationalization of Chinese firms: A critical review and future research. *International Journal of Management Reviews*, 14(4): 408–427.

Di Minin, A., Zhang, J. Y., and Gammeltoft, P. 2012. Chinese foreign direct investment in R&D in Europe: A new model of R&D internationalization? *European Management Journal*, 30: 189–203.

Ding, Y., Nowak, E., and Zhang, H. 2010. Foreign vs. domestic listing: An entrepreneurial decision. *Journal of Business Venturing*, 25: 175–191.

Duanmu, J. L. 2012. Firm heterogeneity and location choice of Chinese Multinational Enterprises (MNEs). *Journal of World Business*, 17: 64–72.

Dunning, J. H. 2006. Comment on "Dragon multinationals: New players in 21st century globalization." *Asia Pacific Journal of Management*, 23: 139–142.

Dunning, J. H., Kim, C., and Park, D. 2008. Old wine in new bottles: A comparison of emerging-market TNCs today and developed-country TNCs thirty years ago. In K. Sauvant (ed.), *The Rise of Transnational Corporations from Emerging Markets. Threat or Opportunity?* Northampton, MA: Edward Elgar.

Dunning, J. H., van Hoesel, R., and Narula, R. 1998. Third world multinationals revisited: New developments and theoretical implications. In J. H. Dunning (ed.), *Globalization, Trade and Foreign Direct Investment*: 225–286. Oxford: Elsevier.

Economist. 2008. Emerging-market multinationals: The challengers. January 10.

Elango, B. and Pattnaik, C. 2007. Building capabilities for international operations through networks: A study of Indian firms. *Journal of International Business Studies*, 38: 541–555.

2011. Learning before making the Big Leap: Acquisition strategies of emerging economy firms. *Management International Review*, 51: 461–482.

Fabian, F., Molina, H., and Labianca, G. 2009. Understanding decisions to internationalize by small and medium-sized firms located in an emerging market. *Management International Review*, 49: 537–564.

Filatotchev, I., Strange, R., Piesee, J., and Lien, Y. C. 2007. FDI by firms from newly industrialized economies in emerging markets: Corporate governance, entry mode and location. *Journal of International Business Studies*, 38: 556–602.

Filippov, S. 2012. Emerging Russian multinational companies: Managerial and corporate challenges. *European Journal of International Management*, 6: 323–341.

Fleury, A. and Fleury, M. T. L. 2011. *Brazilian Multinationals: Competences for Internationalization*. Cambridge University Press.

Gammeltoft, P. 2008. Emerging multinationals: Outward FDI from the BRICS countries. *International Journal of Technology and Globalisation*, 4: 5–22.

Gammeltoft, P., Barnard, H., and Madhok, A. 2010. Emerging multinationals, emerging theory: Macro- and micro-level perspectives. *Journal of International Management*, 16: 95–101.

Gammeltoft, P., Filatotchev, I., and Hobdari, B. 2012. Emerging multinational companies and strategic fit: A contingency framework and future research agenda. *European Management Journal*, 30: 175–188.

Gaur, A. and Kumar, V. 2009. International diversification, business group affiliation and firm performance: Empirical evidence from India. *British Journal of Management*, 20: 172–186.

Ghemawat, P. and Khanna, T. 1998. The nature of diversified business groups: A research design and two case studies. *Journal of Industrial Economics*, 46: 35–61.

Ghymn, K. I. 1980. Multinational enterprises from the third world. *Journal of International Business Studies*, 11: 118–122.

Goldstein, A. 2007. *Multinational Companies from Emerging Economies: Conceptualization and Direction in the Global Economy*. London: Palgrave Macmillan.

Govindarajan, V. and Ramamurti, R. 2011, Reverse innovation, emerging markets, and global strategy. *Global Strategy Journal*, 1: 191–205.

Gubbi, S. R., Aulakh, P., Ray, S., Sarkar, M. B., and Chitoor, R. 2010. Do international acquisitions by emerging-economy firms create shareholder value? The case of Indian firms. *Journal of International Business Studies*, 41: 397–418.

Guillén, M. F. 2002. Structural inertia, imitation, and foreign expansion: South Korean firms and business groups in China, 1987–1995. *Academy of Management Journal*, 45: 509–525.

2003. Experience, imitation, and foreign expansion: Wholly-owned and joint-venture manufacturing by South Korean firms and business groups in China, 1987–1995. *Journal of International Business Studies*, 34: 185–198.

Guillén, M. F. and Garcia-Canal, E. 2009. The American model of the multinational firm and the "new" multinationals from emerging economies. *Academy of Management Perspectives*, 23(2): 23–35.

2012. *The New Multinationals.* Cambridge University Press.

He, W. and Lyles, M. A. 2008. China's outward foreign direct investment. *Business Horizons,* 51(6): 485–491.

Heenan, D. A. and Keegan, W. J. 1979. The rise of third world multinationals. *Harvard Business Review,* 57(1): 101–109.

Henisz, W. J. 2003. The power of the Buckley and Casson thesis: The ability to manage institutional idiosyncrasies. *Journal of International Business Studies,* 34: 173–184.

Hennart, J-F. 2009. Down with MNE-centric theories! Market entry and expansion as the bundling of MNE and local assets. *Journal of International Business Studies,* 40: 1432–1454.

2012. Emerging market multinationals and the theory of the multinational enterprise. *Global Strategy Journal,* 2: 168–187.

Hobday, M. 1995. East Asian latecomer firms: Learning the technology of electronics. *World Development,* 23: 1171–1193.

Hong, E. and Sun, L. 2004. Dynamics of internationalization and outward investment: Chinese corporations' strategies. *China Quarterly,* 187: 610–634.

Hope, O. K., Thomas, W., and Vyas, D. 2011. The cost of pride: Why do firms from developing countries bid higher? *Journal of International Business Studies,* 42: 128–151.

Hoskisson, R. E., Eden, L., Lau, C. M., and Wright, M. 2000. Strategy in emerging economies. *Academy of Management Journal,* 43: 249–267.

Hoskisson, R. E., Johnson, R. A., Tihanyi, L., and White, R. E. 2005. Diversified business groups and corporate refocusing in emerging economies. *Journal of Management,* 31: 941–965.

Islam, G. 2012. Between unity and diversity: Historical and cultural foundations of Brazilian management. *European Journal of International Management,* 6: 265–282.

Jormanainen, I. and Koveshnikov, A. 2012. International activities of emerging market firms: A critical assessment of research in top management journals. *Management International Review,* 52(5): 691–725.

Kalotay, K. and Sulstarova, A. 2010. Modelling Russian outward FDI. *Journal of International Management,* 16: 131–142.

Kang, Y. and Jiang, F. 2012. FDI location choice of Chinese multinationals in East and Southeast Asia: Traditional economic factors and institutional perspective. *Journal of World Business,* 17: 45–53.

Kedron, P. and Bagchi-Sen, B. 2012. Foreign direct investment in Europe by multinational pharmaceutical companies from India. *Journal of Economic Geography,* 12(4): 809–839.

Khanna, T. and Palepu, K. 2000. The future of business groups in emerging markets: Long-run evidence from Chile. *Academy of Management Journal,* 43: 268–285.

2006. Emerging giants: Building world class companies in developing economies. *Harvard Business Review*, 84(10): 60–70.

Khanna, T. and Rivkin, J. W. 2000. Estimating the performance effects of business groups in emerging markets. *Strategic Management Journal*, 22: 45–74.

Khanna, T. and Yafeh, Y. 2007. Business groups in emerging markets: Paragons or parasites? *Journal of Economic Literature*, 45: 331–372.

Kim, H., Hoskisson, R. E., Tihanyi, L., and Hong, J. 2004. Evolution and restructuring of diversified business groups in emerging markets: The lessons from Chaebols in Korea. *Asia Pacific Journal of Management*, 21: 25–48.

Kim, H., Kim, H., and Hoskisson, R. E. 2010. Does market-oriented institutional change in an emerging economy make business group-affiliated multinationals perform better? An institution-based view. *Journal of International Business Studies*, 41: 1141–1160.

Kim, L. 1998. Crisis construction and organizational learning: Capability building in catching-up at Hyundai Motor Corporation. *Organization Science*, 9: 506–521.

Klein, S. and Wöcke, L. 2007. Emerging global contenders: The South African experience. *Journal of International Management*, 13: 319–337.

Klossek, A., Linke, B. M., and Nippa, M. 2012. Chinese enterprises in Germany: Establishment modes and strategies to mitigate the liability of foreignness. *Journal of World Business*, 17: 35–44.

Knoerich, J. 2010. Gaining from the global ambitions of emerging economy enterprises: An analysis of the decision to sell a German firm to a Chinese acquirer. *Journal of International Management*, 16: 177–191.

Kolstad, I. and Wiig, A. 2012. What determines Chinese outward FDI? *Journal of World Business*, 17: 26–34.

Kotabe, M., Jiang, C. X., and Murray, J. Y. 2011. Managerial ties, knowledge acquisition, realized absorptive capacity and new product market performance of emerging multinational companies: A case of China. *Journal of World Business*, 46: 166–176.

Kumar, K. and McLeod, G. (eds.). 1981. *Multinationals from Developing Countries*. New York: Free Press.

Kumar, N. 2009. How emerging giants are rewriting the roles of M&A. *Harvard Business Review*, 87(5): 115–121.

Kumar, N. and Chadha, A. 2009. India's outward foreign direct investments in steel industry in a Chinese comparative perspective. *Industrial and Corporate Change*, 18: 249–267.

Kumaraswamy, A., Mudambi, R., Saranga, H., and Tripathy, A. 2012. Catch-up strategies in the Indian auto components industry: Domestic firms' responses to market liberalization. *Journal of International Business Studies*, 43: 368–395.

Kuo, A., Kao, M. S., Chang, Y. C., and Chiu, C. F. 2012. The influence of international experience on entry mode choice: Difference between family and non-family firms. *European Management Journal*, 30: 248–263.

Laforet, S. and Chen, J. S. 2012. Chinese and British consumers' evaluation of Chinese and international brands and factors affecting their choice. *Journal of World Business*, 17: 54–63.

Lall, S. 1983. *The New Multinationals: The Spread of Third World Enterprises*. New York: Wiley.

Lecraw, D. 1977. Direct investment by firms from less developed countries. *Oxford Economic Papers*, 442–457.

1993. Outward direct investment by Indonesian firms: Motivation and effects. *Journal of International Business Studies*, 24: 481–498.

Lessard, D. and Lucea, R. 2009. Mexican multinationals: Insights from CEMEX. In R. Ramamurti and J. V. Singh (eds.), *Emerging Multinationals from Emerging Markets*. Cambridge University Press.

Li, J. T. and Yao, F. K. 2010. The role of reference groups in international investment decisions by firms from emerging economies. *Journal of International Management*, 16: 143–153.

Li, P. P. 2007. Toward an integrated theory of multinational evolution: The evidence of Chinese multinational enterprises as latecomers. *Journal of International Management*, 13: 296–318.

2010. Toward a learning-based view of internationalization: The accelerated trajectories of cross-border learning for latecomers. *Journal of International Management*, 16: 43–59.

Li, P. Y. and Meyer, K. E. 2009. Contextualizing experience effects in international business: A study of ownership strategies. *Journal of World Business*, 44: 370–382.

Lin, W.-T. and Cheng, K.-Y. 2013. The effect of upper echelons' compensation on firm internationalization. *Asia Pacific Journal of Management*, 30(1): 73–90.

Liu, X., Buck, T., and Shu, C. 2005. Chinese economic development, the next stage: Outward FDI? *International Business Review*, 14: 97–115.

Liu, X., Xiao, W., and Huang, X. 2008. Bounded entrepreneurship and internationalisation of indigenous private-owned firms. *International Business Review*, 17: 488–508.

Lu, Y., Zhou, L., Bruton, G., and Li, W. 2010. Capabilities as a mediator linking resources and the international performance of entrepreneurial firms in an emerging economy. *Journal of International Business Studies*, 41: 419–436.

Luo, Y. D. and Rui, H. 2009. An ambidexterity perspective toward multinational enterprises from emerging economies. *Academy of Management Perspectives*, 23: 49–70.

Luo, Y. D., Sun, J. Y., and Wang, S. 2011. Emerging economy copycats: Capability, environment, and strategy. *Academy of Management Perspectives*, 25: 37–56.

Luo, Y. D. and Tung, R. L. 2007. International expansion of emerging market enterprises: A springboard perspective. *Journal of International Business Studies*, 38: 481–498.

Luo, Y. D. and Wang, S. 2012. Foreign direct investment strategies by developing country multinationals: A diagnostic model for home country effects. *Global Strategy Journal*, 2: 244–261.

Luo, Y. D., Xue, Q., and Han, B. 2010. How emerging market governments promote outward FDI: Experience from China. *Journal of World Business*, 45: 68–79.

Luo, Y. D., Zhao, H. X., Wang, Y. H., and Xi, Y. M. 2011. Venturing abroad by emerging market enterprises: A test of dual strategic intents. *Management International Review*, 51: 433–460.

Madhok, A. and Keyhani, M. 2012. Acquisitions as entrepreneurship: Asymmetries, opportunities and the internationalization of multinationals from emerging economies. *Global Strategy Journal*, 2: 26–40.

Manolova, T. S., Manev, I. M., and Gyoshev, B. S. 2010. In good company: The role of personal and inter-firm networks for new-venture internationalization in a transition economy. *Journal of World Business*, 45: 257–265.

Mathews, J. A. 2002. Competitive advantages of the latecomer firm: A resource-based account of industrial catch-up strategies. *Asia Pacific Journal of Management*, 19: 467–488.

  2006. Dragon multinationals: New players in 21st century globalization. *Asia Pacific Journal of Management*, 23: 5–27.

McCarthy, D. J., Puffer, S. M., and Vikhanski, O. S. 2009. Russian multinationals: Natural resource champions. In R. Ramamurti and J. V. Singh (eds.), *Emerging Multinationals in Emerging Markets*: 167–199. Cambridge University Press.

McGuire, S., Lindeque, J., and Suder, G. 2012. Learning and lobbying: Emerging market firms and corporate political activity in Europe. *European Journal of International Management*, 6: 342–362.

Mendes Borini, F., de Miranda Oliveira, M., Freitas Silveira, F., and de Oliveira Concer, R. 2012. The reverse transfer of innovation of foreign subsidiaries of Brazilian multinationals. *European Management Journal*, 30: 219–231.

Meyer, K. and Thaijongrak, O. 2013. The dynamics of emerging economy MNEs: How the internationalization process model can guide future research. *Asia Pacific Journal of Management*, 30(4): 1125–1153.

Miller, S. R., Thomas, D. E., Eden, L., and Hitt, M. 2008. Knee deep in the big muddy: The survival of emerging market firms in developed markets. *Management International Review*, 48: 645–665.

Morck, R., Yeung, B., and Zhao, M. 2008. Perspectives on China's outward foreign direct investment. *Journal of International Business Studies*, 39: 337–350.

Morilha Muritiba, P., Nunes Muritiba, S., Galvão de Albuquerque, L., Leme Fleury, M. T., and French, J. L. 2012. Challenges for Brazilian MNCs' international human resources management. *European Journal of International Management*, 6: 248–264.

Musteen, M., Francis, J., and Datta, D. K. 2010. The influence of international networks on internationalization speed and performance: A study of Czech SMEs. *Journal of World Business*, 45: 197–205.

Nachum, L., 2004. Geographic and industrial diversification of developing country firms. *Journal of Management Studies*, 41: 273–294.

Narula, R. 2006. Globalization, new ecologies, new zoologies, and the purported death of the eclectic paradigm. *Asia Pacific Journal of Management*, 23: 143–151

2010. *Much Ado about Nothing, or Sirens of a Brave New World? MNE Activity from Developing Countries and Its Significance for Development.* OECD Development Centre.

2012. Do we need different frameworks to explain infant MNEs from developing countries? *Global Strategy Journal*, 2: 188–204.

Narula, R. and Dunning, J. H. 2010. Multinational enterprises, development and globalization: Some clarifications and a research agenda. *Oxford Development Studies*, 38: 263–287.

Nayir, D. Z. and Vaiman, V. 2012. Emerging multinationals: Globalisation paths and management styles. *European Journal of International Management*, 6: 243–247.

Nayyar, D. 2008. The internationalization of firms from India: Investment, mergers and acquisitions. *Oxford Development Studies*, 36: 111–131.

Nguyen, T. D., Barrett, N. J., and Fletcher, R. 2006. Information internalisation and internationalization – evidence from Vietnamese firms. *International Business Review*, 15: 682–701.

Pajouh, M. S. and Blenkinsopp, J. 2012. Knowledge transfer into a developing country: HRM practice in an Iranian hotel chain. *European Journal of International Management*, 6: 283–299.

Pananond, P. 2007. The changing dynamics of Thai multinationals after the Asian economic crisis. *Journal of International Management*, 13: 356–375.

Panibratov, A. 2012. *Russian Multinationals: From Regional Supremacy to Global Lead.* Abingdon, Oxon: Routledge.

Pant, A. and Ramachandran, J. 2012. Legitimacy beyond borders: Indian software services firms in the United States, 1984 to 2004. *Global Strategy Journal*, 2: 224–243.

Pattnaik, C. and Elango, B. 2009. The impact of firm resources on the internationalization and performance relationship: A study of Indian manufacturing firms. *Multinational Business Review*, 17: 69–88.

Peng, M. W. 2012. The global strategy of emerging multinationals from China. *Global Strategy Journal*, 2: 97–107.

Petrou, A. 2007. Multinational banks from developing versus developed countries: Competing in the same arena? *Journal of International Management*, 13: 376–397.

Prashantham, S. 2011. Social capital and Indian micromultinationals. *British Journal of Management*, 22: 4–20.

Prashantham, S. and Dhanaraj, C. 2011. The dynamic influence of social capital on the international growth of new ventures. *Journal of Management Studies*, 47: 967–994.

Puffer, S. M. and McCarthy, D. J. 2011. Two decades of Russian business and management research: An institutional theory perspective. *Academy of Management Perspectives*, 25: 21–36.

Puffer, S. M., McCarthy, D. J., Jaeger, A. M., and Dunlap, D. 2013. The use of favors by emerging market managers: Facilitator or inhibitor of international expansion? *Asia Pacific Journal of Management*, 30(2): 327–349.

Quer, D., Claver, E., and Rienda, L. 2012. Political risk, cultural distance, and outward foreign direct investment: Empirical evidence from large Chinese firms. *Asia Pacific Journal of Management*, 29(4): 1089–1104.

Ramamurti, R. 2009. The theoretical value of studying Indian multinationals. *Indian Journal of Industrial Relations*, 45: 101–114.

2009. What have we learned about emerging market multinationals? In R. Ramamurti and J. V. Singh (eds.), *Emerging Multinationals in Emerging Markets*: 399–426. Cambridge University Press.

2012. What is really different about emerging market multinationals? *Global Strategy Journal*, 2: 41–47.

2012. Competing with emerging-market multinationals. *Business Horizons*, 55: 241–249.

Ramamurti, R, and Singh, J. V. 2009. Indian multinationals: Generic internationalization strategies. In R. Ramamurti and J. V. Singh (eds.), *Emerging Multinationals in Emerging Markets*: 110–166. Cambridge University Press.

(eds.). 2009. *Emerging Multinationals from Emerging Markets*. New York: Cambridge University Press.

Ramaswamy, B., Yeung, M., and Laforet, S. 2012. China's outward foreign direct investment: Location choice and firm ownership. *Journal of World Business*, 47: 17–25.

Rugman, A. M. 2009. Theoretical aspects of MNEs from emerging economies. In R. Ramamurti and J. V. Singh (eds.), *Emerging Multinationals in Emerging Markets*: 42–63. New York: Cambridge University Press.

2010. Do we need a new theory to explain emerging market MNEs? In K. P. Sauvant, W. A. Maschek, and G. A. McAllister (eds.), *Foreign Direct Investments from Emerging Markets: The Challenges Ahead*. New York: Palgrave McMillan.

Rugman, A. M. and Li, J. 2007. Will China's multinationals succeed globally or regionally? *European Management Journal*, 25: 333–343.

Rugman, A. M. and Oh, C. H. 2008. Korea's multinationals in a regional world. *Journal of World Business*, 43: 5–15.

Rui, H. and Yip, G. S. 2008. Foreign acquisitions by Chinese firms: A strategic intent perspective. *Journal of World Business*, 43: 213–226.

Sauvant, K. (ed.). 2008. *The Rise of Transnational Corporations from Emerging Markets: Threat or Opportunity?* Northampton, MA: Edward Elgar.

Sauvant, K. P., Maschek, W. A., and McAllister, G. A. (eds.). 2010. *Foreign Direct Investments from Emerging Markets: The Challenges Ahead*. New York: Palgrave McMillan.

Stucchi, T. 2012. Emerging market firms' acquisitions in advanced markets: Matching strategy with resource-, institution- and industry-based antecedents. *European Management Journal*, 30: 278–289.

Sun, S. L., Peng, M. W., Ren, B., and Yan, D. 2012. A comparative ownership advantage framework for cross-border M&As: The rise of Chinese and Indian MNEs. *Journal of World Business*, 47: 4–16.

Svetlicic, M. 2004. Transition economies multinationals – are they different from Third World multinationals? In C. Chakraborty (ed.), *Proceedings of the 8th International Conference on Global Business and Economic Development*. Guadalajara, Mexico: Montclair State University.

Tan, D. and Meyer, K. E. 2010. Business groups' outward FDI: A managerial resources perspective. *Journal of International Management*, 16: 154–164.

Thomas, D. E., Eden, L., Hitt, M. A., and Miller, S. R. 2007. Experience of emerging market firms: The role of cognitive bias in developed market entry and survival. *Management International Review*, 47: 845–867.

Tolentino, P. E. 1993. *Technological Innovation and Third World Multinationals*. London: Routledge.

2010. Home country macroeconomic factors and outward FDI of China and India. *Journal of International Management*, 16: 102–120.

Tsang, E. W. K. and Yip, P. S. L. 2007. Economic distance and survival of foreign direct investment. *Academy of Management Journal*, 50: 1156–1168.

Ulgado, F. M., Yu, C. M. J., and Negandhi, A. R. 1994. Multinational enterprises from Asian developing countries: Management and organizational characteristics. *International Business Review*, 3: 123–133.

Vernon-Wortzel, H. and Wortzel, L. H. 1988. Globalizing strategies for multinationals from developing countries. *Columbia Journal of World Business*, 23: 27–35.

Voss, H., Buckley, P. J., and Cross, A. R. 2010. The impact of home country institutional effects on the internationalization strategy of Chinese firms. *Multinational Business Review*, 18: 25–48.

Wang, C. Q., Hong, J. J., Kafouros, M., and Boateng, A. 2012. What drives outward FDI of Chinese firms? Testing the explanatory power of three theoretical frameworks. *International Business Review*, 21: 425–438.

Wei, Z. Y. 2010. The literature on Chinese outward FDI. *Multinational Business Review*, 18: 73–112.

Wells, L. T. Jr. 1983. *Third World Multinationals: The Rise of Foreign Investments from Developing Countries*. Cambridge, MA: MIT Press.

Williamson, P. J. 2007. The global impact of China's emerging multinationals. In C. A. McNally (ed.), *China's Emerging Political Economy: Capitalism in the Dragon's Lair*. London: Routledge.

   2010. Cost innovation: Preparing for a "Value-for-Money" revolution. *Long Range Planning*, 43: 343–353.

Williamson, P. J. and Anand, R. P. 2011. How China reset its acquisition agenda. *Harvard Business Review*, 89: 109–114.

Williamson, P. J. and Yin, E. 2009. Racing with the Chinese Dragons. In I. Alon, J. Chang, M. Fetscherin, C. Lattemann, and J. R. McIntyre (eds.), *China Rules: Globalization and Political Transformation*. New York: Palgrave-Macmillan.

Williamson, P. J. and Zeng, M. 2009. Value-for-money strategies for recessionary times. *Harvard Business Review*, 87: 66–74.

Williamson, P., Ramamurti, R., Fleury, A., and Fleury, M. T. (eds). 2013. *Competitive Advantages of Emerging Country Multinationals*. Cambridge University Press.

Witt, M. A. and Lewin, A. Y. 2007. Outward foreign direct investment as escape response to home country institutional constraints. *Journal of International Business Studies*, 38: 579–594.

Wright, M., Filatotchev, I., Hoskisson, R. E., and Peng, M. W. 2005. Strategy research in emerging economies: Challenging the conventional wisdom. *Journal of Management Studies*, 42: 1–33.

Yamakawa, Y., Peng, M. W., and Deeds, D. 2008. What drives new ventures to internationalize from emerging to developed economies? *Entrepreneurship Theory and Practice*, 32: 59–82.

Yang, X. H., Jiang, Y., Kang, R. P., and Ke, Y. B. 2009. A comparative analysis of the internationalization of Chinese and Japanese firms. *Asia Pacific Journal of Management*, 26: 141–162.

Yeung, H. W. C. 1994. Third World multinationals revisited: A research critique and future agenda. *Third World Quarterly*, 15: 297–317.

1999. Competing in the global economy: The globalization of business firms from emerging economies. In H. W. C. Yeung (ed.), *The Globalization of Business Firms from Emerging Economies*. Cheltenham, UK: Edward Elgar.

Yiu, D., Lu, Y., Bruton, G., and Hoskisson, R. E. 2007. Business groups: An integrated model to focus future research. *Journal of Management Studies*, 44: 1551–1578.

Yiu, D. W., Lau, C. M., and Bruton, G. D. 2007. International venturing by emerging economy firms: The effects of firm capabilities, home country networks, and corporate entrepreneurship. *Journal of International Business Studies*, 38: 519–540.

Young, S., Huang, C. H., and McDermott, M. 1996. Internationalization and competitive catch-up processes: Case study evidence on Chinese multinational enterprises. *Management International Review*, 36: 295–314.

Zattoni, A., Pedersen, T., and Kumar, V. 2009. The performance of group-affiliated firms during institutional transition: A longitudinal study of Indian firms. *Corporate Governance: An International Review*, 17: 510–523.

Zeng, M. and Williamson, P. J. 2003. The hidden dragons. *Harvard Business Review*, 81(10): 92–99.

2007. *Dragons at your Door: How Chinese Cost Innovation is Disrupting the Rules of Global Competition*. Boston, MA: Harvard Business School Press.

Zhang, J., Zhou, C., and Ebbers, H. A. 2011. Completion of Chinese overseas acquisitions: Institutional perspectives and evidence. *International Business Review*, 20: 226–238.

Zhao, W., Liu, L., and Zhao, T. 2010. The contribution of outward direct investment to productivity changes within China, 1991–2007. *Journal of International Management*, 16: 121–130.

Zhou, L., Barnes, B. R., and Lu, Y. 2010. Entrepreneurial proclivity, capability upgrading and performance advantage of newness among international new ventures. *Journal of International Business Studies*, 41: 882–905.

Zhou, L. X., Wu, W. P., and Luo, X. M. 2007. Internationalization and the performance of born-global SMEs: The mediating role of social networks. *Journal of International Business Studies*, 38: 673–690.

Zhu, H., Eden, L., Miller, S. R., Thomas, D. E., and Fields, P. 2012. Host-country location decisions of early movers and latecomers: The role of local density and experiential learning. *International Business Review*, 21: 145–155.

Index

Printed in the United States
By Bookmasters